What Editors Do

Chicago Guides
to *Writing*, Editing,
and Publishing

What Editors Do

THE ART, CRAFT, AND BUSINESS

OF BOOK EDITING

Edited by **PETER GINNA**

THE UNIVERSITY

OF CHICAGO PRESS

Chicago and London

The University of Chicago Press, Chicago 60637
The University of Chicago Press, Ltd., London

For more information, contact the University of Chicago Press,
1427 E. 60th St., Chicago, IL 60637.

Published 2017

Printed in the United States of America

27 26 25 24 23 22 21 20 19 18   1 2 3 4 5

ISBN-13: 978-0-226-29983-9 (cloth)
ISBN-13: 978-0-226-29997-6 (paper)
ISBN-13: 978-0-226-30003-0 (e-book)
DOI: https://doi.org/10.7208/chicago/9780226300030.001.0001

Library of Congress Cataloging-in-Publication Data
Names: Ginna, Peter, editor.
Title: What editors do : the art, craft, and business of book editing / edited by Peter Ginna.
Other titles: Chicago guides to writing, editing, and publishing.
Description: Chicago : The University of Chicago Press, 2017. | Series: Chicago guides to
    writing, editing, and publishing | Includes index.
Identifiers: LCCN 2017025411 | ISBN 9780226299839 (cloth : alk. paper) | ISBN 9780226299976
    (pbk. : alk. paper) | ISBN 9780226300030 (e-book)
Subjects: LCSH: Editing. | Publishers and publishing.
Classification: LCC PN162 .W465 2017 | DDC 808.02/7—dc23
LC record available at https://lccn.loc.gov/2017025411

♾ This paper meets the requirements of ANSI/NISO Z39.48-1992
(Permanence of Paper).

For Margaret Williams Ginna

and Robert Emmett Ginna Jr.

who coauthored, and edited, me

CONTENTS

. . . .

INTRODUCTION

. . . .

THE THREE PHASES OF EDITING

People outside the book publishing industry—and even many within it—often wonder: just what is it that editors do? It's a simple question with a complicated answer. This book attempts such an answer. It's intended for readers who are interested in becoming editors themselves, or who have embarked on an editorial career and want to learn more; for those in other jobs within publishing who want to understand their editorial colleagues; for book lovers curious about how the books they loved (or hated) came into being; and not least, for writers who want to know just what goes on inside the walls of a publishing house—or inside an editor's head. To find out how the literary sausage is made, for better or worse, read on.

In today's book business, the role of editor encompasses an enormous range of tasks. Imagine that the whole American publishing industry could be found on one single street. (So much of it was, in nineteenth-century New York, that the expression "Publishers Row" became a lasting metonym for the book business, as "Madison Avenue" did for advertising. Today publishing is more geographically dispersed than ever, but suppose the contrary with me for a moment.) If we could peek in the windows of all the different publishers, here are some of the things we might see editorial staffers doing:

- In this skyscraper, an editor is on the phone with a literary agent negotiating a contract for a new book.
- In the conference room next door, another editor is sitting with an author in front of a pile of photographs, choosing images for a book going into production.
- In the hallway, a senior editor is buttonholing the sales director to tell him why he has *got* to read a memoir that's just been delivered.
- In this ivy-clad building, a university press editor is scanning a new journal, looking out for promising young scholars.
- Across the street, several editors are in a marketing meeting, discussing publicity and sales plans on next season's titles.
- In this cubicle, an editorial assistant is struggling to fit a flap copy description into the two hundred words allotted for it.
- In this one, a copyeditor is checking to make sure that a character who

has green eyes on page 60 of this manuscript didn't have blue eyes on page 14.

- At the textbook publisher's building on the corner, an editor is researching professors who might peer-review a new environmental studies reader.
- In the brownstone housing an independent press, a fiction editor is painstakingly composing a letter asking a famous writer to blurb a debut novel.
- Back at the skyscraper, in the corner office, the editor in chief is . . . actually she's not there, she's on her way to lunch. But this, too, is a very important part of her job! I'll discuss why in the next chapter.

What we probably wouldn't see through these office windows are editors *editing* things—that is, reading manuscripts and suggesting changes and improvements to them. Perhaps the kaleidoscope of other tasks listed above suggests why. Those essential editorial activities require concentration and long blocks of time to do properly—and that's near-impossible to find in the busy publishing workday. If we followed all these editors out of their offices at night, we would see almost every one, as they sit on the bus, or on the sofa after dinner, pull a computer tablet or a stack of pages out of their bag and start to read. And many of them are probably still reading and making comments in the margins deep into the evening.

WHAT EDITING IS

It's ironic that publishing, a business whose essence is words, has some of the loosest, most confusing, and most contradictory terminology of any industry I know. For instance, one very common term, *galley*, could refer to three or four different things.[1] And the very item editors work on continues to be called a *manuscript*, which properly means a document written by hand, when today every author delivers his work by computer.[2]

As the list of activities above suggests, the title *editor* is misleading, too. What the word *editing* connotes to most people—correcting and improving an author's text—is only a part of what book editors do. It's a big slice of the

1. The word is used in shorthand to refer to first-pass proofs, bound galleys, and advance reading copies, three related but quite distinct items—none of which matches the term's original meaning (see the glossary for definitions of each).

2. Our British colleagues might reply in self-defense that they say "typescripts"— but that term is only marginally less obsolete.

. . . .

pie, but far from the whole pizza. The Latin origin of *edit, edere*, meaning "to bring out" or "to put forth," usefully expands our understanding of the role. *Editors take the work of authors and put it before readers.* Another word for that activity, of course, is *publishing*, and another instance of our fuzzy professional vocabulary is the overlap of "editing" and "publishing." (In some languages *editor* and *publisher* are the same word.) Everyone in a publishing company, from the website designer to a picker in the warehouse, is by definition part of that process.

But editors have a special position, as the professionals most closely connected with the book and its author. Editors are responsible for finding works to publish in the first place, and for steering each one through the serpentine pipeline of the publishing house into the marketplace, tending to the author's needs (and psyche) along the way. An old publishing adage has it that an editor "represents the author to the house and the house to the author," and this is true, but incomplete. The editor also represents the *reader* to the author, and vice versa. To edit a manuscript effectively, you must put yourself in the shoes of someone who's picking up the book with no prior knowledge of the author or the project's history. At the same time, you must grasp what the writer is trying to accomplish in the book; sometimes this will be more evident to you than to the author. And to publish a book well, you must combine that understanding of the author's vision with your knowledge of the marketplace—of what readers are looking for and how they find it.

The editor, then, is a connector—a conduit from writer to reader—but also a translator, improving the communication from each to the other. As our snapshots from Publishers Row revealed, editing takes in a wide variety of activities. Sometimes one person carries out all of them; sometimes they are distributed among multiple individuals, depending on the type and the size of the publishing house.

Our time has seen enormous and still-ongoing changes in the industry of book publishing—the technology has been revolutionized, the retail landscape has been transformed, and even as commercial publishing has increasingly become the domain of huge corporations, small publishers and self-publishers have greater presence in the marketplace than ever before. A "publisher" now might be a multinational corporation like Penguin Random House; a small not-for-profit literary firm or university press; or even an author publishing his own e-books from his kitchen table.

Some have wondered whether in this brave new world editors will become obsolete. I doubt it, because whatever form publishing takes—unless it is defined downward to be something like blogging or handing out photocopies—the editorial functions explored in this book will always be critical to it. That self-publishing author doesn't have a business card saying "Editor," but as soon as he reads over his work to get it ready for uploading, or when she writes a description for her Amazon page and wonders how to make it sound appealing, she is one.

THE PURPOSE OF THIS BOOK

For all the transformations mentioned above, some aspects of publishing remain little changed since the nineteenth century, such as the way people in the industry learn their craft. Almost no American publishing house has any formalized instruction program. Training for most publishing jobs, certainly those in editorial positions, is in effect a classic apprenticeship system where junior people learn on the job by working as assistants to more experienced professionals.

A small but increasing number of universities offer publishing classes for undergraduate or graduate students, or intensive summer courses for aspiring editors; those at Columbia, New York University, and the University of Denver are among the best known.[3] But they train a relative handful of applicants. Perhaps that's why there are virtually no textbooks or manuals for book editors, not counting those covering specialties such as copyediting and proofreading.

One standout exception to this was the essay collection *Editors on Editing*, in which the veteran editor Gerald Gross gathered contributions from many leading practitioners discussing aspects of their work. First published in 1962 and still in print, *Editors on Editing* is an excellent resource. I read it avidly when I started out in publishing in the 1980s, and I still find it valuable.[4] But the contents focused almost entirely on trade publishing, offering little practical information for editors in academic or small press settings. Also, it was last updated in 1993—a time when Amazon did not exist, very few Americans were online, and the cutting-edge technology in publishing was the CD-ROM. *What Editors Do* aims to perform a similar service for publishing in the era of Amazon, downloadable e-books, and social media.

The figure of the editor has often been romanticized or glamorized (or,

3. A more complete list of these programs can be found within the resource list at the end of this book.

4. The resource list also includes the titles of other useful reading material, in print and online.

. . . .

in some quarters, demonized). Another goal of this book is to demystify the editor's job and put it in context within the publishing process. I have used the subtitle *The Art, Craft, and Business of Book Editing* because I believe all those nouns fit together. The *art* of editing lies in exercising taste and making aesthetic judgments, and in attuning oneself, in a slightly different way each time, to the sensibility and psychology of an author. The *craft* involves learning techniques and best practices, which range from the rules of grammar and style mastered by copyeditors to the diplomatic ways of phrasing suggestions that good line editors learn by experience. Finally, the editor, even in a not-for-profit press, is part of a *business* that sells a product and must generate revenue. Understanding how that business works, and learning how to guide one's projects through the publishing process and into the marketplace, is a prerequisite for serving your authors well.

Like many of my colleagues, I was drawn to editing initially for the art of it: the opportunity to read for a living, the chance to help creative people shape their work, the hope of contributing to literature. Happily, I found all that as an editor. But I also found that I enjoyed learning the craft of editing. Some of that learning came from generous mentors, much from my own curiosity and sometimes painful experience, but whatever the source, there is always satisfaction in improving one's skills. And the craft is difficult and complex enough that the journey up the learning curve can last a long time. Once I got far enough along, though the pace of learning new things diminished, I took satisfaction in teaching the craft to others. But most unexpectedly to me, I discovered over time that I actually loved the business of publishing. I came to relish the perpetual challenge: starting with a book you're excited by, how can you operate the equipment of the publishing house to realize the author's vision as fully as possible and put it in the hands of the greatest number of readers?

This volume attempts to capture each of these aspects of book editing, in essays contributed by some of the most effective practitioners and insightful observers of publishing at work today. Inevitably the shape of this collection reflects my own experience: although I have worked in a small literary press and a large academic one, most of my time has been spent in trade publishing, where editors tend to have the broadest responsibilities. Therefore I tend to conceive the job in those terms. But those who have more specialized functions, from in-house production editors to freelance developmental editors, are no less crucial to the process. They too are represented in these essays. Furthermore, as I noted above, a significant share of the titles in today's marketplace comes from authors who publish themselves, and sometimes become publishers of other kindred writers. So a chapter here is devoted to editorial best practices for the self-publisher.

To cover every variety of editor and editing would require a multivolume encyclopedia rather than a handbook, so I have not attempted that here. These essays amount to a mosaic that I hope will give the reader a clear understanding, if not a complete image, of the editor's place in the publishing ecosystem. Nor have I attempted to address every kind of book publishing, a vast and diverse industry that bleeds into fields such as journals in one direction, database publishing in another, and comic books in yet another. This book focuses mainly on core sectors of publishing with which most readers will have at least some familiarity. These include the following:

- *Trade publishing.* Of all counterintuitive publishing terms, this may be the commonest—it's as if the industry aimed to trip up laypeople at the door. While a trade *magazine* is one that covers a particular industry, aimed at readers in that industry, a trade *book* is the opposite: a work aimed at a general audience. The usage arose because these items were sold in the "book trade"—that is, bookstores.
- *Mass market publishing*—paperbacks sold through drugstores, newsstands, and the like—was once a separate category but has now largely been absorbed into trade publishing as trade and mass market houses merged, partly because their readers overlap so much.
- *Juvenile publishing* is the antique-sounding term for children's and young adult books. While a huge category in market share, it too falls under trade publishing, as kids' books are also found in general bookstores.
- *Academic (or scholarly) publishing.* This includes both university presses and commercial firms that publish for the academic market. Their books are aimed at specialist readers and the research libraries that serve them.
- *Textbook publishing.* Textbooks are written and published for use by students in the classroom, whether in elementary and high school (K–12 or "el–hi" in industry jargon) or in colleges.
- *Reference publishing.* Reference works span everything from a desktop dictionary to a massive online resource. Many reference titles are now published purely online; still, most publishers have some print and e-book titles on their lists that qualify as reference.

- *Self-publishing.* Together, the technological breakthroughs of printing on demand, e-book publishing, and online bookselling have allowed authors to publish their own work competitively with much larger companies, though few receive bookstore distribution. Self-published titles now number in the hundreds of thousands annually. Most of them have small to minuscule audiences, but in some popular genres such as fantasy, thriller, or romance, self-published books routinely become bestsellers.

The specifics of an editor's job may vary considerably from one of these categories to another. For that matter, even within the same category no two houses have identical procedures: a children's book editor at Dell may do her job quite differently from one at Scholastic. Nonetheless, across all these categories, even self-publishing, some fundamental features of the editor's role persist.

THE THREE PHASES OF EDITING
In a typical workday, an editor may "touch" anywhere from a few titles to a score of them, and (as that peek in the windows of our imaginary Publishers Row showed) carry out dozens of activities, some momentous and some menial. But overall, the editorial process consists of three overlapping phases, and every editorial task can be grouped into one of them. Some editors, such as copyeditors or freelance book doctors, perform one of these functions exclusively. But most, especially in trade publishing, will be involved in all of them. This book begins by exploring these three basic kinds of editorial labor.

The first is *acquisition*—finding new works to publish, which includes not just screening submissions from authors and literary agents but also scouting for promising new writers or even seeking the right author for a project the editor thinks up. In textbook or reference publishing, this phase usually begins with the editor identifying an opportunity in the marketplace.

Acquisition is a "sales" job too—it includes the crucial task of persuading one's in-house colleagues to invest in a new project, and of selling the house to an author who may have other publishers to choose from. Finally, to use a current-day buzzword, acquisition is the art of curation. One important way in which an editor contributes to both his business and our culture is helping the public find books worth reading. The very developments that some predicted would make editors obsolete—the technology allowing anyone to publish a book with a few clicks—has created an explosion of titles that has only made the editor as curator more valuable.

The techniques of acquisition vary from one market segment to another, as the essays in part I make clear. In trade publishing, the vast majority of projects come to editors from their network of agents, the cultivation of which is a key ongoing task. In academic publishing, an editor develops a network of scholars in her field. In textbook and reference publishing, the process often begins with the editor working backwards from a subject and seeking authors for it. The title of Peter Coveney's chapter on textbook acquisitions, "The Lords of Disciplines," might also apply to the academic editors described in Greg Britton's essay: in both markets, a lively understanding of one's designated scholarly field is essential. In every category, the acquiring editor must advocate for a new book with enthusiasm, but temper that enthusiasm with a pragmatic understanding of the book's prospects in the marketplace. Jonathan Karp's "The Alchemy of Acquisition" wryly offers some guidelines for doing so from the viewpoint of a seasoned trade-book publisher.

The second phase might be called *text development*; it is sometimes referred to as "pencil editing" after the time-honored tool for the job. This is what most people think of when they hear the word *editing*: the core task of working with the author, from proposal or first-draft manuscript, to make his manuscript as good as it can be and ready it for publication. Today, of course, much "pencil editing" is in fact done electronically, allowing quicker exchanges between author and editor and greater efficiency in later stages. In this way, technology has enhanced rather than threatened a traditional process. (Like many colleagues, I still prefer to edit "old school," with pencil on paper, but I'll often transcribe my comments into an author's electronic manuscript to make it easier and faster for him to respond.)

Text development takes place along a continuum from the big-picture, conceptual level—such as when an editor and author talk through the outline of a book over a lunch or a telephone call—down to the level of phrases, words, and punctuation marks. I refer to the most fundamental, "macro" interventions as *conceptual editing*—this is not a common industry term, perhaps because a conversation over lunch doesn't seem like "editing" and indeed a pencil may be nowhere in sight. But sometimes the most important contribution an editor can make is to help an author frame her approach to a topic in a compelling way or steer away from a poorly chosen subject. In *Avid Reader*, Robert Gottlieb's memoir of a brilliant career at Simon & Schuster, Knopf, and the *New Yorker* (highly recommended for all aspiring, or practicing, editors), he jokes that all editors' accounts of their work take the form *"So I said to him, 'Leo! Don't just do war! Do peace too!'"* That's conceptual editing. By definition, it takes place early in the creative process. Quite a lot

....

of conceptual editing may be done by the author's agent before editors even see a proposal, as editor-turned-agent Susan Rabiner explains in her essay in part II.

Developmental editing is a term often used for input a step or two further along, usually when the author has a complete draft or most of one. At this stage an editor may reorder chapters or restructure within them, suggest different writing approaches, or retool an introduction, for example. This kind of work bleeds into *line editing*, where the editor works her way literally line by line through a manuscript and makes comments on every aspect of the text, down to word choice and punctuation. *Copyediting* is the final and most fine-grained step of the editing process, in which the manuscript is combed for any technical errors or lapses in consistency, marked up with design specifications, and otherwise prepared to be set into type by a compositor.

Nancy Miller's "The Book's Journey," which begins part II, traces the path taken by a typical book from the moment an author delivers a draft manuscript to the time a printed copy leaves the publisher's warehouse. Other chapters in part II, by Scott Norton, George Witte, and Carol Fisher Saller, walk us through each of these kinds of edits in more detail. As Miller points out, these are different *levels* of editing, not necessarily discrete *stages* that a book passes through in sequence. They can happen simultaneously—a developmental editor won't hesitate to correct a misspelling, and on rare occasions a copyeditor may suggest a chapter-level overhaul.

In trade publishing, usually the acquiring editor does everything through the line edit, while in academic presses the sheer volume of titles to be published often means books get only a high-level developmental edit with little line-by-line work. But no serious publishing house, nor even a self-respecting self-publisher, sends a title into the marketplace without a meticulous copyedit: grammatical errors and other obvious flubs instantly put readers off and damage a writer's credibility.

Notwithstanding my comments earlier that pencil editing is only part of the editor's job, shaping the book in this way—working through it with close attention both to what is on the page and to the author's vision, and bringing them back together when they diverge—is still the essential and defining task for members of our profession. We are called "editors," after all, not "acquisitionists" or "flap-copyographers." And a publishing professional who is involved only with the text, like a copyeditor, is still an editor; one who's involved only in marketing is not.

The publishing house as a whole should serve the author in many ways. But engaging with the author's ideas and their expression is often the place where the editor personally can have the most direct impact. It is probably the part of our work most greatly valued by authors, and for that reason often the most rewarding. For the editor, it's the most creatively stimulating part of the job, and the most intimate. For that very that reason, it's often the most psychologically fraught. Agent Betsy Lerner, a gifted author herself as well as a former editor, gives us a bracingly honest look at the author–editor relationship in the second chapter of part II.

The third phase of the editor's job is what we usually understand by *publication*—the complex and demanding effort to get the book into the marketplace and put it in the hands of readers. This effort includes both the nuts-and-bolts tasks of production (turning the work from a manuscript into a printed and/or electronic volume, or perhaps an app or audiobook) and the wide range of activities that constitute sales, publicity, and marketing. Unlike acquisitions and text development, the editor is not usually directly responsible for these functions, but she is essential to them. In trade houses the editor is in effect the project captain at the hub of all these processes; at a small indie house the editor may wear several of these hats herself; in academic or reference publishing the editor may be further from these functions but will still be responsible for funneling key information to all the players and communicating with the author.

This phase of the editor's job, marketing the product, is sometimes looked down on as mere commerce or, worse, hucksterism, but no good editor is ashamed of it. It brings us back to the essence of what editors do: connect writers with readers. What service is more important to the author, or to our culture, than bringing a good book into the lives of as many readers as possible?

Part III of this volume looks into the intricate machinery of twenty-first-century publishing and what it takes for editors to utilize that machinery on their authors' behalf. To begin, Michael Pietsch, who rose from editing some of America's most acclaimed writers to become the CEO of a Big Five publisher, writes incisively of "the editor as manager" and the skills of communication, organization, and teamwork that make an editor effective.

One particular form of communication is essential for editors to master: persuasion. To say that an editor must be a manager does *not* mean that he is a bloodless functionary. The best editors are passionate about their books, and have learned how to spread that passion through the publishing house and out into the world. Calvert Morgan explains this mission—the editor as evangelist—in "Start Spreading the News."

Pietsch and Morgan write from the perspective of the big corporate houses that constitute much of the publishing business. But vital publishing is also being done in small to mid-sized independent presses all over the country. Unconstrained by corporate pressures, sometimes explicitly not for profit, these houses often take more chances and nurture more daring and innovative work. One such publisher is Minnesota's Graywolf Press. Jeff Shotts, Graywolf's executive editor, offers a glimpse of how an editor in an indie house operates, making an eloquent case for what indies have to offer authors: a keen sense of community and the gift of patience.

If the fundamental principles of publishing and editing hold true across diverse sectors of the market, from college texts to paperback thrillers, each content category has its unique features, too: the kinds of authors you work with, the editorial skills you need, and the ways you reach audiences will vary from one to the next. Part IV, "Categories and Case Studies," gathers essays from eight editors with expertise in varied fields: Erika Goldman on literary fiction (with echoes of Shotts on the value of independent publishing); Diana Gill on genre fiction; Matt Weiland on general nonfiction (a category far more interesting than its name, as he rightly observes); Nancy Siscoe on children's and young adult books; Wendy Wolf on biography and memoir; Susan Ferber on scholarly nonfiction; Anne Savarese on reference publishing (it still thrives, even in the age of Google); and Deb Aaronson on illustrated books. All of these editors discuss one or more projects they've worked on, giving us several vivid illustrations of what editing is in practice, not just in theory. Together, these essays suggest both the wide variety of issues that editors must grapple with and the underlying similarities in what all of them do.

THE PROFESSION OF EDITING

Finally, book editing is not only an art, a craft, and a business—it is also a career. Part V explores several aspects of editing as a profession.

When we speak of publishing careers, the elephant in the room—and it is, unfortunately, a white elephant—is the industry's lack of diversity. As of 2017, surveys show American publishing houses are roughly 80 percent white, and editorial staffs even whiter. This is almost 20 percent higher than the share of white Americans in the 2010 census. African Americans and Latinos make up only 2 to 4 percent of editors—somewhere between one-eighth and one-fourth of their share of the general population.

I personally suspect this doesn't reflect conscious racism so much as the tradition-bound thinking of the industry. (One tradition, I'm afraid, is snobbery, such as the knee-jerk tendency to hire students from prestigious schools and look no further.) But that is only another way of saying that publishing shares in the structural racism of American society, and it is certainly no ex-cuse for accepting the status quo. Publishing's lily-whiteness is not only a failure of social justice when minority candidates are denied opportunity. It's a problem for the industry, as the works editors choose to publish become demographically out of step with an ever more diverse customer base. And it's a loss to the culture that publishers should be serving.

In his chapter, Chris Jackson, an African American editor who has pub-lished a diverse list of authors and in 2017 restarted the multicultural One World imprint at Penguin Random House, looks back at his own career to draw some lessons from it for publishers. His piece offers inspiration for any-one interested in becoming an editor, especially those from nontraditional backgrounds. And it offers a challenge for those in the business who make hiring and promotion decisions to widen their field of vision.

But let's suppose you are a talented applicant who has landed an entry-level position: what's it like? A few people move into editorial positions from other departments or even other media, such as magazines or television. But to reiterate a point made earlier, most of us learn the trade by apprenticeship. The best first step toward becoming an editor, then, is to be a good editorial assistant. Katie Adams's "The Apprentice" explains what EAs do and what sets the best ones apart.

Meanwhile, some editors make a career working for themselves—usually, but not always, after gaining some in-house experience. The increasing pres-sure for houses to publish more titles with fewer staffers and the surge in self-publishing have created new opportunities for freelance editors. Copy-editing and proofreading, because of their piecework nature, have long been outsourced by big publishers. Today, developmental and line editing work, too, may well be sent to freelancers. Katharine O'Moore-Klopf, a freelance editor for two decades, explains the dynamics of freelance work and how one might go about building an editorial solo practice in "This Pencil for Hire." Some self-publishers, of course, don't want or can't afford to hire freelance services. Yet at some level every self-publisher must be responsible for the editorial quality of his work. Arielle Eckstut and David Henry Sterry's chapter, "The Self-Publisher as Self-Editor," is an invaluable guide to what that means.

The final essay in part V, by publishing expert and consultant Jane Fried-man, steps back to offer a wider, synoptic view of the changing publishing marketplace and the editor's place in it. While the e-book's threat to disrupt publishing has been overblown, many related developments—including the growing market share of Amazon and other e-tailers, the explosion of new titles from self-publishers, and the consequently critical problem of helping

. . . .

readers find books—have caused the business to change more in the past fifteen years than the previous fifty. If most of the other essays in this collection focus on what editors do now, Friedman's offers a glimpse at how those roles might—and might not—evolve in years to come.

A passing word about technology: Readers may notice that, for all my emphasis on change in publishing, this book does not include a chapter on technology per se, nor on such burgeoning product categories as e-books or audiobooks. This is not because these topics are unimportant—exactly the contrary. Every part of the publishing process, from writing and editing to marketing and distribution, has been reshaped by electronic tools and the internet, and each chapter here reflects how editors now work in a networked digital environment. But the principles and best practices of editing laid out in these essays are largely identical whether the editor scribbles on paper or taps on a tablet, and whether the book is delivered on paper, via e-reader, or through headphones.

Book publishing undoubtedly confronts many challenges as this book comes into being: not just technological but demographic, economic, and cultural. But the death of publishing has been proclaimed on a regular basis, seemingly since Gutenberg, and as I point out in my conclusion to this volume, the continuities in the profession are just as striking as the changes. I believe now is an exciting, dynamic time to be an editor, whether inside a publishing house, as a freelancer, or even as a hybrid creator-publisher of your own work. Compiling this book, and exchanging observations about editing with some of the smartest publishing people I know, has reinforced my optimism about the profession. Regardless of why you picked up this book, I hope that once you have read it, you will find reasons to share that optimism.

PART ONE

Acquisition

· ·

FINDING THE BOOK

1 WHERE IT ALL BEGINS

· ·

PETER GINNA

Every acquiring editor knows the feeling: I call it *the spark*. You're reading a manuscript or book proposal, and something about it quickens your pulse, makes you turn the pages a little more eagerly: *this is the real thing*. Whether you're looking for picture books for children, self-help, scholarly monographs, or poetry, you've found a work that catches your attention. And when you turn the last page you think, *I can't wait to tell someone about this*.

The power of that feeling is something outsiders often don't understand. Critics of traditional publishing, who include, understandably, many rejected authors, focus much disapproving attention on the editor's function of "gatekeeping," with its image of turning authors away like a surly bouncer at a club. But editors don't live to turn books down. They live to find books they believe in and to bring them to readers. Simply put: it is acquisition, not rejection, that drives the engine of publishing.

Acquisitions is the *primum mobile*, the activity from which every other task in publishing springs. New books are the lifeblood of a publishing house, and finding new titles that the house can publish successfully is the most important task anyone in it can have. To be a brilliant manuscript editor or a genius at marketing—these skills are invaluable, without doubt. But in purely pragmatic terms, the ability to find books worth publishing—new voices, provocative arguments, captivating original stories or old ones freshly told—is prized above all, because without new projects to fill its pipeline, a publishing company withers away.

This was a lesson that I, for one, took far too long to learn as I made my way in my career. Like many eager new recruits, I imagined I would move up the career ladder as I demonstrated my ability with my editorial pencil. In fact, when it comes to advancement (and salary), nothing counts as much for the editor as an acquisitions track record. Just as law firms reward the "rainmaker" partners who bring in the biggest clients, publishers are quickest to hand promotions and raises to the editors who bring in successful authors.[1]

---

1. As explained in the introduction, some editors have no acquisitions responsibility. But for all editors whose job descriptions include acquisitions, that role will typically be considered their most valuable one.

Even in houses that are not primarily commercial, editors are measured on their acquisitions. University presses and other not-for-profit firms need new titles just as much as big trade houses. In many houses, editors will have explicit "signing goals"—sometimes a specific number of titles acquired per year, more often a minimum dollar value of projected sales for the titles signed. In others the target is left vague, but you can be sure someone in management is keeping track. When I worked at Crown Publishers, a division of Random House, I was never given a signing goal, but I remember the head of another division remarking, "A senior editor at this place has to bring in a million dollars a year to pay the rent." That was in the 1990s; the number may be higher now.

In the aggregate, acquisition is important because it determines the success of a publisher's list. No matter what magic its editors can work on manuscripts, they must first find books to publish that will fulfill the house's mission—and please an audience. Alas, no amount of brilliant editing can turn an unsalable book into a winner. My former boss and mentor, Tom McCormack of St. Martin's Press, liked to quote a line from the film *Chariots of Fire*, where a canny veteran track coach says to a would-be Olympic sprinter, "I can find you two steps in the hundred."[2] Two steps in the hundred is often all that editing can add to a manuscript. The valuable editor is one who builds a stable of Olympic-caliber writers.

Acquisitions also determine the identity of a publisher's list—or in market terms, its brand. Some houses are known for bestselling commercial fiction (Putnam, for instance); some for high-quality literature (FSG, Knopf, and indies like Coffee House and Graywolf); some for elegantly produced lifestyle and cooking books (Clarkson Potter). University presses tend to have strengths in certain disciplines. Repeated success in a category has multiple benefits for a firm. It builds up the house's skill sets for publishing in that area—its knowledge of what works and doesn't, and its relationship with that community of readers. And this success burnishes the house's reputation for such books with media, booksellers, and consumers. Thus begins a virtuous cycle, attracting more submissions from authors and agents in the same field.

At the other end of the scale, one single title can change the fortunes of a company. Bloomsbury was a respected but small house in London when it bought J. K. Rowling's first Harry Potter novel; before the Potter series ended,

2. McCormack cites the scene (and acknowledges slightly misquoting the script) in his insightful book *The Fiction Editor, the Novelist, and the Novel* (Philadelphia: Paul Dry Books, 2006), 160.

. . . .

Bloomsbury's annual sales had risen 500 percent and it had become one of the five largest publishers in Britain. The not-for-profit New Press, which publishes a cutting-edge list of progressive books and struggled for years to do better than break even, found a long-running *New York Times* bestseller in *The New Jim Crow*, which put the company solidly in the black and allowed it to plan for the future.

THE PROCESS

When publishers speak of "the acquisition process," they usually mean the specific procedures within a house for making a contract offer on a given work. In truth, the process of acquiring books begins long before an editor brings a project to an editorial meeting. The dynamics and techniques of acquisition vary somewhat from one category of publishing to another, and the chapters that follow will discuss some of those differences. But broadly speaking, most acquiring editors do similar things, beginning with the hunt for exciting books and for authors who show the promise of writing them.

Step 1 might be called "Schmoozing and Scouting." An editor spends a lot of time networking with writers and people who can connect him to writers—especially, in the case of trade editors, with literary agents. It is, I must report, untrue that Manhattan editors spend most of their time having three-martini lunches in elegant restaurants, but breaking bread (and hoisting a glass) with agents is in fact part of the job, because having good relationships with your key source of projects is vitally important.

Academic editors, of both monographs and textbooks, will deal with agents occasionally, but more often they get out among academics themselves, visiting campuses and attending scholarly conferences. They are hoping professors will tell them about their own works in progress and also provide leads to other books and authors (their graduate students, for instance).

No matter how many agents they know, the best editors don't sit at their desks waiting for the next bestseller to arrive in their email; they go scouting for it. Scouting takes many forms. It may be attending writers' conferences or visiting MFA writing programs. It may be reading literary magazines or surfing the web, looking for a story or essay that catches your eye, then contacting the author. (Since the advent of social media, many books have originated when an editor or agent queried the writer of a blog or even a Twitter feed.) It might be pursuing a public figure or celebrity and persuading her to write a book. In the early 1990s an editorial assistant at Bantam, Rob Weisbach, reached out to a hot young comedian/actress, Whoopi Goldberg. She had turned down more established editors' invitations to write a memoir, but Weisbach found she was interested in doing a children's book. Weisbach signed Goldberg's *Alice*; his initiative soon led him to acquiring a string of bestselling titles by TV stars like Jerry Seinfeld, Ellen DeGeneres, and Paul Reiser and propelled him from an assistant's desk to the helm of his own imprint.

The most satisfying form of scouting may be coming up with your own idea for a book, then seeking out someone to write it. An enterprising editor can usually find at least two or three potential book ideas in one day's edition of the newspaper. During the intense public debate around the 2007 surge of American troops in Iraq, I was surprised to find that there was no current book for a general audience that offered a historical perspective on counter-insurgency warfare. I contacted an experienced military historian, James R. Arnold, who swiftly delivered an excellent proposal for just such a book. It was published in 2009 as *Jungle of Snakes: A Century of Counterinsurgency Warfare from the Philippines to Iraq*. Creating a project from scratch this way has other advantages: the editor can tailor it with the author more directly than is possible otherwise, and by originating the idea, the editor can usually avoid the sort of competitive bidding situation that drives up the cost of acquisitions.

THE PUBLISHING DECISION

Once you have succeeded—whether by networking, prospecting, or dumb luck—in attracting a submission, the trickiest part of the process begins: making the publication decision. This begins with the editor's gut response: the spark I spoke of earlier. The editor must ask, *Do I want to invest my time and energy in this project?* As many of the contributors to this book point out, unless you're passionate about a book, publishing it is a mistake. To champion a book effectively among one's colleagues and in the world demands a high level of enthusiasm and commitment. It's readily apparent in an editorial or sales meeting when an editor is presenting a title without conviction. Furthermore, an author wants, and deserves, to have a publishing partner who's thrilled to bring her work to readers. And finally, publishing any book is a long, intensive, sometimes exhausting process. To undertake it on behalf of a book you're *not* passionate about is a recipe for burnout. All this is why trade publisher Jonathan Karp of Simon & Schuster lists as his Rule #1 simply "Love it."

In fairness, "love" may be too much to ask from someone in a textbook house or a university press weighing, say, a monograph on population genetics. Yet even in these specialized fields, there some projects that strike a spark—books that are intellectually exciting, that are written with special verve, or that deliver something of particular value to their readers.

. . . .

Beyond the editor's personal enthusiasm, there are larger issues to consider. How does this title fit into the house's mission and strategy? In scholarly publishing, titles are expected, in the traditional phrase, to be a "contribution to knowledge." This is part of the mission of any academic publisher, and a major purpose of the peer review process is to ensure that each book published meets the standards of its discipline and has something new to offer. But even those titles that pass muster academically may or may not fit well within the area where the publisher wants to concentrate. As noted above, most presses have areas of strength, or they may wish to develop others. Greg Britton of Johns Hopkins University Press, in his essay here, explains this in more depth.

At an independent literary publisher, the sense of mission may be defined in terms of "the ways these literary works might contribute to important cultural conversations" and with a "vision for social impact," as Jeff Shotts writes of his own house, Graywolf. But even large commercial houses have (in degrees varying by size and corporate culture) some guiding notion of what they seek to publish and what they're most effective at. A celebrity memoir, no matter how titillating, is unlikely to be a good fit on the upmarket literary list of FSG.

But let's assume the potential acquisition is right for the house and the editor is ablaze with passion. Now comes the nitty-gritty question: what is it worth? Every acquisition is a financial investment. The house must decide what advance against royalties to offer the author. In theory this would equal a sum the publisher is confident will be earned out over time, but in practice he may be competing with several other houses, and the winning bidder may need to offer more, even much more, than the book's projected royalty earnings.

Royalty schedules are complicated and vary among categories of publishing, but typical royalties range from about 10 percent of total sales to 25 or 30 percent; in trade books these are, confusingly, often computed on the stated (list) price of a book rather than the publisher's actual (net) receipts after accounting for discounts to the retailers or wholesalers who sell the book. It is quite possible for the publisher to earn a profit even if the author's advance goes unearned—the million-dollar advances that are often reported in the media are seldom earned out. It is also true that overpaying on the advance is the commonest reason for a book's losing money.

In small press or academic publishing, advances may be small or even zero, for publication itself may be the most valuable currency for a scholar. But even with no advance, the publisher must be sure that a title's sales revenues will exceed the costs of bringing it to market (which include some share of overhead—staff salaries, rent, and the like—as well as title-specific expenses such as advertising). So every publisher, for every potential acquisition, must ask, *How many copies of this can we sell, and at what price?*

Editors use a fairly simple spreadsheet tool called a profit-and-loss worksheet, or P&L, to make this calculation. Editors often run several variations on the P&L to arrive at one where the numbers (a) are plausible enough to persuade the management and (b) at the same time project enough royalties to justify a competitive advance.

What makes publishing unusually challenging as a business is that every new title is a unique product. One book is not the same as the next, even within categories. This cozy mystery novel may be completely unlike the hardboiled one beside it on the shelf; a gluten-free cookbook sits next to a German one. The marketing or publicity campaign for one title on a publisher's list cannot be replicated to sell another one (with some important exceptions, discussed below). Thus each new publication is, in a sense, reinventing the wheel. For the same reason, predicting the sales of a prospective new book is highly difficult. For every publisher, it amounts to an exercise in educated guesswork.

This is not to say it's a matter of picking numbers out of a hat. There are several sources of information that can help an editor assess a project's sales potential. The first is the author's track record. This is by no means an infallible guide, especially if his new book is unlike its predecessors. But today editors as well as buyers at every book retailer have ready access to each writer's sales history via industry sales databases such as Bookscan, and the buyers use them to make *their* sales estimates, so these numbers tend to set the range of expectations.

More broadly, editors refer to "comp titles" (short for comparable or competitive)—other works that are similar to the new book in terms of their content, likely readership, or expected sales history. Selecting the right comps is a key task for an editor lobbying for an acquisition, and editors spend a surprising amount of time mulling these choices—chewing them over with colleagues, scanning the shelves of bookshops, and looking up online to see "customers who bought this title also bought _____."

There are also data points external to the book itself—for instance, the author's "platform." This term has become an industry cliché and mocked as such, but publishers, quite reasonably, have always been attuned to the prominence of an author. Platform simply means an author's ability to command the attention of readers, or in some cases of intermediaries, such as the media, that can do so. Today this may be easier to measure, at least in terms of social media followers, which is why popular bloggers or YouTube sensations get book deals. But an author's platform includes intangibles such as his credentials. If the author is a doctor at a leading medical school who has pioneered a new treatment for obesity, that's a significant element of his platform; if the same doctor has appeared frequently on television to discuss it, that adds another dimension. For a chef writing a cookbook, a really hot new restaurant may be enough of a platform to sell a book—but a hugely popular Instagram account would enhance it.

Such credentials may not be directly translatable into sales figures, but they help give the publisher confidence that the book will earn favorable media exposure, which is a crucial part of attracting readers. Platform tends to be most relevant, and easiest to understand, with well-defined nonfiction subjects, but a memoirist or a crime novelist may have a platform too—a lively fan following on Facebook or a network of influential supporters in his field. (In part IV, Diana Gill discusses how this may be valuable for genre fiction authors.)

Mind you, for a small number of prospective acquisitions it's possible to project sales with a high degree of confidence—for example, those by authors with consistently bestselling track records, and especially those who write in a series or follow a consistent formula. It was a pretty good bet that the sales of Sue Grafton's Kinsey Millhone mystery *T Is for Trespass* would be very similar to those of *S Is for Silence*, featuring the same sleuth. What makes publishers covet titles like these is that they offer the rare opportunity *not* to invent the wheel: in these cases you have a clear idea of who the audience is, and you know that previous marketing campaigns have worked to sell something almost identical. Perhaps you'll make a few tweaks in the hope of improving the sales, but starting off with a winning template is a leap forward in both efficiency and confidence. Such predictability is so valuable, especially when the revenues are large, that a publisher will often willingly accept very modest profits on a bestselling title, paying the author an advance much larger than she would earn at the contractual royalty rate.

External data can get you only so far, though, in evaluating a project. Even an author with an impressive track record may, unfortunately, come in with an uninspiring manuscript or proposal: her novel may be misplotted or his reportage focused on too esoteric a subject. Conversely, a first-time writer, or one who has never had a major success, may suddenly deliver a book in which everything comes together. An editor should take account of track record, platform, and other factors, but always judge the book itself on the merits.

I often think acquisitions can be assessed along three axes: author, subject, and execution. Obviously, the ideal acquisition combines a bestselling author, an exciting subject, and superb writing. But a project that ranks high even on two out of three of these can be a viable one to publish. For instance, the lives of families in a Mumbai slum might seem a topic doomed to modest sales. But journalist Katherine Boo wrote about them so vividly and empathically that her book *Behind the Beautiful Forevers* became a bestseller. Though Boo was a first-time book author, her stature as an award-winning journalist helped her publisher, Random House, to attract reviewers to her work; the quality of her writing did the rest. Or imagine a popular historian with an outstanding track record. If he writes about a relatively obscure subject, but does so brilliantly, the resulting book is likely to find an audience. Ditto if he chooses a hugely popular topic—the founding fathers, say, or World War II—even if he turns in a mediocre manuscript. (If the same author picks an offbeat subject *and* writes a subpar book, that spells trouble.) So perhaps editors should pin the immortal lyrics of the song by Meat Loaf to their corkboards: *Two out of three ain't bad.*

The most important question the editor must answer about any acquisition is *Who is the audience for this book?* It's not enough to be excited about a book—the publisher's job is to put that book in the hands of readers, and that begins with having some idea of who they are.

It was working at a university press that brought this point home to me. Academic publishing, because it's organized by disciplines, focuses with great clarity on who the readership is for a given work: will scholars in *this* subject area need to read *this* book? The peer review process helps answer that question—it's not just a quality check but a valuable form of market research. Textbook publishing typically begins with the intended audience, students in a specific course, and works backward to a proposal, as Peter Coveney explains in his essay here.

In trade publishing, editors are sometimes swept away by "the writing" and pursue a project without focusing on who it will be marketed to, or with a vague idea that it will appeal to "general readers." This is dangerous. I once heard my former colleague Michael Denneny, a shrewd and experienced editor, say, "There's no such thing as a 'general reader.' There are 473 kinds of specialized readers!" His random number was meant to suggest that every reader has a bundle of interests—for one it might include architecture,

....

baseball, sixties music, Asian travel, literary fiction, and so on, while for another it might be gluten-free cooking, social justice, queer theory, and mystery novels. Both of those people would be "general readers," but they are unlikely to walk out of a bookstore with the same titles. Marketing a new book means identifying and reaching out to the right constituencies.

Even outside of academic disciplines, sometimes identifying a work's audience is straightforward: think of a Civil War history, a quilting guide, or *Personal Finance for Dummies*. But for a literary novel, or many works of narrative nonfiction, the audience may be harder to pin down. This is another place where comp titles are important. A title like *Behind the Beautiful Forevers* should be of interest to readers of *Maximum City*, a successful earlier book that offered a gritty portrait of Mumbai; but it could also appeal, less obviously, to readers interested in the struggles of ordinary people elsewhere in the developing world, such as those who made a bestseller out of *A Long Way Gone*, the memoir of a boy soldier in Sierra Leone. (Note, by the way, that these comps might lead you to both the Asian-travel enthusiast reader I conjured above and the social-justice believer, respectively.) Recognizing this sort of potential allows an editor to pitch the book more effectively in-house during the acquisition process, and ultimately to readers as well. In an online universe, all of the potentially marketable aspects of a book (#Mumbai, #families, #slum, #deeplyreported, #socialjustice, and so on) can be made searchable as metadata—digital tags that carry information about each work—to aid in its discoverability to readers. This is a capability publishers are only now beginning to master and another way in which the internet is a boon to them.

Do I seem to be talking about marketing here, rather than acquisitions? In fact, the two are inextricable. If the first rule of acquisitions is *Never buy a book you don't love*, the second rule is *Never buy a book unless you know who the audience for it is, and how you are going to sell it to them*.

Start describing your would-be acquisition to a veteran sales rep, and he'll cut right to the chase with this question: *What's the handle?* I love *handle* as a term of publishing art because it's such a clear image: the thing you grab onto to explain why someone would buy a book. The author's platform, or the comp titles, might be part of the handle: "Beginner-friendly seafood recipes from the 2016 winner of Top Chef" or "A probing, dystopian literary novel in the tradition of *The Handmaid's Tale* or *The Children of Men*." But the handle may also express other unique elements of the book: "A groundbreaking new study of the connection between gun laws and violent crime" or "A graphic novel that brings the anarchic spirit of Captain Underpants to the world of paranormal romance." A good handle not only conveys something about the content of a work but suggests why certain readers will be drawn to it.

At some houses where I've worked, before having a contract approved, editors were required to draft a marketing tipsheet for the title, beginning with the handle (or "keynote," as such documents often call it). It was a chore to do this paperwork when one was in hot pursuit of a book, but I was invariably glad, once it was acquired, to have gone through the exercise. Even if you don't distill the handle of your prospective acquisition down to a few pithy lines, it's invaluable to have a clear sense of the marketing strategy when it comes time to publish.

After the What and Who questions comes the equally critical How. That is, *How are we going to get this in front of readers?* The editor should think about how the house can launch this particular title into the marketplace. For instance, popular fiction is an intensely competitive category, but if a novel is a potential book-group choice, it may be a candidate for mass-merchandise programs such as Pennie's Picks at Costco. (Independent stores and other chains also target book groups in their marketing.) How-to books can sometimes reach huge readerships through special sales channels like gourmet shops or sporting goods stores. And as suggested earlier, the publisher's experience in such markets can be a powerful asset, encouraging acquisitions in those niches. When a title has no such obvious channel—literary fiction, for instance, often doesn't—the editor looks for an interesting story behind the book that might attract publicity: the author was once a roadie for the Allman Brothers! Or an intriguing plot element or setting: a novel taking place in a beautifully realized Tuscany or Thailand is ripe for promotion via travel blogs and magazines.

CLOSING THE DEAL

So far I have described what might be called the prehistory of an acquisition: the trawling for properties that brings a project to the editor's desk and the thought process an editor and his colleagues go through in deciding to pursue it. Now comes what may be the most exciting part, or the most frustrating: reeling the book in.

How this unfolds will depend on whether the editor is competing with other houses or negotiating one to one with an author or agent. The latter is most common in scholarly publishing or with textbooks, where the editor may well have initiated the project. In trade publishing, a literary agent is usually involved, and when one is, there is typically a "multiple submission" to several houses at once.

. . . .

When the agent expects strong interest from publishers, there may be a formal auction held (by telephone or email) on a specific day. These may be simple "best bid" affairs, where each house makes one single offer, but really hotly contested ones often go in multiple rounds following rules prescribed in advance. These are the events that sometimes earn multimillion-dollar contracts for authors and make industry news—though auctions are inherently unpredictable. Some agents today tell me that frenzied auctions are less common than they were in the 1980s or 90s: they blame the mergers of commercial houses, which have reduced the number of players; the difficulties of the marketplace and flattened earnings across the industry, making publishers more cautious; and the much better sales information (on author track records and comp titles, thanks to tools like Bookscan) that force editors to be more realistic in their projections. But the concentration of commercial houses also means the quest for "big books" is still powerful, and hot properties still command huge numbers.

No matter how many houses are competing, buying a book actually requires an editor to sell—in two directions at once. First, the editor must sell the project to her colleagues. Unless she's the owner of the house, she will need to persuade a publisher to authorize a bid, and in most companies this begins with generating enthusiasm and support from her colleagues. In an academic press, support from outside peer reviewers will also be required. Some houses have formal editorial or publishing boards, typically composed of representatives from editorial, marketing, and sales, that meet regularly to consider new acquisitions. In smaller houses—or larger ones under competitive time pressures—decisions may be made in an ad hoc meeting in someone's office. Regardless of procedures, though, the editor's task is get the rest of the house to share her excitement about a book and to see the opportunities it presents.

At the same time, the editor is selling her company to the author— convincing the writer that this house is the one he should choose to publish with. Often, and especially in an auction, this may just come down to offering the highest advance. For most authors a difference of even a thousand dollars is significant, and the advance is the most measurable index of publisher commitment. Still, savvy authors and their agents will also be concerned about other things, including how, and how well, the house promises to market the book or even to design it; how responsive the house will be to author input; and the publisher's past history with the author or with similar books in the category. (Publishers have track records too.)

Editors may go to great lengths in wooing authors, bringing them in to meet marketing and publicity staffers and writing up multipage marketing plans with details of author tours, social media campaigns, and the like. For one celebrity author I pursued at Crown, we not only mocked up a dust jacket for her memoir but created a full-color cardboard floor display loaded with dummy copies of her book to show how we intended to merchandise it in the chain stores.

One key point the author may be concerned about is how much the editor can help develop the manuscript. This is where editorial skill can become an acquisitions asset. It's not common, but I have known authors to turn down higher advances in order to work with an editor they thought "got" their book in a way her competitors did not. And editors known for being particularly gifted at a certain genre—Oxford's Sheldon Meyer in history or Faith Sale of Putnam in literary fiction, to name two legends—attract authors who want that editorial acumen, or simply that editor's imprimatur.

I have been speaking of the author as the editor's "customer" in this scenario. Yet especially in trade publishing, the sale is often brokered by a third party—the agent. Many authors rely heavily on the agent's seasoned judgment in making their final decision—especially when confronted by financially similar offers from different houses.

Publishing people love to complain, and literary agents are high on the list of editors' finest whines. Life would certainly be simpler for us if we didn't have agents forcing us to compete for books and driving up author advances. Also, since every percent of profit the agent adds to the author's share comes out of the publisher's, and vice versa, there's necessarily some adversarial element to their relationship.

Yet the good agents perform an essential role, both in supporting the careers of writers and in helping editors find quality work. Anyone who has read through the slush pile of unsolicited proposals in a publishing house will quickly understand why agents earn their keep. The best agents have clout with publishers because they consistently submit books well suited to those publishers' lists. Their intermediary function serves both parties: they can interpret the publisher's concerns to the author, making sure both sides understand what's being negotiated, and prevent the awkwardness that could arise if an editor, who needs to have an intimate working relationship with the author, has to haggle with him or her over royalties or contract boilerplate. The agents I admire most are tough negotiators but straight shooters, and they add value for both the author and the publisher in the process.

The final phase of the acquisition process is less glamorous than power lunching or battling through an auction, but no less crucial: the editor must negotiate a contract for publication—again, either directly with the author or with an agent. Publishing contracts, even in the digital age, are almost quaintly simple—typically ten to fifteen legal-size pages, almost all of which is standard boilerplate. (In contrast, movie contracts may be hundreds of pages.) The publisher's accepted offer will have spelled out a handful of deal points—advance, royalty rates, the length and delivery date of the manuscript, which territories the publisher has rights in, and some other items such as how house and author will split subsidiary rights income. The contract boilerplate will cover many other details of the publisher-author agreement, such as who is responsible for costs like maps, illustrations, or indexing; who indemnifies whom in the case of a lawsuit against the book (a key question for any nonfiction work about living people); and how soon the house must publish the book once it's delivered.

The one essential rule for negotiations: PUT IT IN WRITING, the motto long printed on the notepaper at the venerable William Morris Agency. Any provision that isn't carefully recorded is subject to the vagaries of recollection and may lead to acrimony later. In an auction I prefer to make at least my first bid by email, putting all the deal points on the written record; if I improve terms by telephone in later rounds, I keep written notes of the calls and confirm by email afterward.

Both because publishing still maintains a tradition of gentility and because most publishers and agencies have settled on boilerplate terms in prior contracts, I have rarely found contract negotiating to be contentious—though there always exceptions, sometimes memorable ones. On occasion—most often, and ironically, when there has been little bargaining over the advance—agents will choose to pick a battle over some minor contract clause simply to show their clients they're fighting for them. But in general, by the time the fine print is being negotiated, publisher and author have decided to commit to one another, so both sides are motivated to agree. And rather than grabbing every possible nickel off the table, a good editor wants the author to be happy with the contract.

Finally the moment arrives when all the clauses have been thrashed out, the contract is signed, and a check is winging its way to the author. The book has been acquired! This is always one of the high points in an editor's working week. The editor can bask in her job well done—for a moment. Then she turns and opens the next submission.

2 THE ALCHEMY OF ACQUISITIONS
TWELVE RULES FOR TRADE EDITORS

· ·

JONATHAN KARP

When I think about the alchemy of trade book acquisitions, I recall two conversations—one with a tenacious editor and the other with a billionaire investor.

The tenacious editor was feeling anxious. He'd been acquiring books for several years, and hardly any of his beloved discoveries had become best-sellers. Several had sold in only minimal quantities, though many had received favorable review attention. I tried to lift his spirits by noting that having three commercially successful books for every ten published would be considered a great track record. "How are you going to feel the other seven times?" I asked him. "Is every book that misses the mark going to feel like a public death?"

"Yes," he said. "Each book that misses feels like a personal failure."

The billionaire investor had a different view. When I told him that a successful acquisitions editor might average three hits for every ten books published, he said, "That sounds right. It's about the same for my business."

In other words, a book editor can succeed three times out of ten and feel like a professional loser, while an investor can succeed three out of ten and become a billionaire. It's all a matter of perspective.

Let's acknowledge that devoting a good part of your career to acquiring books is a strange way to earn a living: being the first filter through which books pass. The acquisitions editor serves many roles—cultural gatekeeper, personal shopper for the leisure class, talent scout, trend sniffer, crusader, rabble-rouser, proselytizer, muse, keeper of golden-egged geese and flatulent turkeys, profit loser and profit center.

There is no single way to become an acquisitions editor. Many rise after

JONATHAN KARP began his publishing career in 1989 at Random House, rising from editorial assistant to editor in chief over the course of sixteen years. Since then, he has worked at the Hachette Book Group as the founding publisher and editor-in-chief of Twelve, and at Simon & Schuster as president and publisher of the company's flagship imprint. His writing has been published in the *New York Times Magazine*, the *American Scholar*, *GQ*, *Slate*, and the *Washington Post*.

beginning as editorial assistants. Others enter the business after working for magazines or other journalistic and literary enterprises. No matter how they got to where they are, there aren't many of them. All of the editors acquiring for the five major adult trade publishers wouldn't even fill a Broadway theater, and if you asked them afterward what they thought of the show they just saw together, they would probably disagree on just about everything—the quality of the work, whether it was too long or too short, whether the leading man was annoying or charming, and whether the show would run for a week or a year.

I've been acquiring books for twenty-five years, and there are times in the acquisitions process when I don't even agree with myself! Years ago, I derided a competitor for publishing a book on the history of the potato, a subject for which I couldn't imagine much of a readership. This view did not prevent me from approving the acquisition of journalist Jonathan Waldman's history of rust, an even more arcane subject. We bought it because all of us who read the proposal were so enthusiastic about the author's approach to telling the story that we decided to ignore the question *Who wants to read a book about rust?* To our collective delight, the book earned many favorable reviews and has sold respectably enough to cover our costs.

On visiting my local bookstores, I have found equally questionable endeavors: *Aging Backwards: Reverse the Aging Process and Look 10 Years Younger in 30 Minutes a Day* (it takes *chutzpah* to put a scientific impossibility in your book title with no irony); *The Internet Is Not the Answer* (but what *is* the answer?); and *Lesser Beasts: A Snout to Tail History of the Humble Pig* (clever subtitle, but I suspect the vast majority of readers will keep kosher). I could cite numerous other examples, but then again I'm the guy who published a book about rust, so I'll stop casting stones. Instead I'll offer some general rules for thinking about trade acquisitions, with these underlying assumptions:

- The target audience is the typical book browser (not a toddler, or an accountant seeking to study tax law, or a philosopher researching theories of esotericism).
- The key objective is to sell enough books (and earn enough revenue) to keep both the author and the publisher financially solvent while making some incalculable contribution to culture. Your place on the art-to-commerce spectrum will depend on your company's mission and financial condition, your supervisor's management philosophy, and your sense and sensibility.

RULE #1: LOVE IT

This is the most common advice given by acquisitions editors, but it raises questions. Is it possible to love many books at the same time without winding up in a polyamorous predicament? Would it be easier on the editor's heart to arrange a few marriages of convenience?

Some editors fall in love too easily. Others withhold their love with such discipline that it's an event whenever they want to buy something. Regardless of whether the editor is a puppy dog or an ascetic, the inescapable truth is that each new acquisition marks the beginning of a relationship, one in which you will be reading an author's work closely and engaging in what is usually an extensive conversation and collaboration. If you don't begin that relationship with enthusiasm or desire, the project is likely to become a grind or a burden.

Love at first sight isn't necessary. Arranged marriages can succeed; you can grow to love your partner. But if you don't feel intrigued or excited by the prospect of the book, and if you don't think you'll feel a sense of accomplishment at seeing the result of your work on your bookshelf in the future, then you shouldn't acquire it, no matter how much business sense it might seem to make. There are better ways for the company to make money.

RULE #2: WAIT FOR AUTHORITY

Whether the work is fiction or nonfiction, readers respect authors who deeply understand their subject. It's apparent when a writer is in command. The voice is more assured, the details are precise, the momentum builds, and there is meaning between the lines. Often there is wit, because the author knows the material well enough to relax and show a sense of humor. There is a point of view.

It can take some authors years to develop authority, and this command is the surest justification for asking readers to devote hours of their time to a book.

It's possible for someone who deeply understands a subject to write an authoritative book in less than twelve months, but it's unlikely. Many works of award-winning caliber take at least eighteen months to research and write, and often the time is measured in years rather than months. The 2015 and 2014 winners of the Pulitzer Prize for fiction, Anthony Doerr and Donna Tartt, each took about a decade to write their books. Editors should learn to recognize when a book will be worth the wait, contractual due date or not.

....

RULE #3: IF YOU CRY, BUY!

I once asked Jamie Raab, a publisher at the Hachette Book Group, why she had the confidence to spend a vast sum to acquire a first novel. She responded, "I cried at the last page." Her reaction was purely emotional, and she was right not to overthink it. *The Notebook* by Nicholas Sparks went on to become a phenomenon and launched Sparks's career as a bestselling author.

Often the books readers most enthusiastically embrace are the ones they experience emotionally, not just intellectually. Trust your emotions (as long as you're not an overly emotional or weepy person).

RULE #4: MAKE A PROMISE, HAVE A PURPOSE

Although there might be some altruistic readers out there who hope to better the world through their book purchases, many potential consumers are probably asking, "What's in it for me?" as they search for something to read next. The works most likely to appeal to them are the ones that make them the most direct and appealing promise. *How to Win Friends and Influence People*: Who wouldn't want to know how to do that? *What to Expect When You're Expecting* is at once reassuring and prophetic—just what anxious parents-to-be need before their lives are thrown into upheaval.

In 2015 the nation's number-one nonfiction bestseller was *The Life-Changing Magic of Tidying Up*—an inspired promise, because it is within every lazy slob's reach and does not strain credulity.

In the case of fiction, the promise might be escape or artistry.

Assiduously researched works can make a promise or have a purpose, too. The author might be offering a definitive account or the answer to a persistent mystery.

Ultimately, you should be convinced that the author has as strong a purpose for writing the book as readers would have for buying it.

RULE #5: RESIST THE URGE TO ACQUIRE IN SLOW PERIODS

One of my colleagues, when asked by strangers what he does for a living, tells them, "I read bad books so you don't have to."

But what happens when the book isn't bad? What if it's good but not great? The most frequent comment I hear from less experienced acquisitions editors is "I'm on the fence."

If you're on the fence, get off, don't buy it, and find something else to read. To paraphrase Sky Masterson in *Guys and Dolls*: you'll know when your love comes along.

If you're like me and capable of talking yourself into falling in love, I offer this cautionary tale: One weekend I didn't have many submissions to read, and I didn't have many books lined up for publication the next year. An agent sent me a proposal for a nonfiction book on the number seven. On the surface it seemed like a thin idea for a book (why would anyone want to read an entire book about a number?), but the author made an excellent case for the primacy of seven in our lives, and it seemed like it could be a fun, breezy read that could be produced quickly. I acquired it.

Ultimately, my first instinct proved correct. Though it was an interesting and attractive work, our book on the number seven sold about that many copies. The lesson I learned was to resist the temptation to acquire in idle periods, even though that temptation can be strong. Book editors are paid to come into the office to acquire books, just as Pentagon officials are paid to come into the office to defend the United States of America. Consequently the military-industrial complex continuously expands, and so do publishers' lists. We each have a bias to action, and financial targets to meet, and yes feels better than no. The result is bloat.

RULE #6: DON'T BE CYNICAL

There are certain books for which there is almost always an audience. If you promise immediate weight loss, ecstatic sex, or grounds for impeaching the president, your books have a better chance for broad distribution. A competitor who specialized in mass-market paperbacks once told me, "Sometimes we have to check our brains at the door." This perspective is soul-crushing at best and pernicious at its worst (when the publisher reinforces malignant tropes in the culture).

There are certain books with great visceral appeal, but they have to withstand scrutiny. Maybe there's an author capable of convincing me that *The Macaroni and Cheese Diet* will reduce my waistline and boost my productivity while also improving my sex life, but the evidence would have to be compelling.

Don't assume that a book will sell because the author is famous, or connected to someone famous, or capable of getting publicity. A personality in search of an idea is a waste of time.

Be wary of sequels, especially in memoirs and other works of nonfiction. It's generous and egalitarian to believe that each of us has a good book in us. Whether or not that's true, it seems unlikely that each of us has *two* good books in us.

A prominent literary agent once tried to convince me to pay a large advance for an author's second memoir, even though the conventional wisdom in the publishing industry is that second memoirs sell about half of what the first memoir sells. When the agent insisted our sales would increase for memoirs #2 and #3, I asked him to name one author whose subsequent memoirs had outsold his first book.

After a long pause, he finally responded: "Proust."

RULE 7: TELL ME SOMETHING I DON'T KNOW

Chris Matthews always used to end his Sunday-morning TV show with a segment called "Tell Me Something I Don't Know," in which his guests had to offer one piece of news. On an elemental level, books serve the same purpose. The "tell" should be apparent.

On some hot topics, such as abortion or gun rights or immigration, readers can't be told anything because they've already made up their minds. Other topics may not seem urgent enough to require their attention. An agent once submitted a book proposal on procrastination to me, and I decided not to acquire it on the assumption that readers would never get around to buying it.

It may seem unlikely that there's anything "new" to be said about great historical figures who have been the subject of many biographies, but a talented writer with a keen eye and a commitment to examining the subject with close scrutiny can provide a fresh perspective. We've published works on Julius Caesar, William Shakespeare, and Abraham Lincoln which provoked conversations. The authors had devoted years of their professional lives to studying their subjects. Their conclusions were not front-page news, but scholars and other close readers found value in their perspective. If you read enough book reviews, you'll come across this line: "Every generation gets the biography it deserves."

RULE 8: KNOW THE AUDIENCE

One reason editors tend to specialize in certain categories is that they become familiar with the tastes of the most active buyers in those categories. An experienced editor of crime fiction might have a more sophisticated understanding of when a novel is too wild or too mild for the intended audience. A sophisticated reader of literary fiction will have a sense of which authors write the kind of novels likely to command attention among the influential reviewers. A history editor will know whether the week's "new" Lincoln biography on submission says anything distinctive enough to spark commentary.

Conversely, an editor who really knows her market may spot a niche that hasn't been filled. As the publisher of the Amistad imprint at HarperCollins,

Dawn Davis pursued an opportunity to acquire the first book by radio personality Steve Harvey. He was not yet a well-known name among New York City book editors, but Dawn knew how popular he was among African American listeners. She also helped him come up with the title *Act like a Lady, Think like a Man.* The result was one of the bestselling books of 2011. She knew the audience.

RULE #9: HAVE YOUR OWN IDEAS...

Great acquisitions editors are always thinking of books they'd like to publish. Ann Godoff suggested to her author Ron Chernow that he write a biography of John D. Rockefeller. At Random House, Kate Medina pursued Tom Brokaw for a long time before he wrote *The Greatest Generation.* Scribner publisher Nan Graham sent her favorite fiction to Don DeLillo for many years, in the hope he would eventually join her at Scribner. He ultimately did.

In the early 1980s Simon & Schuster editor Alice Mayhew was sharing a cab home with a young magazine reporter. She asked him to write a group biography of the men most responsible for America's international leadership after World War II. The writer was Walter Isaacson, and that book marked the beginning of an editorial relationship that's lasted more than thirty years and included such bestsellers as *Benjamin Franklin, Einstein,* and *Steve Jobs.*

John Kilcullen was a sales rep for Bantam Books when he heard an anecdote about a bookstore customer who had asked for a basic introductory book on a computer language, DOS, that would give an explanation simple enough for a dummy. Kilcullen founded IDG Books Worldwide, publisher of the For Dummies series, which has since sold over 150 million copies.

RULE #10: ...BUT DON'T THINK YOUR IDEAS
ARE BETTER THAN THE AUTHOR'S

If your vision for the book is stronger than the author's, don't acquire the book—unless you're planning to rewrite it on your weekends.

A good editor can cut excess while also seeing gaps. Ultimately, though, it's up to the author to fill those gaps. If the author can't provide the necessary perspective, it's unlikely that you will, and it isn't your responsibility to do so. You're also unlikely to be able to fix work that's inherently flawed. Editors with a messiah complex are likely to see their books crucified by reviewers.

I once had an idea for a comic murder mystery called *Dead Housewives of New Jersey*, in which participants in a noxious reality TV show would get bumped off by an unknown killer. As brilliant as I think my idea is (it's hard to be objective about one's own ideas), I'm certain that the novel would succeed only if the author were even more imaginative.

RULE #11: BEWARE OF MOVING TARGETS

I once heard that a prestigious publisher refused to acquire any biography of a living person because it can't be definitive or impartial until the subject's life is over. Unfortunately, this publisher has since issued many biographies of people who seem very much alive, so the rumor is false, but there's still wisdom to be gleaned. It's possible to write an interesting book about a living figure, but unless you believe people don't change, it seems unlikely that the biography will be the one that endures. Sources tend to be more cooperative when the Elvis in question has left the building.

Similarly, proposals for nonfiction books on stories-in-progress or works in which the narrative will be built entirely from the author's observations are risky. It may be a worthwhile risk, especially if the characters are complex and the story has an inherent narrative arc, if you can see the opportunity for a dramatic resolution. But if you're unsure where the story might go and the writer is unproven, there's no reason to be confident things will end well.

Finally, beware of hot topics. By the time the book has been researched, written, edited, copyedited, designed, manufactured, and distributed, that "hot" topic will have probably be as cool as a bowl of gazpacho. Also, you'll be competing not just against other book publishers but against the news media and anyone with capable of posting a coherent sentence online. Proceed with such endeavors only if your author has an exclusive angle that you're sure readers will want badly enough to pay for even in a sea of free or competing information.

RULE 12: HAVE CONVICTION

Great editors push hard for the works they want to publish. Robert Gottlieb had to rally support behind Joseph Heller's *Catch-22* when he was a young editor at Simon & Schuster. Years later another young Simon & Schuster editor, Morgan Entrekin, had to lobby on behalf of *Less than Zero* by Bret Easton Ellis. In both of these cases, editors championed fresh generational voices and helped to shape the literary consciousness of their era.

I wasn't at Simon & Schuster when Gottlieb and Entrekin advocated on behalf of their novelists, but I have been an eyewitness to books acquired by many current Simon & Schuster editors. One of the very best, Editor in Chief Marysue Rucci, felt such conviction about a novelist named Matthew

Thomas that we did not hesitate to make an offer for his first novel, *We Are Not Ourselves*. She knew the audience (readers of sophisticated fiction who love books with a strong female protagonist). She had a purpose (to give voice to an indelible portrait of the impact of Alzheimer's disease on a family). And to top it all off, the novel made Marysue cry, so she was certain of its emotional power. Upon its publication, *We Are Not Ourselves* was an instant bestseller and one of the best-reviewed books of 2014.

If you're a new editor, your fresh perspective is the one advantage you'll have over the weathered veterans who have been evaluating manuscripts for years. If a new voice speaks to you, persist in your crusade on behalf of that writer. The lack of a successful precedent is often used as a reason for not publishing a book, but it can also be the reason that a book will connect with the public: precisely because no writer has ever done it quite this way, and quite this well, before. Carolyn Reidy, the chief executive officer of Simon & Schuster, recalls the tentative feelings colleagues expressed when Frank McCourt's memoir *Angela's Ashes* was being considered for acquisition. "We were hesitant at that point because the belief was the Irish don't buy books about themselves. And this was a memoir of harsh poverty, told through the child's point of view. But the writing was so gorgeous and the point of view so unique, we persuaded ourselves that spending $125,000 for it was okay."

Since then *Angela's Ashes* has sold over 2.5 million copies.

To this point I've refrained from addressing my own accomplishments as an acquisitions editor because I'm mindful of how one of my former Random House colleagues, Jason Epstein, described himself when accepting a National Book Award medal for "distinguished contributions to American letters." He characterized his relationship to literature as "that of a valet." Our work is supposed to be in the margins, and while I feel a sense of accomplishment about certain acquisitions, I have had many more misses than hits, just like the colleague to whom I alluded at the start of this essay. Nevertheless, most editors have a few favorite tales we like to tell, so here are my top three:

The best discovery I ever made was *Seabiscuit*, the first book by Laura Hillenbrand. I had no idea it would become such a fixture on the best-seller list. All I thought at the time was that the story had an inherently good dramatic structure: the horse kept winning against all odds. Laura brought expertise and focus to the subject—it was clear she felt a personal connection to the material—and ultimately she wrote the book with remarkable perception and feeling.

My most fortuitous acquisition was Bruce Springsteen and Frank Caruso's illustrated western *Outlaw Pete*, the tragic tale of a bank-robbing baby. Other publishers passed, but I was thrilled by the prospect of publishing a great songwriter whose work has meant so much to me, and the book itself was beguiling. Two years later, because Simon & Schuster had enthusiastically published *Outlaw Pete*, we were offered the exclusive opportunity to read the completed manuscript of Bruce Springsteen's autobiography, *Born to Run*—the best memoir I've had the privilege of editing.

Similarly, I was given the opportunity to publish my favorite novelist, John Irving, after repeatedly declaring my love for his work to anyone who asked (for more than 20 years). Eventually, through a passing remark I reflexively made to someone I barely knew, he heard, and gave me a chance. In these instances I was like Charlie, the boy in Willy Wonka's chocolate factory: good rewards come to you if you truly love the chocolate.

I don't see a sweeping pattern to explain why some of my other acquisitions succeeded and others failed. There are data scientists who are trying to create a computer program capable of determining a work's commercial appeal. Even if they succeed—and some claim they already have—I hope such a program becomes just another tool in the acquisitions process, along with sales data and social media metrics. The personal impulse will remain the most powerful factor because book buying is an impulsive act. We are attempting to create desire among readers with the publication of each new book. To remove desire from the process, to reduce acquisitions to the mechanics of big data, would remove the beating heart from publishing's life force.

So we will proceed with our impulses, our "gut," our quasi-arbitrary rules, our own pattern recognition. Like billionaire investors, we will fail more than we succeed, and many of us will come to believe that other than "I love you," the most satisfying words in life are "You were right." We will read thousands of submissions a year and reject most of them. We will pay so much money for some "bestsellers" that they will be unprofitable, and we will come to regard them as personal disappointments even though they look like cultural triumphs to the rest of the world. We will publish many books that are assailed, ignored, or forgotten.

Yet every now and then, we will read something that knocks us out and enlightens us or moves us or elevates us in a way no other book has quite done. And it will all be worth it.

3 THINKING LIKE A SCHOLARLY EDITOR

THE HOW AND WHY OF ACADEMIC PUBLISHING

· ·

GREGORY M. BRITTON

Universities exist to create and transmit knowledge. They employ scholars, researchers, and teachers—and those who support them—to think about ideas and to share what they think. These are fundamentally liberal institutions that believe in free inquiry, creative expression, and the life of the mind. Scholarly publishing exists to support this activity in its many iterations. We publish books of these ideas, fix them in enduring forms, and disseminate them as widely as we realistically can. In fact, it is this challenge that brings us back to campus each day.

Scholarly editors sometimes hear new ideas as they are just forming. We see prototypes of inventions that can be dazzling. We see the products of enormous creativity as they are being created. By its very nature, acquiring scholarly books can be a heady job. Our role is to help it all happen, to bring our professional acumen to the table and publish all this great stuff.

What we mean by "publishing" in this context is selecting, shaping, vetting, and producing books and then connecting them with their readers— mostly other scholars who need them—in a way that is responsible and sustainable. This is harder than it sounds because as important as this work may be, it rarely reaches an audience big enough to support its publication in a purely economic sense. This means that scholarly editors need to be creative, strategic, and opportunistic.

To put it in less idealistic terms, what editors do is acquire intellectual property that will make both an important scholarly contribution and a return on the publisher's investment. We make bets on certain projects—proposals

GREGORY M. BRITTON is editorial director of Johns Hopkins University Press, where he oversees the publishing of the press's 170 new books annually. He also acquires its list in higher education studies. Greg serves on the management team that oversees the press's substantial book and journal programs, distribution service, and Project Muse. Prior to his appointment at Hopkins, Britton directed Getty Publications at the J. Paul Getty Trust, the largest museum publishing program in America. He is active in both the Association of American Publishers and the Association of American University Presses, which presented to him its 2016 Constituency Award.

and manuscripts—in hope that those bets will pay off. Editors assemble portfolios of this property, which we call *lists*. We protect that property with legal instruments called contracts. Publishers market, sell, and license that property, all in hopes of delivering impact for these ideas while generating revenue for the press and author. As a group, scholarly editors are entrepreneurs and take chances on new authors, novel projects, and groundbreaking ideas that we hope will deliver those returns. Some of us are careful, methodical, and strategic in our moves. Some of us are just plain lucky, although luck is not an acquisitions strategy.

Editors cannot rely solely on intuition; we work to develop a keen sense of what might work and what probably will not. Scholarly editors develop this skill by doing our homework: We read articles. We talk with authors and scholars. We attend academic conferences and workshops. We look for college course syllabi online and audit online courses. We poke around campus bookstores. We monitor trends in disciplines to see where the intellectual core is and what might be emerging on its margins. Acquiring a project at a discipline's core might have one type of impact, while picking one on the leading edge of a field will have a very different pattern of influence and, possibly, sales.

Scholarly editors know that we have two bottom lines. One measures the scholarly merit of a project, how well it is reviewed, and how great its impact might be in its field. The other measures its commercial viability, how well it sells. Although many scholarly publishers are nonprofit organizations, the books they publish need to return some portion of their cost (preferably all of it) in sales. This is not for crass commercial reasons—no one is getting rich from scholarly publishing—but because even nonprofit publishers need to make enough money to sustain their activity. This is our mission: publish excellent work in a way that allows us to do it again. Book sales, then, are an imperfect measure of impact and a more perfect measure of viability.

This is also true for a wide array of for-profit scholarly publishers. Working without the tax advantage of nonprofit status or the support of institutional subsidies or grants, these publishers are even more dependent on the commercial success of the books they publish.

This dual bottom line is one of the differences between scholarly editors and our colleagues in the trade. Both strive to acquire the best books we can, works readers want to read, but the scholarly editor is also looking for books that will contribute to the development of a scholarly field. These books advance an argument, expand what we know, or overturn what we thought we knew. They may synthesize, integrate, and interpret a vast array of research. These are books that create knowledge, make it public, and fix it in a form that allows it to be shared over space and time.

For scholarly authors, this recognition of the commercial aspects of scholarly publishing might be disquieting. Their work, the product of years of preparation, teaching, thinking, and research, is not simply a commodity. It is the result of their intellectual effort and creativity, plus the often painful process of writing, rewriting, and being reviewed. For a scholar, her work is totally unique. When asked to name books comparable to their own, many authors simply cannot. Editors think differently. We know past performance is no guarantee of future returns—but it may be the best predictor.

The reality is that a scholarly book may be unique, but it exists within a larger context of other books in its field. These books are in conversation with others, they advance arguments, they test ideas and may overturn them, they bring different perspectives on previously accepted wisdom. Scholarly books exist in dialogue with other scholarly books.

Books, of course, are only one way in which scholars communicate. They also write journal articles and book reviews, speak at conferences and workshops, and participate in other collaborative endeavors. They communicate by email, listservs, and blogs, and on social media. Some scholarly disciplines—the sciences and some social sciences in particular—have long since shifted away from books as the primary medium of communication. These are fields that have developed rich and fast-moving journal economies, in which articles are the preferred currency. For scholars in these fields, publication in the right journal can be a career-making move. In the humanities, at least for now, the book remains the gold standard, but books are really just one way scholars connect within an increasingly networked and interlinked world.

GOING WHERE THE ACTION IS

Understanding this hints at how scholarly editors find authors. Some academic editors have advanced academic degrees, but others do not. Regardless, these editors immerse themselves in their fields, and the more senior ones become sought-after informal advisers to scholars in a field. Editors understand where a field has been, what the current issues and arguments are, and what the seminal books are. Editors, given their vantage point, can also see trends across disciplines. By keeping up with conference papers, journal articles, and symposia, we hope to see where the field is headed. Getting to know leading senior scholars in our discipline is important, but so

....

is learning who are the midcareer powerhouse scholars, and who might be an emerging young academic with real potential. In short, we go where the action is.

This does not always require travel. Although nothing surpasses personal contact and quiet conversations at a conference book exhibit or over coffee, scholarly editors can and do connect with authors online. Webinars, online forums, and social media sites like Facebook and Twitter are places where savvy editors can follow academic trends in their fields. The best editors monitor those and actively participate in them. Scholarly editors become part of the community of scholars we serve. I think of us as embedded in the community, bringing a professional expertise and a distinct perspective to the conversation.

For scholars, this also means that they should go where the editors are likely to spot them. Scholars who are active and outspoken in a field, who participate, speak, write, and contribute, are scholars who have developed an audience that will increase their book's impact. Books by these "public intellectuals," even if only in their own subfields, will have a greater impact than those whose authors have not developed a following. The academy has always been a social network, one built around ideas, argument, and discussion.

What about literary agents? This is another difference between trade and scholarly publishing. Agents make their money by selecting authors and projects that can command substantial returns on investment and placing them with publishers willing to pay for those properties. Few scholarly books fit this category, simply because their potential readership is not large enough to deliver that return. This is not true of all books, of course, and scholarly publishers do work with agents, but those books tend to be on the trade end of the spectrum. Trade books, which are discussed elsewhere in this volume, can be an important part of many scholarly editors' lists. Mostly, we scholarly editors are out there hunting and gathering on our own.

Scholarly editors, especially those with well-established lists in humanities and some social science fields, get many unsolicited proposals for books. These can come by the hundreds every month. Sometimes even complete manuscripts arrive. Wary of such projects, editors often relegate them to the slush pile for review at some later date or assign them to an assistant for a quick assessment. Every editor has her own strategy for dealing efficiently with this material, but most have some system of triage: quickly dividing projects into "yes," "no," and "maybe" piles. Only the most promising get more than a few minutes of review.

How can an editor decide so quickly which projects it is worth spending more time on? Because most editors come to understand fields and lists quite intimately, the first question is one of fit. We ask, *Does this book fit the list I am trying to build? Does it advance the discipline in an important way?* An excellent book from a first-rate scholar might not pass that test if it falls outside the editor's subject area. Think of it this way: an acquisitions editor is an architect and has sketched out the building she envisions. Is this proposal a brick or beam that will help build that structure? If not, beautiful as it might be, she may set it aside for another use.

The architectural metaphor has other applications here as well. Most scholarly lists have foundational books, those that define disciplines and support entire lines of inquiry. They include books that are structural, such as textbooks and course books, designed to help teachers and students. A list might also include professional and reference titles that aid researchers in their work—researchers who also teach and rely on those course books. Groundbreaking new works, either monographs or big idea books, are a third supporting type that forms the list. That list might also include some ornamentation, trade books in any field that display creativity and add sparkle to a publishing program. Few scholarly editors want just one type of book or another; rather, we strive to have integrated lists of books that support each other.

In this way, scholarly editors are strategic. We have a clear idea of the types of books we need, books that will fill our list-building goals. The best editors are also opportunistic and always looking out for chances to expand our building with another floor or interesting wing. Being immersed in a scholarly community allows editors to take advantage of such opportunities.

Waiting for the right project to walk through the door or land in the email box simply is not enough, however. Most scholarly editors also *commission* works—that is, we conceive a book and seek an author to write it. We see a hole in the wall we are building or a roof that needs support. An emerging field may need an initial book or a contributed collection of first voices. A new question, spurred by current events or a new discovery, may reinvigorate an old topic. Because editors may see this before others, we go looking for an author to fill the need in the discipline.

Commissioning books requires a different set of skills for the editor. Selecting projects is reactive, while commissioning is proactive. Most scholars work independently on the topics and ideas that most interest them. They want to work on *their* idea, not an editor's. Here, too, it helps if an editor has developed a substantial network of scholars, advisers, and colleagues willing to point to the right person to write the book he needs. Next, it is the editor's job to convince this person the topic is worth her time, and that it would be in *her* interest to write the book.

Why would it be in a scholar's interest to say yes? Most scholars make very little money publishing scholarly books. (This is not always the case, of course, and there are exceptional books that break out of their fields to find a large, welcoming audience.) Why then would do they do it? The reasons are multiple: scholars publish books because they can have intellectual impact on their field; because they want to influence a conversation or debate; because they want to stake a claim to an idea or perspective. In short, scholarly authors write because they have something to say.

It is not only for intrinsic reasons, however. Because of the way academics in the United States, Europe, and much of the developed world are assessed, publishing can be financially rewarding. Universities and colleges make hiring, promotion, and tenure decisions based on many things, but a record of publication is a substantial component. Publishing a book (or journal articles, in many disciplines) is a ticket to career advancement. Few academics these days progress very far in their career without a record of publication.

On the editor's end, commissioned books require a substantial amount of planning, communicating, and working with an author, and because of this, they can be expensive in both time and money. They require substantial homework from the editor, and because the author may need an incentive to take up a commissioned project, the publisher may proffer the author an advance. Publishers commission books only after considering the market needs and a book's potential for success. Why do it then? Editors do it because we understand what a field (or market) might need, and we seek to fill that demand. Instead of picking from what authors happen to offer her, the editor gets exactly what she wants.

GETTING EXPERT ADVICE

Once a scholarly editor has found or commissioned a promising project, how does she know it's the one? Editors are good at acting on instinct—a sense informed by experience and market knowledge, but a hunch nonetheless—and we then second-guess ourselves. In fact, we are so careful about this critical appraisal that most scholarly publishers have an institutionalized system for it. It is called peer review.

All American university presses—the Association of American University

Presses has more than 130 members—and many scholarly societies adhere to rigorous standards of peer review.[1] Some for-profit scholarly presses also perform peer review in one form or another. The ideal is for the editor to solicit no fewer than two single-blind reviews (meaning the reviewer knows the identity of the author but the author doesn't know the identity of the reviewer, at least at the time of the review). These are prepublication reviews solicited by the editor to help determine the strength and quality of a manuscript or proposal.

A peer is an expert in the field, with credentials equal to or better than the author's, who can advise the press on the work. In larger fields, such as American history, the selection of peers is easy because of the large number of scholars available to review projects. In more esoteric fields or subfields, finding a peer can be difficult. Also, readers need to be as objective as possible, but it can be difficult to find ones who do not have some connection to the author. Especially in our networked time, editors might ask a potential reader to disclose any conflicts of interest before taking on a review.

Usually peer review—and the offer of a contract if the review is favorable—occurs on a complete manuscript. In some cases a press may instead offer a contract based on an initial peer review of a book proposal. When the author submits the final manuscript, the press may then send it out for a final peer reading. This ensures that the author accomplished what he set out to do and the manuscript meets the field's standards.

Editors, in reality, use peer review to do two things. First, the review helps determine whether the book deserves the press's imprint—basically, that it is worth publishing. This gatekeeping aspect of peer review, however, may not be the most useful. The best peer reviews do something else. They suggest improvements to the work, they offer constructive criticism of the author's argument, and they point out any errors or gaps in the work. They may also alert authors to other sources that could help refine the book's argument. This prepublication review is invaluable. Occasionally authors will bristle at the suggestions or react with embarrassment to the criticism. To this I respond that it is better to be criticized privately than after publication in the pages of the key journal in the author's field. The purpose of the review, ultimately, is to give the editor and the press confidence that this book will make a meaningful contribution to scholarship.

There is a third element of peer review that can be invaluable to an editor.

1. An excellent resource on the practice of peer review is the AAUP's *Best Practices for Peer Review*, http://www.aaupnet.org/policy-areas/peer-review.

. . . .

The reviewer sometimes offers qualitative market research on the book: "Everyone in this field is going to have to read this book," or "I hope to assign this to my class when it is ready." Conversely, a reviewer might warn, "As good as the writing is, the subject is just too narrow—I can't imagine who will buy this book." We editors are responsible for making our own guesses about sales, but it is reassuring to have someone corroborate those estimates.

Sometimes a reviewer who doesn't realize that projected sales are a factor in scholarly publishing can overstep while trying to be helpful: "This is an excellent book written for a large popular audience. This isn't the type of book *your* press should publish." A good scholarly editor knows to sign this book immediately!

What about the book's financial picture? As the book is undergoing peer review, the editor will prepare a publication plan for the book. How long is the manuscript? How many illustrations, charts, or graphs will it include? Does it require any special formatting or presentation? More importantly, how many copies of this book can the press realistically sell and at what price? Will it need to be a hardcover original, a paperback, or a split-run of both? Will this be a born digital project or be included in digital aggregations to be sold to libraries? The editor will bring his own substantial experience and the press's sales history with similar projects to bear on these decisions, in addition to consultation with colleagues in the production department and sales and marketing team. With that, the editor will create a preliminary financial plan or profit-and-loss statement (P&L) for the book. This document is based on a best guess about how the book will perform, and it asks the editor to consider whether the project is a viable investment for the press.

Equipped with a supportive set of peer reviews, the author's response to them (which may include a revision plan for the manuscript), and an acceptable publication plan, the editor will present the project to the press's editorial board. At most university presses this is a committee of senior faculty at its home institution. At others it might be a caucus of senior managers at the press along with the director. This committee will review the project, the editor's sales projections, advice from the peer reviewers, and the financial plan before making a decision about whether the book should be put under contract. Given the amount of time and money invested in the project by this point, the stakes are already high.

With the board's approval, the editor will offer a book contract to the author.

Once the contract has been executed, the scholarly editor can feel satisfied that she has signed the book. At most presses editors have specific goals for the number of titles and their net value (based on projected sales) placed under contract in a given year. The signed book now counts toward that quota. The editor is not done with that book, of course. She is still responsible for ensuring that the author delivers an acceptable final manuscript, illustrations, and permissions, all ready to be transmitted into production, where it will begin its next steps toward the finished product.

When we think of an author creating a book, we often imagine a solitary pursuit: the lone scholar working away at a desk. In reality, books begin their lives as part of a larger scholarly conversation, and they come to fruition as group projects touched by editors and peer reviewers, copyeditors, designers, and compositors, marketers and salespeople. In scholarly publishing especially, books are collective efforts.

The editor, however, is the book's real champion. She might pick the book out of hundreds of other manuscripts because of something special about in it. The editor convinces colleagues and the publisher that the book is worth the investment, and sometimes she needs to coax the author into reworking a manuscript long after the author thought it was complete. She is the book's first salesperson, pitching it to the editorial board and later to the sales team itself. She may even draft the jacket, catalog, and website copy for the book, and later maybe write award nomination letters. All of this continues something begun by the author. The editor and the scholar work together to deliver the greatest impact possible for the book. If they do their work right, the scholarly conversation they spark may ignite into something that generates both heat and light.

4 THE LORDS OF DISCIPLINES

ACQUIRING COLLEGE TEXTBOOKS

. . . .

PETER COVENEY

It's easy to romanticize the publishing process, but ultimately it helps to bear in mind that a publishing company essentially makes something and then has to sell it: some people acquire the raw material (the content), others turn that material into a finished product (the book), and still others market and sell it. Virtually every job in a publishing house is some version of one of these three things. But nothing happens if there's no manuscript in the first place, and that's why the acquiring editor's job is considered primary.

Like many, I came to textbook acquisitions after traversing other jobs in publishing; my path may have been a little less traditional than others, but the other kinds of experience I gained along the way all proved invaluable to the task of acquiring. Having been exposed to hand-set type and letterpress printing in my Indiana junior high school, I gravitated to the book design and production workshop of the six-week Radcliffe Publishing Procedures Course that I took the summer after college graduation. My first job was production manager of a small university press, where I did everything from casting off manuscripts and purchasing typesetting, printing, and binding, to corresponding with designers, liaising with suppliers, and generally acting to insure that the books were published on time, within budget, and looking great.

Following that, I became the managing editor for the business and economics imprint of a New York–based college textbook publisher, managing the production of a much larger list of much more complexity. In those days the editorial director and I would sit down together about once every six weeks and calculate, based on estimates I had gathered from suppliers,

PETER COVENEY has spent over forty years in college publishing, most recently as executive editor for history at John Wiley & Sons. Previously he worked as executive editor for history at Blackwell; senior editor at Oxford University Press, M. E. Sharpe, Greenwood/Praeger, and Paragon House; editor and marketing manager at Harper & Row; managing editor at Holt, Rinehart & Winston / Dryden Press; and production manager at Northern Illinois University Press. He has spoken at seminars and courses at several universities and is the author of nearly two dozen articles and reviews on book collecting, publishing, design, and production.

whether the various books on that year's list would be profitable. This is all done now with preprogrammed software, but back then we simply used a calculator and a pencil and paper. I little knew at the time how well that experience would serve me when I became a textbook editor myself. In weighing an acquisition or solving problems in the production process, having a sense of the interdependence of design, typeface, and type size, and how these can influence page count, printing costs, and unit cost—thereby pushing profit margins up or down—is a necessity for editors.

Next I was hired as a marketing manager for a major college textbook publisher, a position that involved not only writing, editing, and in some cases designing direct-mail pieces and dealing daily with sales reps and college professors on the phone, but also making presentations of the various lists for which I was responsible to large audiences at sales meetings. So by the time I was offered a job as an acquiring editor for college textbooks, I knew how such books were made, and I knew how they were sold; all I had to do now was figure out how to get them under contract and written.

College editors, I quickly learned, are evaluated annually mainly on three measures: the number of book contracts signed (and their dollar value); the number of titles published; and the number of manuscripts handed over to the production side of the house (which may publish in the current year or the following). College textbook editors are responsible for a particular discipline, or related disciplines, within the college curriculum, such as biology, or mathematics, or history and political science. An editor's job is to acquire and publish textbooks within that discipline that will sell successfully enough to make a profit. In a different industry, this person might be called a product manager; in publishing he or she is called an acquiring editor.

In order to work effectively in a publishing company, you have to be aware of both process and product: the book is the result of a collaboration among various people both inside and outside your company, and the more you know about other parts of the process (especially production and marketing) the better you will be at finding solutions if problems arise. You'll be limited as a publisher by any lack of knowledge, so the more you know the better you'll be at recognizing opportunities and publishing books.

KNOW YOUR MARKET

Unlike trade books, reference books, or academic monographs, textbooks are rarely found in bookstores or libraries—except for campus bookstores. They are written and published for use by students in the classroom, whether in elementary and high school (K–12 or "el–hi" in industry jargon) or in colleges.

While the acquisition and development process is similar, a fundamental—and critical—difference between books for college courses and those for the K-12 market is that while the content for the former is roughly based on aggregated syllabi from colleges across the country, the content of el-hi texts is often dictated either by local school districts or by Common Core standards. Further, the adoption of a college textbook is a matter of a professor's individual discretion, while el-hi textbook selections are often district-wide and based on a committee vote, highly subject to local politics. As a result, winning an el-hi adoption can be extremely lucrative for the publisher, but the pursuit of one can be uncertain and sometimes stressful.

While having a university degree in the field in which you are acquiring textbooks can be helpful, it's not a requirement. What *is* essential to acquire effectively is to know your market, which includes having a grasp of what your competition is doing. Fortunately, the field of college textbook publishing operates in an open environment: college professors post their syllabi and reading lists online, and it's relatively easy, given enough time, to see what the most popular texts for a given course are, and the institutions and professors that use them. Formerly (I hate to use the phrase "before the internet," but there you have it) an editor would have to rely on the reports, written and oral, from campus sales representatives, or, in many cases, include an obligatory stop at the campus bookstore when calling on professors in one's discipline. Once you were in the bookstore, the relative size of the stacks of various textbooks told you all you needed to know. This has become less reliable now that so many textbooks are purchased online, but there are other ways to assess markets and the relative popularity of particular textbooks.

The markets in college textbook publishing can easily be learned with a little application: companies such as CMG publish catalogs of their mailing lists, broken out by discipline, and these are further broken out by course title. The numbers next to each list represent college professors who say they teach such a course, and so function as relative indicators; it's not a huge leap to extrapolate an average class size, multiply by the number of professors teaching, and come up with a rough estimate of the total student population for most courses within one's discipline.

Market knowledge accumulates over time, and speaking with those who teach the various courses in your discipline, whether via email or phone, or in person at conventions or during visits to campuses, is one of the most effective ways to build this knowledge. It's not enough to know that X is the bestselling text nationwide for a particular course; you'll want to know why and gain a sense of what that book has—and also what it might lack, what its vulnerabilities are. The world may not need another thousand-page four-color Principles of Economics survey that retails for $199.95, for example, but there might be a place for a cheaper, shorter text that covers substantially the same ground. Your job is to find the college professor who can write that book.

Textbook publishing also differs from trade and certain other kinds of publishing in that rather than an author coming to you with an idea for a textbook (though this does happen), it's more often the case that you as an editor have to come up with the idea for a textbook and then find and commission someone to write it. Textbook editors work far less often with agents than do their counterparts in other types of traditional publishing.

Most textbooks are revised regularly. For the largest courses this can be every three years; for smaller courses higher up in the curriculum it can be every five years or so. The ostensible reason for revisions is to keep the material current, but in fact, for the large introductory level courses it can serve as a way for the publisher to reinvigorate a declining sales curve and wash used books out of the market. In any case, if the textbook you publish is successful, you will want to revise it regularly, and this can mean that you will be working with a particular author or team of authors for years to come.

Another characteristic of college textbook publishing is that the professor is everything—he or she is your author, your peer reviewer, and the eventual adopter of your book. So it's essential that you get to know and cultivate those in your discipline who can help you, because you are going to have to call on their expertise time and time again (usually in return for an extremely modest stipend or honorarium). These can sometimes turn into rewarding friendships or at the very least professional relationships that extend over a long period; I have known some of my authors and reviewers for twenty-five years or more.

For many years college textbook publishers maintained a field force of sales representatives dispersed across the country, each rep (or "college traveler," as they were called) responsible for a particular territory that included a number of campuses. The rep's job was to present the most recent texts to professors who might adopt particular books for their courses. Because the nature of the job involved being familiar with one's own titles as well with competing books, cultivating professors in different departments, working with the college bookstore, and generally taking the pulse of various departments and disciplines, the college traveler's job was ideal training for an aspiring editor, and many people made their way into acquisitions this way.

....

There are fewer field sales reps today, but it remains a great way to pursue a career in textbook publishing.

GETTING TO A CONTRACT

Once you think you have the right person to write a textbook, you have to test the idea—no sense going to the trouble to commission, write, and publish the book if no one will ever use it in a class. So the first step is to have your author write a proposal, one that you will send out to various people who teach the course, asking them to answer a battery of questions that will help you assess the author's plan and refine what you think you know about the market. The larger the course (and potential student audience), the more detailed the questions. You then use the information from these peer reviews to help the author refine the proposal.

Once the two of you have agreed that it represents what you both intend, it's time to present the book to your editorial board. In most publishing companies this is the body that approves the project and its anticipated costs and agrees on a realistic sales forecast as well as your proposed contract terms. Once you have the blessing of the editorial board, it's time to draft a contract, send it to the author, reconcile any lingering issues or differences, and secure the required signatures.

I often tell people starting out in publishing that one of the best ways to get to know one's company and the overall editorial process is to simply read through a standard contract. Contracts all basically say the same thing: the author agrees to write the book to certain specifications, and your company agrees to publish it, subject to the following terms and conditions—which then can go on for twelve to fifteen pages or more. But it's good to know what the negotiable parts of a publishing contract are: they include the delivery date for the manuscript; the length of the work (text and illustrations); the royalty rate; any advances, grants, or other things the publisher agrees to pay for; which rights the author retains and which ones the publisher retains; the versions in which the book will appear (hardcover, paperback, e-book, etc.); how many free copies the author receives on publication; and what happens if the author never delivers the manuscript.

MANUSCRIPT DEVELOPMENT

Assuming your author delivers as planned, you will want to get the full manuscript reviewed, as you did with the proposal, in order to help you and your author arrive at a version that is optimally suited to the market for which it is intended. Once again, you will call on those professors who teach the course, ideally some of whom use the text or texts that you have by now identified as your primary competition. The questions you will now be asking will be more detailed than those you asked at the proposal stage. Then it was just an idea; now it's a real (though first-draft) manuscript, and people can see what the author is really up to. As an editor you have to choose your reviewers carefully at this point, and once you get their written reviews back, you also have to help your author make sense of them, telling him or her which points and suggestions for revision you feel are important and which remarks it isn't necessary to respond to.

These reviews are known as *developmental reviews*, because their intent is to help the author develop the manuscript to the point where it addresses the market that you both intend. For larger market books the developmental reviewing can go through several rounds before a manuscript is deemed ready. And you have to allow for this in your timing when planning a publication date—depending on its size and other factors such as the number and complexity of the illustrations, the development phase can take from three to six months. Smaller-market titles might go through only one round of reviews, or they might be edited and revised by the acquiring editor. The latter course is becoming increasingly rare in larger publishing houses, where many of these tasks are highly segmented and manuscripts are often sent out to free-lancers who specialize in this. It is still the acquiring editor's responsibility to monitor this process, as by this time the book will have begun to show up on the screens of various sales and marketing people within the company, even though it may not yet even be handed over to the production side of the house.

FROM MANUSCRIPT TO MARKETPLACE

Once you and the author agree that the manuscript is ready to publish, it's time to formally hand it off to the production department, who will cast it off (estimate its eventual length in printed book pages by applying the type-setting specifications to the overall word count) and confirm the schedule. Someone in production (called a production editor or project editor) will get in touch with the author about matters of copyediting, proofreading, and cover design—although as the acquiring editor you will always be an interested party in all of this and will often have the final say. Soon enough (generally six to nine months after production has commenced) the happy day arrives and you will email your congratulations to your author, who shortly will have a copy of the finished book in hand.

. . . .

Although this is when the sales begin, the marketing activities will have been launched well in advance of publication. If your company has a dedicated sales force that represents your book to professors at various college campuses, you will likely have to present your book to these reps at an annual sales conference, suggest effective strategies for getting your book adopted as a classroom text, and convince them that it's worth their while. You will also want to display your new book at one of the several scholarly conferences each year, which professors attend to present papers and connect with others in their discipline, and also where they peruse book exhibits looking for new titles that might be useful in their own classes. These meetings are opportunities for you to expand your circle of acquaintances in your area, as these are potential adopters of your text and also your reviewers and possible future authors. And the process can start all over again.

If you're interested in becoming a textbook editor, there is no one single established path. Entry-level positions in sales, marketing, or editorial, as an intern or editorial assistant or sales assistant, will expose you to the jobs that others do and provide you with an entrée to colleagues in your own area as well as others throughout the company. So I often suggest getting started wherever you can, do a great job at whatever you're hired to do, survey the landscape once you're there, and be on the lookout for someone who can act as a mentor. Be professional, set good goals, don't give up easily, have a sense of commitment, and try not to see the job that you're doing solely as a path to something else. And remember that you can do everything right but you still have to have a little bit of good luck.

Finally, I've always found the following observation from Max Schuster (cofounder of Simon & Schuster) both inspiring and true:

> Editing can, and should be, not only a life-enhancing profession but also a liberal education in itself, for it gives you the privilege of working with the most creative people of your time: authors and educators, world-movers and world-shakers. For taking a lifetime course for which you would be willing to pay tuition, you are paid, not merely with dollars, but with intellectual and spiritual satisfactions immeasurable.[1]

1. M. Lincoln Schuster, "An Open Letter to a Would-Be Editor," in *Editors on Editing*, ed. Gerald Gross, 3rd ed. (New York: Grove, 1993), 28.

PART TWO

The Editing Process

· ·

FROM PROPOSAL TO BOOK

5 THE BOOK'S JOURNEY

. . . .

NANCY S. MILLER

After acquisition, editor and author embark on a journey that takes the proposal or first-draft manuscript to a finished book.

To be a book editor is to work at the intersection of art and commerce. Editors are passionate about reading, about books—and yet their job involves not only falling in love with an author's work and working with that author to make the best book possible, but also selling the book to colleagues and to the world, making sure it finds a readership, *publishing* it. Publishing is a business. Without the commerce part of the equation, the most beautiful book in the world is like the proverbial tree falling in the forest with no one to hear, which is why most editors embrace the aspects of their job that involve selling. But it is the editing, the work with their authors, the birthing of new books, that brings many editors the greatest pleasure.

Despite the commonly heard lament that editors just don't edit anymore, editors pour their heart and soul and weekends and evenings into the task. Editing is time-consuming, labor-intensive work—work that often cannot be done in the office, where days can be consumed by meetings, emails, preparing materials for sales or marketing meetings, and communicating with those in other departments. The editing process can take a year or much more from the time the first draft of a manuscript is delivered until publication. But it is at the heart of an editor's job, and most editors find it tremendously rewarding, both because of the satisfaction of seeing a book achieve its potential and because of the gratification that can come with the close work involved in the author–editor relationship.

Essential as it is, the labor of editing is only one part of the book's journey from writer to reader. That journey is not just an artistic collaboration but the

NANCY S. MILLER is associate publisher and editorial director of the adult trade division of Bloomsbury Publishing, where she works with such authors as Gail Godwin, Mark Kurlansky, Roz Chast, Daniel Handler, and James Hansen. She started her career at Farrar, Straus, and Giroux, as assistant editor to the legendary Robert Giroux, and has also held editorial positions at Washington Square Press and Pocket Books at Simon & Schuster; Ballantine, where she was editor-in-chief; Random House; and HarperCollins. She is a member of the Freedom to Read Committee of the Association of American Publishers.

creation of a physical or digital product. Every book passes through many stages and is touched by many people in a publishing house before it reaches the marketplace.

This chapter gives an overview of what is involved in turning a manuscript into a finished book, from the earliest developmental stages and a completed first draft through to "setting copy" delivered to a typesetter, and thence to page proofs and a printer-ready file or e-book. The publication process is the same whether the finished product is a hardcover, a paperback, or an e-book.

Many editors work on only nonfiction or only fiction, and some work exclusively on narrower categories within those two divisions—say sports books or thrillers. Some editors have more eclectic lists that may include novels, stories, memoirs, and narrative histories. Some may work on books that are more literary, some on books that are more commercial, others on academic texts. Whatever the category, the editor's work follows similar paths to publication.

DEVELOPMENTAL EDITING

Fiction and nonfiction books often begin their journey to publication at different points. Depending on whether a book is nonfiction or fiction, it can be a long road from acquisition to the delivery of a first-draft manuscript. While editors tend to acquire fiction on the basis of a complete first-draft manuscript, they acquire most nonfiction books on the basis of a book proposal consisting of a brief overview, a detailed outline, and one or two sample chapters. An author might take months or even years to deliver a nonfiction manuscript, depending on the due date specified in the contract.

And yet even if the editor has only an outline and sample material in hand at the time of acquisition, the editing process can begin immediately, sometimes even before the book is acquired, in the first meeting or exchange between author and editor. The editor might start the editorial conversation at this early stage by discussing, for example, any questions about the proposal, issues with how the book is conceived, or problems with the organization. The editor will want to address these issues straightaway so that the author can set forth with a vision for the book that author and editor agree upon from the beginning.

Once the editor has the first-draft manuscript in hand, either upon acquisition if the work is fiction or upon the author's delivery if the work is nonfiction, she can focus on developmental editing. At this stage the editor tackles such big-picture matters as structure, focus, pacing, plotting, shaping an argument, gaps in the narrative, believability of characters, enhancing or

....

cutting subplots, excising extraneous material, and interweaving strands into a cohesive whole—all this in order to get the "bones" of the book in their proper shape. Depending on the publisher and the needs of the manuscript, this type of editing may instead be handed off to a separate developmental editor, either on staff or freelance.

This is a moment when the editor may want to focus on the book's title and subtitle as well. Does the title best convey what the book is? Does the subtitle amplify and clarify the title?

From the editor's perspective, the developmental editing stage involves the most intellectually challenging tasks of the process. Each time an editor edits a manuscript, she or he must grapple with a fundamental question: what makes a good book? There are no absolutes of course, although stellar writing and a great conceit are always a good start. A novel has to have a beginning, a middle, and an end; believable, memorable characters; a compelling narrative arc. A nonfiction book has to have an engaging core idea, a framework that makes sense, a well-shaped argument. But at its most basic, a book has to have a reason to exist—and it's the editor's job to make sure that reason is evident to the reader on every page.

As curious as it might be to consider, there is no real training for this editorial work. In a 1982 talk on the education of an editor, legendary editor Robert Giroux stressed the intuitive aspect of editing. "There are three qualities that cannot be taught and without which a good editor cannot function—judgment, taste, and empathy. Judgment is the ability to evaluate a manuscript and its author. Taste is subjective and difficult to define, but we all recognize it when we encounter it. Empathy is the capacity not only to perceive what the author's aims are, but to help in achieving their realization to the fullest extent."[1]

It is empathy that is perhaps the quality most crucial to the editing process: the ability to help an author make the book the best book it can be—via comments, suggestions, queries, notes, and rewrites—while keeping in mind that it is always the author's book. This means the editor must always be prepared for an author to find his or her own solutions to any issues raised.

There's a problem-solving aspect to the editing process that can feel almost like doing a crossword or jigsaw puzzle, complete with the satisfaction of seeing things ultimately fall into place. It's a mysterious process, and even when a first draft requires heavy rewriting and seems a complete mess,

---

1. Robert Giroux, *The Education of an Editor* (New York: R. R. Bowker, 1982), 11.

when the finished product shines in the end, a good editor usually feels the achievement is the writer's.

A manuscript may require two, three, four, or even five rounds with an author—or it may be nearly pristine and require only one round of light edits. Either can result in a terrific book.

LINE EDITING

After receiving a revised draft of the manuscript from the author which satisfactorily addresses most of the general issues raised in the developmental editing stage, the editor tackles the next stage: line editing. In practice, these stages often overlap, as many editors can't help themselves from line editing at the same time they are puzzling through larger problems and questions in a first draft. Line editing addresses such issues as phrasing, word choice, and syntax on the sentence level. When line editing, the editor may

- suggest deleting or transposing words or phrases or entire paragraphs
- query the chronology or any inconsistencies of style, tone, or content, or (with fiction) whether dialogue rings true
- ask the author to clarify material that confuses or to add needed information
- note transitions that need work
- suggest rewrites on the sentence level
- correct punctuation, spelling, and grammar, and make sure tenses agree (primarily the responsibility of the copyeditor, but many editors reflexively correct such errors)

The editor must always respect the author's voice when making line-editing suggestions that pertain to style, while adhering to the goal of making the book the best it can be.

The editor usually marks up line edits on the manuscript itself—whether in pencil on a hard copy or electronically via a change-tracking tool—by suggesting rewrites directly in the text and adding comments and queries in the margins. If the editor is editing on hard copy, the editor marks up the manuscript using the editing symbols (e.g., carats) and terminology (e.g., "stet") found in the *Chicago Manual of Style*. Whatever the technology—whether pencil or computer—the essence of what an editor does is the same.

COMMUNICATING WITH THE AUTHOR

For each draft of the manuscript, the editor will usually send the author an editorial letter laying out general thoughts, suggestions, comments, and queries. Such a letter often begins with praise for what the author is trying to achieve and for what is working in the manuscript, and then brings up general developmental issues that need to be addressed. The editor may also refer to line-editing issues in the editorial letter.

Depending on how much developmental work the author needs to do in each draft, the editor may or may not send an edited manuscript along with the editorial letter—with suggestions for rewrites and deletions marked on the page and comments and queries in the margins, and perhaps with line edits as well. Here too, an editor must remember that his or her job involves being not only a critic but also a cheerleader. A few positive comments here and there in the margins can go a long way.

There are times when an author will disagree with an editor's comments or suggestions. Often a back-and-forth can find common ground. If not, the editor must decide whether the issue being raised is important enough to continue pressing the point. Making sure the author recognizes that the editor is the author's advocate is key. The editor must be skilled at conveying criticism in a supportive, positive way. The bond between editor and author can be a strong one, with the editor taking on the role of friend, adviser, confidant, parent, and therapist over the course of a manuscript's journey to finished book.

It can often be helpful as well to have a discussion with the author by phone or in person to go over some of the developmental issues and even some of the line-editing questions. An author may be wedded to phrasing something a particular way, and talking this through can help both author and editor understand the other's intent. Again, the author–editor relationship is based on trust, and clearly communicating respect and admiration for an author's work while conveying the issues that need to be addressed is a delicate task that if handled well can help strengthen and reinforce that bond.

PERMISSIONS AND LEGAL VETTING

The editor acts as a safety net for the author, not only in terms of the actual writing but also in terms of legal issues. At the developmental editing stage, the editor must call to the author's attention any quoted material that might need permission (anything not considered "fair use") from the rights holder—whether epigraphs, lines from songs or poems, or long excerpts from other works. Illustrations (artwork or photographs) need permissions from rights holders as well—and the process of seeking clearance for these can be even more laborious. Often the editor will help guide the author through the permissions-seeking process, though the responsibility for clearing and paying for permissions usually rests with the author. It's important to begin this process early, as clearing permissions from rights holders can take some time and the task must be completed before the book is ready to go to press so that sources can be credited in the finished book. Permissions charges for using lines from songs or poems can be steep; the author may decide to delete the lines rather than pay an expensive charge. This is another reason permissions should be sought early; it's best to make any text deletions before the book is set into type.

The editor must also judge at this early stage whether the manuscript will need a legal vetting. Might there be any legal issues with the manuscript? Did the author base a particular character in a novel on a real-life ex-boyfriend who may sue? Should the author's relatives in a memoir be disguised? Could the way a sentence is phrased be deemed libelous? If there are concerns, the editor will engage a lawyer to vet the final edited manuscript. If the publishing house does not have an in-house lawyer, the editor will usually need to get approval from higher-ups before sending the manuscript to an outside lawyer, as a legal vetting can be expensive. Sometimes the entire manuscript will have to be vetted; occasionally only a section of the manuscript will need to be looked at. The legal vetting takes place while (if not before) the manuscript is being copyedited, and any changes the lawyer suggests are usually incorporated into the manuscript before it is typeset. (To incorporate them later increases typesetting costs and also the danger of unvetted text circulating outside the house, when early galley proofs go out for publicity and promotion.)

THE "TRANSMITTAL" MANUSCRIPT

Once the back-and-forth between author and editor has produced a manuscript that is "satisfactory"—the word used to describe an acceptable manuscript in most publishing contracts, though it's certainly a bit tepid (most editors aim higher than mere "satisfaction" in what they publish)—the editor prepares to "transmit" the manuscript to the managing editorial or production editorial department.

In order to do so, the editor must create a transmittal manuscript that contains all the elements that will appear in the finished book. These elements include *front matter* (the material—such as the title page, copyright page, and contents page, and a dedication or epigraph, if desired—that appears before the actual text of the book begins) and *back matter* (the material, such as a bibliography, notes, or appendices—that might follow the actual text of the book). An index, if necessary, is usually prepared by a professional indexer, or by the author, later in the process, from the first round of page proofs.

....

If there are images to be included in the book, either throughout the text or to appear in one or more inserts, the editor will at this stage supply an art log. The art log indicates where the images are to be placed, any captions (from the author), and the camera-ready artwork (again, from the author). Each publishing house will have its own requirements for creating an art log.

The editor may have some special instructions to the copyeditor ("watch out for repetitions"; "double-check the chronology"). The editor should convey these to the managing editor at the time the manuscript is transmitted.

The editor, consulting with an art director, may also need to make some design decisions before transmitting the manuscript. For example, will there be running heads at the top of each page? If so, what information (chapter or book title, author, page numbers) should appear where? Should chapters always begin on a right-hand page? If there are illustrations, will they be grouped into inserts or placed throughout the text? (In the case of full-scale illustrated titles—whether a coffee-table art book or a picture-heavy cookbook—the design process begins very early, even at the conception of the project, and can involve page-by-page discussion of each layout.)

At some publishing houses, transmitting the manuscript is the final interaction the editor will have with the text; the managing editor will shepherd things along from here. At most houses, though, the editor will continue to be involved at least to some extent with the next stages: the copyedited manuscript and page proofs.

After the manuscript has been transmitted, the managing editor will give the transmittal manuscript to a designer, who will take into consideration the editor's design requests and generate sample designed interior text pages. The editor will often share the sample designed text pages with the author and may convey any comments the author has to the designer.

The managing editor will also send the transmittal manuscript to the copyeditor, who may be either on staff or a freelancer.

COPYEDITING

The copyeditor corrects spelling and grammar and punctuation. In addition, the copyeditor makes further line-editing suggestions, checks for consistency, makes sure that timelines make sense, that there aren't repetitions, and that any proper nouns are correct, and queries anything that doesn't quite make sense. Copyeditors are not fact checkers—publishers as a rule do not employ fact checkers—but the best ones often catch factual errors. The copyeditor usually works with an electronic version of the manuscript, using change-tracking software.

The copyeditor spends a few weeks reviewing the manuscript. Once the copyedits are completed, the copyedited text will be sent to the author—again, usually electronically. The author will have one to several weeks to review the copyeditor's work, approving or stetting any changes and answering any queries. Sometimes the original editor goes over the copyedits with the author; sometimes it's the managing editor who does this. This is often the last chance for the author to make any substantial changes in the manuscript, as making significant changes after the manuscript is typeset can be expensive. If the author does substantially revise the copyedited text, the editor and managing editor will review the revisions.

SETTING COPY AND PAGE PROOFS

When the author has answered all the copyeditor's queries and has responded to all the copyeditor's changes and any legal changes have been incorporated into the text, and the manuscript has been marked up with design specs, the manuscript goes to the compositor for typesetting. This version of the manuscript is known as the setting copy, and it's at this stage that the manuscript really starts "becoming a book."

The compositor, or typesetter, usually needs at least two to three weeks to produce the first round of typeset page proofs, sometimes referred to as first pass pages or galleys. Author and editor now have a chance to read the typeset pages, which can allow them to view the text with a fresh eye. A proofreader should also review the first pass pages, reading them carefully against the setting copy to check for any errors—including typographical errors, "widowed" lines, and bad line breaks. (Bound galleys or advance reading copies are often produced from first pass pages to be sent out to media, reviewers, and potential blurbers—well-known authors, celebrities, acknowledged authorities on the topic, or other public figures who might lend the book some of their own renown—in advance of finished books.)

Once the first pass pages are marked up with corrections from the author and the proofreader (and perhaps the editor), they are returned to the compositor, who creates a corrected version of the text in the form of second pass pages. The author and editor often don't review second pass pages unless there have been major changes or corrections made to the first pass pages, but the proofreader or someone from the production editorial department will carefully review the second pass pages to check for further errors. Any corrections will again be sent on to the compositor, who will now generate a third pass. This will continue until the text is (theoretically) without errors, at which point the book will be ready to go on press, if a hardcover or

....

paperback—or if also an e-book, to be transformed into digital files suitable for the many electronic reading platforms.

SCHEDULE

Throughout the book's journey from manuscript to finished book, the editor has to keep in mind the schedule in terms of the production process: will there be time for editing, copyediting, typesetting, proofreading, corrections, printing and binding, shipping—and creating e-book files and uploading them—in order to meet the publication date? Once the book has been transmitted, the managing editor can create a realistic production schedule for the book with dates for when the copyedited manuscript and then first pass pages can be expected; when the book is scheduled to be on press; and when finished copies will reach the publisher's warehouse.

At the same time that the book is chugging along the production track, it is also moving on a parallel route through the sales and marketing process, and so there is another schedule the editor must keep in mind: the "selling" schedule. Having materials such as sample chapters or even a finished manuscript for sales and marketing colleagues many months ahead of publication, and sometimes a year or more, has become a necessity in some areas of publishing. A comfortable production schedule for a book from finished manuscript to publication can be as little as nine months, but the sales and marketing schedule typically exceeds a year. Of course there are exceptions. Faced with a dramatic news event or a timely celebrity bio, a publisher may opt to "crash" a book on an abbreviated schedule. The editor's work from draft manuscript to transmittal manuscript may then be telescoped into a matter of days or weeks.

Even while the book is still in the editing stage, the marketing machinery of the house is beginning to turn to the rhythm of a seasonal publishing cycle that applies to all the books on a publisher's list. While the production schedule for each book is uniquely tailored to that project, for practical reasons houses group titles together in "seasons" of three to six months, putting out catalogs that list all their books for that period. These lists help make the unceasing river of titles manageable not just for workers in-house but for people downstream—distributors, booksellers, and media.

It's the editor's job both to supply information to sales and marketing colleagues about each title—via tipsheets, catalog copy, launch meetings, and databases (meeting the deadlines for that season's publishing schedule)—and at the same time to generate excitement by sharing sample material from the manuscript, soliciting and circulating blurbs, calling attention to news pegs, writing to booksellers, buttonholing colleagues in the hallway, and so on. The editor must help to "position" the book relative to other ones on the publisher's list and the marketplace at large. Because positioning is so important, the fate of a book can be decided, or nearly so, even before the final draft manuscript is delivered. The editor's contribution to this process may be just as important as—or more important than—her shaping of the manuscript, no matter how brilliantly she edits.

JACKET AND COVER COPY

Some publishers have copywriting departments that handle writing jacket and cover copy. At most publishing houses, however, it is the editor's responsibility to write jacket copy (for hardcover books) and cover copy (for paperback books). Writing copy is part of an editor's job as chief cheerleader and salesperson for the book; the copy is meant to persuade prospective readers to buy it.

For hardcover books, the editor must prepare jacket copy for the flaps and the back of the dust jacket; this may share space with the author's photo or blurbs—endorsements from noteworthy early readers. For paperbacks, all copy must fit within the confines of the back cover, though the editor may also prepare "quote pages" featuring blurbs or excerpts from reviews to appear at the front of the book. The editor will usually make sure the author has a chance to weigh in on jacket and cover copy and suggest changes—a process that, with finicky writers, can become a tricky negotiation.

Jacket and cover copy is usually due several months before the book's publication, to allow time for the jacket or cover to be designed with the text in place. But back-cover quotes are often "TK" (to come) at the time copy is due, so copy for the back usually comes in just a few weeks before the book goes to press.

AT LAST: PUBLICATION

Finished books usually arrive at the publisher's office (and warehouse) four to six weeks before the official publication date. E-books generally become available on retail sites on publication date.

The finished book represents a true collaboration between author and editor, who can take tremendous pleasure in seeing all of their hard work come to fruition. This is a time for celebration and anticipation as the book now begins a new journey—into the hands and, with luck, the hearts of readers.

6 WHAT LOVE'S GOT TO DO WITH IT
THE AUTHOR–EDITOR RELATIONSHIP

. . . .

BETSY LERNER

Once a middle-aged man at a writer's conference asked me how editors know when a manuscript is good. He seemed without guile or agenda. It was a simple question, but no one had ever asked it of me. I fumbled an answer, saying something about experience, taste, and conviction. "But how do they *know*?" he repeated, and this time I could hear behind the question the desperation and frustration of an aspiring writer whose work had met with a fair amount of rejection. "Isn't it all subjective?" His voice was now mixed with disgust and accusation.

Another writer weighed in that she couldn't stand it when rejection letters said "I just didn't love it," "I didn't fall in love," or "Alas, I wanted to love this . . ." The woman looked wounded and irritated at the same time: "Why can't they just say no instead of bringing love into it?" *What's love got to do with it?* I saw her point. To the writer it sounds disingenuous and weirdly upbeat. More, wouldn't it be better to be rejected on practical terms than to be rejected like a girl at a dance sitting alone near the punch bowl?

Thing is, editors don't acquire books that they think are *pretty good* or *good enough*. Acquisitions editors are in it for the high, for the feeling that something amazing is happening when they start to read fresh pages. Pheromones might even be involved. No matter how many manuscripts an editor reads, it is always there: the hope. This could be the book that hits the best-seller list, or wins a Pulitzer Prize, or, rarest of all, changes someone's life.

The author–editor relationship begins on the page. The first sentence. The first paragraph. Does it hold up twenty pages in? Fifty? A hundred? Is it quirky or elegant, funny or baleful, familiar or just strange enough? Is it deceptively simple or brilliantly complex? Does it move you?

I've met many writers who disagree with me. They believe editors choose manuscripts on the basis of the bottom line, the author's track record, or

BETSY LERNER is the author of *The Forest for the Trees: An Editor's Advice to Writers*, *Food and Loathing: A Lament*, and *The Bridge Ladies*. Her blog on the agony of the writing life is www.betsylerner.com.

what's fashionable or trendy. Publishers only want to pluck young things out of MFA programs or sign the next comic with a special on HBO. They don't believe their pages are as important as their "platform." And who can blame them, when the writing-industrial complex has been bludgeoning writers with the same questions: how many Facebook friends do you have, how many Twitter followers? In this climate the author–editor relationship often seems like the smallest part of the equation. Plus writers can self-publish with a few keystrokes. Editors might go the way of dodos.

And yet.

No matter how disenchanted writers may become, every one I've ever met has what I call the Maxwell Perkins fantasy—hoping for the editor who will pluck you from obscurity, who will lend you money when you drink away your advance, who is brilliant with a blue pencil, and who has launched the writers we will still be reading decades from now. In fact, fantasy infuses almost every idea an author has about getting published. After all, that's when you go from being a writer to an author, when you finally win the respect of friends and family, when you allow yourself just enough hope to believe in a writing career and giving up the day job. The Maxwell Perkins fantasy doesn't stop there: Your editor is handsome, picks up the checks, introduces you to fancy writers, and throws you a publication party in his apartment overlooking the Hudson River, lights twinkling across the way in distant New Jersey. Your editor peppers your manuscript with compliments and has a light touch. Contract in hand, you now dream of riding atop the best-seller list, donning your tux for the National Book Awards. The next day, still high from your win, you're on NPR, chatting with Terry Gross.

Terry: Thanks for being on the show.
You: Thanks for having me.

Most writers feel the one thing standing between them and their dream of publication is the editor. For the writer, having your work rejected is like being told you have an ugly baby or being broken up with. Behind every rejection looms the question *why?* Why didn't they fall in love? Why that book and not mine? No one wants to be told that his book isn't ready, that it's at least six drafts away. No one wants to hear *scrap this one, start over.* Or *take a writing class.*

It takes tenacity, endurance, and years of work for a writer to hone his craft, to find his story, to develop his voice. And then he has to figure out how to market himself, perhaps engage an agent's services, which in itself can be a brutal process. And getting an agent doesn't guarantee finding a publisher. Every rejection is like a referendum on his life.

Editors are not ogres. Yes, they are gatekeepers, yes they hold the purse strings, and yes they have the power of rejection. Are they aloof, or do they only seem it? Do they get off on rejecting manuscripts? Do they enjoy killing hopes and dreams? Do they love writers or resent them? Are they in competition with them, either overtly or unconsciously? Are they, as some suggest, failed writers themselves? Does the Woody Allen quip apply: "Those who can't do, teach. Those who can't teach, teach gym"?

How does one become an arbiter of taste? What makes an editor believe that just because he loves a book others will too? There are no licenses, courses, guidebooks, or manuals. There is some mentoring but no real supervision where editing is concerned. Sometimes a great editor on the page has no bedside manner. Sometimes the most charming editor has no discernible skill with sentence structure. Editors need clout to acquire, a proven track record of successful books. Young editors have to work even harder than their older, more experienced counterparts. They have to prove their case, implore the editor in chief to take a chance on younger writers. In order to acquire books, they need to diplomatically campaign among the different departments and research comparison titles with strong sales figures. They need to come up with "handles," elevator pitches that make the book sound salable. *Godzilla* meets *The Help*. And they need to schmooze agents, and impress writers, and navigate the politics of publishing. Although editors seem to have all the power, they too, like the author, are caught in their own Darwinian struggle to get the best books and launch them into the world. It takes passion, perseverance, smarts, savvy. In fact, love really isn't enough. *Is it ever?*

Another writer at another conference asked: "Do you think there are extraordinary novels out there that will never be published, that will remain in someone's drawer?" The "great lost novel" theory is in reality another veiled condemnation of editors who clearly "miss" the great projects. In this version, the world isn't unfair to writers, it's blind. If we believe that great work, maybe even the best work, is going undiscovered, then it stands to reason that maybe our own rejected novel just might be that work of genius. I might be Emily Dickinson! And there are enough stories in publishing lore to keep this fantasy alive. In fact, it's a badge of honor for an editor to find the diamond in the rough. Or stick with a project left for dead that ends up winning a major prize. Writers and editors have this in common: they are underdogs. The editor desperately wants to discover the next great novel. The novelist is desperate to be discovered.

Back on earth, editors don't always return calls or emails promptly, sometimes they take months to read manuscripts and provide comments, sometimes they provide feedback that can be helpful and astute or, just as easily, withering and vexing. Some make an author feel welcome, plenty of room at the inn. Some are like the little old lady who lived in the shoe: there doesn't seem to be any room left over for you. Some are hurried, hassled, and distracted. Others are such good listeners that authors feel as if they should pay by the hour.

For some author–editor relationships, unfortunately, it's all downhill after the acquisition. These editors are all about the chase. Once they have acquired a book, they're on to the next one. Sometimes the writer finds himself vying for the editor's attention. The author is automatically cast in a sibling situation with fellow writers on his editor's roster. Who does Mommy love the most? How important am I in the scheme of things? Writers frequently ask editors with terrific nonchalance, "What else are you working on?" It's a loaded question: *Where am I in the pecking order? Which author will get the most marketing money? Whose writing is the best? Not that I'm competitive.*

When it works best, it's the back-and-forth on the page that defines the author–editor relationship. It's the perfect tennis match where each player brings out the other's best game. It's the golf coach saying *Keep your head down, eye on the ball, follow through.* It's working in synchronicity like figure skaters, ballroom dancers: you lead, I follow. There is no greater feeling for me than when a writer takes my notes, then ups the ante, making the passage or paragraph not just better but brilliant. Author and editor form a mutual appreciation society. The author feels inspired and inspires in return. Email exchanges are delightful, hysterically funny. I hate to use that word again, but it's a love fest.

I always felt that there was nothing more intimate than working on a writer's pages. The writer is extremely vulnerable. All of his hopes are in the editor's hands. The writer hopes this person understands and appreciates his work in both the most general and the subtlest way possible. Similarly, the editor hopes the writer is challenged, inspired, and buoyed by the editing. That the editorial letter in tandem with a line edit convinces the writer to make whatever changes are necessary: plot restructuring, killing off a character, changing the point of view, turning short stories into a novel or changing the ending. Just before she died, Harper Lee revealed that it was her editor who suggested she rewrite *To Kill a Mockingbird* from Scout's point of view as a girl. *Good call.* The editor fights the author's battle inside the company and shepherds every aspect of the physical book. It's not a baby, but you made it together.

There's a flipside, too. Sometimes the work on the page does not go well, or the chemistry is just wrong. Communication can break down when a writer feels misunderstood, when his editor rips into his pages and requests a new version, or worse, takes months to respond. Editors become beleaguered by authors who never stop revising, handing in new drafts every day, or who return the manuscript with only cursory attention to the editorial advice, sending the process back to square one.

Editors often feel underappreciated and undervalued. Sometimes an editor is on a losing streak. She has lost every book she's tried to acquire to another publishing house. Sometimes an editor has a string of books that utterly fail in the marketplace. No sales, no reviews, no recognition whatsoever. Editors are not impervious to pain or fear of job loss. They are the closest possible person to the writer, and they are inextricably bound up in his defeats and victories. In the olden days, editors were known for sticking with authors for five, six, seven books even if they didn't particularly sell. The rope is no longer quite as long, and most authors are cut loose after just one or two books if they fail to sell well. Conversely, sometimes an author will leave his editor/publisher just as his work begins to take off, believing another publisher can do a better job with marketing, sales, or distribution.

Some years ago when I was still an editor, I heard a colleague in the next office sobbing at her desk. I poked my head in to see if she was all right. Her most beloved author was moving to a new publisher with her next project. The editor was inconsolable. She had discovered this writer, helped her grow from a tiny acorn to a mighty oak. She had called in every favor she had to help promote the writer, finding blurbers, setting up readings, sending galleys to her media contacts. She gave up vacations to work on her manuscripts. She had loaned the author money when she cried poverty. She even gave her a room in her own apartment to write in . . . the Max Perkins fantasy come to life.

"I'm such a fool," she said. "What did I do it for?"

The question hung in the air.

Love?

If writers sometimes act like babies or belligerent toddlers, it is often because they have been infantilized by the publisher. When I was an editor, it became clear to me that publishers largely felt that the less the authors knew the better. Things like marketing and sales were kept from them like state secrets. At two publishing houses where I worked, even the editors were excluded from the sales and marketing meetings. Authors were deemed the least likely to know what a good title, subtitle, or jacket would be for their book, as if they were surgeons who dare not operate on themselves. (Social media is changing all this. Some writers are geniuses at building or reaching their own constituency; some are even better at it than the publishers. It's no small thing when a writer can fill a bookstore via a post on Facebook or generate enough Amazon preorders to land the book on the best-seller list the week it launches.)

Writers are a lot of things: depressed, funny, paranoid, anxious, competitive, compulsive, surly, sorry, ambitious, brilliant, insightful, perceptive, intense, psychologically acute, dreamy, and indefatigable. They love to fight and seek forgiveness. They want to be alone and loved by all. They will push an editor to the edge and then over it. They love to procrastinate. They love to send emails in the middle of the night. They need to make sure you are thinking about them. Writers cry, complain, gnash. Authors let their freak flags fly. They are insecure because everything about their lives is insecure. Make a living writing? Put their life's work in the hands of publishers? Even the most successful writer lives out on a limb. It's a deeply risky and precarious way to live. It can be equally thrilling and demoralizing. It's life on a high wire and there is nothing like it: creating original work. Making something out of nothing, pulling rabbits from hats. However much power it feels like the publisher has, it's the writer, ultimately, who has the power to create.

In my final days as an editor before I became an agent, I hoped to acquire a new project by an author I had worked with on three previous books of nonfiction. I was usually drawn to brash writers who were emotionally volatile and exciting, their lives a perpetual rollercoaster and their prose high-octane. This woman was reserved. She was incredibly strong and smart, but her affect was gentle and soft-spoken. I marveled at her keen eye, her surprising descriptive details, and the way she let character reveal itself incrementally. I loved her writing! I loved her! When it came time to acquire her next book, I was called into an acquisition meeting. Until that point, all I'd had to do in order to acquire a book was tell my boss how much I loved it, and he would let me make an offer. Only now there was a new regime that ushered in a publishing board comprising people from the sales, marketing, and publicity departments. These meetings, as far as most editors were concerned, were the death of publishing. In the olden days, editorial passion for a project was the only imperative. Now market forces and bean counters were influencing acquisitions.

I looked around the conference room at what I expected to be friendly faces, but it was more like a tribunal than a meeting. I took my seat, my folder in front of me, numbers crunched, reviews xeroxed, book proposal shiny and new. Before I could say anything, the publisher asked who had read the proposal. Hands went up. He called on a woman to give her opinion. She was in charge of selling to the national chains, and her opinion had sway. She tried to smile, but her lips turned down as if a moldy smell was coming off the pages.

"Well," she said, "I don't see it."

Then she glanced at me and shrugged as if to say, *Don't be mad.*

A marketing manager chimed in: "Who's going to buy it?"

And the final stake through the heart of the project came from the editor-in-chief, supposedly my ally: "It seems more like a magazine article."

This was bad. I wanted to put my head on the table. I loved this author and I had stumbled before getting out of the gate. It was all going south before I had a chance to make my case, the skirt of my stupid little Ann Taylor suit was crinkled into accordion pleats, and I felt the backs of my pumps digging into my heels. This wasn't even me in this getup, rather someone I thought the publisher wanted me to be. Everyone was looking at me, possibly taking pity on me. I realized then that it had all been decided. This was a puppet court.

"What do you want to do?" the publisher asked me in a tone that implied *Wrap it up.*

Did I have a choice?

Against my better judgment, I launched into my presentation as if I were a defense attorney and it was my turn to sway the jury—my author's life in the balance. I read some of the wonderful review quotes that showcased her as an up-and-coming writer. I spoke about the idea for this new book and how I believed that universal themes ran through it. I was emboldened by an anecdote from Maxwell Perkins's biography about how he fought to keep Fitzgerald, upbraiding the powers that be for failing to grow new talent.

It wasn't exactly a filibuster, but I'm sure I annoyed the publisher with my tireless enthusiasm, my stubborn belief. Finally, when I was finished, he said, "If you really want it, you can beg."

I'm not saying my soul died that day, but I said, "Okay, I'll beg, I'm an editor."

I was authorized to make a bid so low the agent screamed at me. He sold the book to another publisher, and a few months later I quit my beloved profession and became an agent.

As an author myself, I've had three editors. The first one took three months to read my manuscript. I was a mess, every fingernail shredded, my face a splotch of anxiety. When her notes came, they blew my mind and not in a good way. She seemed to hate the book, large loopy handwriting saying as much in the margins until her notes ended in a crescendo of frustration, "Who would want to read this, it's so negative!!!" It took a while to be resuscitated, but I realized she was right. The book was an ironic take on publishing wrapped in a sardonic point of view. I rewrote it, balanced the negativity with hope and encouragement. She was right and the book so much better for it. *Love hurts.*

My second editor was polite. She was younger than I—that might have had something to do with it. She was extremely respectful and an excellent line editor, but she didn't say very much about the most revealing scenes, which left me feeling a bit uncertain.

My third editor wasn't afraid to push me. Maybe her method provides the best definition I can come up with in the end: a good editor asks the right questions, makes you better than you are, or more willing to stretch even when you resist. It's a known fact that the comments you hate the most are the most important to grapple with.

As I was leaving a conference, I was bombarded by three participants who kind of scared me. One woman trapped me in the ladies' room and demanded to know why I never answered her query letter. Out in the hallway, a man with bulging eyes and sweat soaking his denim shirt lowered his voice to tell me he was working on a book about meth labs in rural Oklahoma, from what appeared to be firsthand experience. Another woman told me a terrible tale of how her mother fell out of a Ferris wheel and plummeted to her death; could I help her write her story?

I packed my bags and headed out. As I was crossing the quad, the rollers on my suitcase thunking over the brick pavers, I spotted a young woman in overalls sitting under a tree writing in a notebook. She must have felt me looking at her, because she glanced up. I wondered what she was writing.

7 THE OTHER SIDE OF THE DESK

WHAT I LEARNED ABOUT EDITING WHEN
I BECAME A LITERARY AGENT

. . . .

SUSAN RABINER

When I made the move to agenting after more than three decades as an editor, I presumed that the editorial skills and judgment calls that made for a successful editor would make for a successful agent. I was right—but only to a point. There were important editorial questions that editing hadn't prepared me for but that agenting required I figure out. Strangely, the most important would make me not only a better agent but a much wiser editor.

As an ex-editor, I knew immediately when an author hadn't really addressed all the questions editors need to have answered in a proposal or when authors were confused about which audience their book was addressing. These issues were easy to identify, if not always easy to fix. But I was neither prepared nor particularly skilled at dealing with what soon became the key editorial issue of agenting: *is this project convincingly conceptualized?*

What's "conceptualization"?

It's the value added by the author to what is essentially a set of facts, stories, and commentary in search of a larger meaning. To conceptualize is to link these facts, stories, and commentary to a compelling point. A successful book proposal offers to take the reader on a journey. It may be one he has taken, in some form, many times before. An author's concept for the book is her promise is that with the benefit of new research, new stories, new insights, and her authorial guiding vision, the reader will see new things on the journey and arrive at a new destination—and even, at the end, be changed by the experience.

Conceptualization goes back to the very simple idea that we read books to make us think, or feel, or question our understanding of ourselves or our

SUSAN RABINER cofounded Susan Rabiner Literary with Alfred Fortunato, with whom she cowrote *Thinking like Your Editor: How to Write Great Serious Nonfiction—and Get It Published*. Previously she was senior editor at a number of major New York publishing houses and editorial director of Basic Books. Authors represented by her agency have won numerous awards, including two Pulitzer Prizes.

universe, or to shake us out of our complacent notions. Facts, stories, even ideas do not, cannot, in and of themselves do that. Only an author can magically transform that raw material into something meaningful. If in doing so the author suggests an exciting journey and good payoff at the end, the book is on its way to publication. If not, it's likely to be stillborn.

It will be clear in this essay that I'm speaking of nonfiction, the field in which I have always worked. The issue of conceptualization doesn't arise in fiction in the same way. But fiction editors and agents would tell you that some of the same lessons apply in their field: a novel must also take the reader on a journey, one that is different from any journey the reader has taken before. If the novel is going to find a publisher, the author must convey what will make this story unique and have a clear structure for it in mind. And as with nonfiction, this critical thought process usually takes place before the book ever reaches the editor's desk.

You might think that as a longtime editor, I had thought long and hard about conceptualization, but I'm not sure the word entered my vocabulary as an editor. My colleagues and I spent little time discussing or thinking about the issue, because we didn't have to. If a project came my way that didn't define its journey in a way I found seductive, I just moved on.

Nor did editing manuscripts force me to learn. While I and most other editors will cheerfully work incredibly hard to identify and fix a good manuscript that falters at times, even if it falters repeatedly, once I sensed a systemic conceptual problem with a manuscript, my editing stopped. Early in my career I had been trained: once that happened, you put down your pencil and shipped the manuscript and the problem back to the two people whose problem it was at the beginning and must once again become—the agent and the author.

But now I *was* the agent. Even if my own sense of pride had not made it impossible for me to send out a poorly conceptualized project, the practical consequences of doing so would soon have jolted me to my senses. For the price of coming up short can be very high. A critical section of any publishing contract is the "acceptance" clause—a misnomer if ever there was one, because the clause deals with the very harsh consequences of nonacceptance. If the editor sends the manuscript back to the author and the latter can't satisfy her with a revision, the author (and agent) must return the advance. Best to prevent that from happening by making sure any conceptualization problems were worked out before I let go of a project.

This proved to be a difficult and time-consuming task, because a surprisingly large number of good potential authors queried me with proposals that had been written before they had any real idea what their book would say. They knew their subject matter, but not necessarily what point they wanted to make with this material. The "draftiness" of these initial submissions was just stunning. You could feel the wind rushing through canyon-size holes in both argument and narrative as you read. I found myself asking basic questions I had never asked before, like "What is the story you want to tell?" because I had no idea what the pages and pages of facts added up to. Or "Whose story is it?" when a memoir author was trying to combine her story with a parallel narrative and it wasn't clear how the two melded. Even "Aren't you telling the wrong story?" when a dual-character book came in and the author chose to tell the story from the perspective of the character who left more written documentation, rather than focus on the person who made it an interesting and counterintuitive tale.

These authors hadn't sent me these drafty proposals because they were lazy. They just didn't understand how much thinking has to go into a book before it is ready to be shown to editors. Part of the problem is that we have all been trained to think about crafting books in terms of *writing*. Conceptualization is about *thinking*.

After a couple of bad decisions on my part, I realized I needed to develop a way to sort out those authors who had a vision but didn't know how to express it from those who didn't. And that meant that I had to steel myself against the allure of other factors.

For an agent, it is very easy to trick yourself into taking on a project by counting up a series of "pluses"—fabulous author credentials, tantalizing bits and pieces of what seems like an unbelievably good story, exceptional command of a topic you just know the public is interested in hearing more about. As those pluses mount up, your initial editorial skepticism somehow weakens, and you talk yourself into the idea that you can always figure out the conceptual part later. But the truth was I often couldn't. And more important, I shouldn't.

I finally came to understand that there is one question every author must be able to answer in order for me to work with him or her: *Why do you want to write this book?*

You might think that those authors who went silent in response to this question, or who scrunched up their faces the way we all do when we realize we don't have a good answer, were the ones I walked away from. Or that the very smart author who slyly looked up at me and asked, "Does my book actually have to say something?" was an automatic reject. Ditto the very talented writer who replied, "You tell *me*. Why *do* I want to write this book?"

To the contrary. These turned out to be the authors I stayed with. Why? Because they took the question seriously. The ones I walked away from were those who started rat-a-tat-tat blurting this answer and that, defensive the whole time and hoping to hit upon one that satisfied me. They never got that this exercise wasn't about me.

Of course, in order to get to a satisfactory answer, very often I had to walk these authors through a series of other questions that would retrace their own journey of discovery. The discussion went something like this. "You are not the first person to have looked at this issue. Think back to what troubled you about the accepted view of this time and place and caused you to question it. What exactly was it you questioned? And what was it you learned on your journey of discovery? Now explain why that journey is going to be as meaningful and compelling to me as it was for you." Or as I sometimes put it, "I get why you want to write this book. Tell me why I want to read it."

Did all the authors eventually come back to me with satisfactory answers? Alas, no. But that was in its own way just as helpful. Why? Because that questioning process did a very good job of selecting those who really had something to say and a compulsion to say it. As important, it took power out of the hands of the agent and put it into the hands of the writer. And it made me much more comfortable asking authors to revise and re-revise their proposals, knowing that the end result would be worth the effort.

Here are a few other editorial insights I have gained from agenting.

Editors rarely talk about genre, but when they evaluate proposals they are subconsciously aware of it in a way that I never understood while I was still an editor.

By "genre" I don't mean some obscure literary taxonomy created by some French writer whose name no one remembers. Nor do I mean broad catch-all categories like "literary fiction" or "travel." To me, speaking of genre is a way of saying that there must be a tight match between the sensibilities of the writer and the preferences of her audience *in terms of how the project is executed.*

Editors rarely even use the word *genre.* I've never had an editor write back to me about a project I submitted that the proposal was "out of genre"—but that doesn't mean they're not aware of it. I've come to realize that editors carefully scrutinize every proposal they read to see if the author truly understands what readers who read this type of book want (for example, do they want to get inside the head of a character, or do they prefer a finely grained dissection of an issue?) and, even more so, how they want their stories told (for example, through an omniscient third-person voice, or the more personal "I" voice, or the points of view of the various characters).

When a proposal makes an editor nervous about the author's feel for his readers' preferences, she is going to be very cautious about bidding on the project—and many won't bid at all, because if the concerns are real, the manuscript is likely to have systemic problems. And systemic problems, as I've already said, can't be resolved through editing.

What editors don't realize—but I have become very aware of as an agent—is how many would-be authors are truly clueless about the need to work within the rules of a genre. "Who are you trying to talk to?" I have often asked these authors, because the material they sent me didn't seem to be speaking to any audience I could define. The editor version of this question is "What *is* this? I don't get it."

People often ask me why the process of who gets published and who doesn't seems to be so opaque. As I tell them, it's because subconscious concerns influence how editors think. It was only agenting that revealed to me that genre was one of those concerns—rarely discussed or defined as such, but nonetheless determinative.

Content matters, more than editors admit—and "filler" is not content.

When I first became an agent, all I heard from the editors was the same line over and over again: *I only want to see the work of really good writers. A-list writers. It's all about the writing.* I believed them—until I started to make submissions, only to learn that when they made that decision to bid or not to bid, what drove the decision and the level of their bids was not the fluency, wit, or eloquence of the prose but the power of the content. I will never forget the editor who called me to say, "We don't frequently see proposals as well written as this one," and then proceeded to turn it down. You'd never know from the way editors talk that this is a content-driven industry. I'm not saying that they will buy a poorly written manuscript--no one wants that. But substance matters.

To put this another way, "good writing" means *compelling ideas clothed in words.* Writing that is merely eloquent, or entertaining, but that does not further the message of the book or feed the storyline or develop the characters is not going to work. Why, you ask, isn't this apparent to most authors? Because of the lure of what I call "filler."

Filler, again, is not an industry term. It is my way of describing proposal material that is very nicely written but devoid of real content. It's there because the author is trying to write his way out of the fact that he doesn't yet know what he wants to say.

Let me acknowledge that filler has an honored place among all kinds of writing. I write tons of it. It's what you produce when you can't abide staring at an empty screen one second longer but you can't get your brain into deep thinking mode. So you tell an anecdote or make a big deal out of some little point, or say the same thing two or three different ways, just to feel productive while your real thoughts are a jumbled mess. And because what you put down on the page is, shall we say, content light, it flows easily and reads well.

And therein lies the problem.

Filler charms. It relaxes. It's likely salted with a dramatic or humorous episode or two, and because the author isn't struggling with both content and language, it's often the best-written part of the proposal. *What a pleasure*, you think initially. But eventually the content bug bites you. For the agent, it might not happen until you have to write the cover letter to editors and you find that you can't articulate what this author wants to say. Or it might not happen until editors pass on the project en masse, saying things like "I just don't know why I'm not more excited about this project. The topic is terrific, the writing is great, but there is just something not compelling me here."

So what began as charming eventually leaves a bad aftertaste. And if an author doesn't have enough to say to fill up a twenty-something-page proposal, how is that author ever going to have enough to say to fill up a book?

Chronology is not narrative. This is why I will never again give short shrift to a fully developed table of contents.

Every compelling book tells a story—and this is just as true for nonfiction as for fiction, even for academic works of ideas. This notion is confusing, or even disturbing, to many academic authors. They think of "story" as the domain of fiction, books that focus on people rather than ideas or events. Or they say, "My book is full of anecdotes—why are you telling me it needs more of a narrative?"

But as already noted, a book has to take the reader on a journey. In a history, it may be from one point in time to another when the world has changed—and also from an old explanation of that event to a new one. In a book on parenting, it may be from one understanding of what children need to a better one. In a political book on inequality, it might be from one model for what causes inequality to a new one based on new data. Each of these journeys is a story.

. . . .

The table of contents shows how that story unfolds. While the conceptualization laid out in the proposal has to promise an exciting destination and lay out the high and low points on the journey, the table of contents has to demonstrate in a much deeper way that the journey itself will be an exciting, powerful experience. The reader needs to gain a sense of momentum, almost of inevitability, as the book moves toward a conclusion. A series of anecdotes, no matter how entertaining, or of ideas, no matter how original, doesn't make a story unless it builds from one to the next. And in order to achieve that, the author needs to understand point by point, chapter by chapter, how he is going to move the reader along the road.

It is only by having an author write a long, thick table of contents that an agent can see that structure developing and ideally identify problems with it up front, so that they won't hobble the author when it's time to write the book. I now ask all my authors to think in terms of a table of contents of around fifty pages, with each chapter summarized in five to ten pages. Writing clarifies thinking, never more so than in a table of contents.

It's not a business decision for editors; it's personal.

It took becoming an agent for me to understand something that always makes me smile now. In the end, no matter how hard management tries to turn publishing into a business, it remains an affair of the heart. Editors are passionate people, not statheads or game theorists. They wouldn't pass Negotiation Strategy 101. Why do I say this? You would think that when an editor loves a project, the last thing he would do is reveal this to the agent. He should hold his cards close to his chest to keep down the price of the book, right? But the opposite happens. If a project has a powerful emotional impact, editors will email us to say that the material "made me cry," or "It's so uplifting," or "Oh my god, a book with new ideas."

Similarly, if a proposal raises editors' hackles—if, for instance, an author comes across as petty or smug—you'll hear about it. "I don't even like this author," as one editor put it to me. And woe to the author whose ideas rub editors the wrong way: then I'm on the receiving end of incredibly long and detailed letters arguing with the author, when the easiest response would have been to just write the standard platitude, "Sorry, not for me."

All of which is to say that the single most important piece of advice I give to would-be editors is this: Don't go into publishing cynically. And once in, don't do it cynically.

Here's what agenting has made even clearer to me than all my years editing. Books remain the last bastion of the truly reflective mind. In the age of social media, there are endless opportunities for those who want to rant to do so. There is now a free and universally available way to access any bit of information you want, rehash any event or experience. But there is only one reason to write books or publish them: to go on that journey of discovery, and to share it with other people who will care about it the way you do—if you have told your story well.

8 OPEN-HEART SURGERY, OR JUST A NIP AND TUCK?
DEVELOPMENTAL EDITING
....

SCOTT NORTON

As an acquiring editor, your day is filled with a plethora of distractions. You're playing phone tag with an agent who's closing the bidding today on a major trade book; your edits to the online seasonal catalog are overdue; a new financial policy requires you to update all of your profit-and-loss statements; one of your authors has had an allergic reaction to her copyediting and must be administered some verbal antihistamines. In the midst of all this activity, it can be hard enough to find the time to give a new proposal your full attention, let alone think strategically about how the project should be developed to ensure a successful book.

Yet if you're like most acquiring editors, development is at the heart of your sense of vocation. You got into publishing because you love books: how they can immerse you in stories of subtle complexity or lead you through a thicket of evidence to yield illuminating insights. And your authors, when submitting a proposal for your consideration, are planning to devote hundreds of hours to writing in the hope that they will achieve the enlightening effects of their own favorite books.

Elsewhere I've defined *developmental editing* as "significant structuring or restructuring of a manuscript's discourse" and mapped out a detailed process for extracting a publishable book from a completed manuscript that has structural flaws.[1] And I've provided a synopsis of those procedures for new academics revising their dissertations into first books.[2] Acquiring editors use

SCOTT NORTON is director of Editing, Design, and Production at the University of California Press, where he has been on staff since 1995. He is the author of *Developmental Editing: A Handbook for Freelancers, Authors, and Publishers* and a contributor to Beth Luey, ed., *Revising Your Dissertation: Advice from Leading Editors*. He currently serves as president of the Publishing Professionals Network, which hosts, among other activities, an annual daylong conference for book-publishing staff and freelancers.

1. Scott Norton, *Developmental Editing: A Handbook for Freelancers, Authors, and Publishers* (Chicago: University of Chicago Press, 2009).

2. Beth Luey, ed., *Revising Your Dissertation: Advice from Leading Editors* (Berkeley: University of California Press, 2004).

the same basic techniques. But because you often first engage with a project as a proposal or partial draft, you have an opportunity to shape the book in a way that is especially intimate and satisfying.

In some sectors of the book industry, the acquiring editor can rely on help with developmental editing. In textbook publishing, for example, full-time in-house developmental editors work with authors to ensure their books remain competitive in the marketplace and meet state curriculum mandates. Developmental specialists also play strong roles in the publishing of medical, technical, legal, public policy, and major reference works. But in trade and academic publishing, most developmental editing takes place at the hands of either the acquiring editor or—when schedule requires and budget allows—a freelance professional.

In this chapter I distill the hard-won wisdom of four accomplished colleagues from the Acquisitions Department at the University of California Press: Naomi Schneider, editor in sociology; Niels Hooper, history; Maura Roessner, criminal justice; and Blake Edgar, science and wine. Their areas of subject expertise are diverse, their editorial styles highly individual—yet they all follow the same basic tenets when guiding an author from proposal to finished manuscript.

THE EDITOR'S ROLE

Effective editors bring three main assets to bear: subject expertise, to ensure that they see where an author is coming from; market knowledge, to allow them to understand the interests and needs of a book's target audience; and the tenacity and tact to hash out solutions when an author's preferences and the market's needs are in conflict.

Maintaining subject expertise is an ongoing commitment. Many acquiring editors have academic degrees in the subject areas in which they publish, but they must keep up their knowledge base postgraduation to remain effective. Just as you wouldn't want to have bridgework done by a dentist whose methods are decades old, an author seeks an editor who has kept abreast of news in the field. In academic publishing this means reading journals and competitors' books, following online blogs and chats, and attending meetings; in trade publishing it can mean following a current-affairs topic in the media and attending summits or protests. For an editor acquiring in general-interest trade, this mandate is equally important, if more elusive: such editors log many armchair hours earning the epithet "widely read."

Marketing knowledge also requires constant maintenance. This insight can come from some of the same sources as subject expertise—conferences,

....

periodicals, online conversations—but the wise editor supplements these re-sources for specific projects by consulting expert readers and surveying the market (see "Conducting Market Research," below).

When an author's vision for her book conflicts with your knowledge of the audience's needs, you must "stick to your guns," says Hooper. These conflicts are often about leaving content in or out: if the content you wish to excise rep-resents an author's laborious research or emotionally charged personal narra-tive, she may have a difficult time parting with it. During these tough moments, it is important for you to constantly demonstrate to the author your enthusi-asm for the project, your investment in its message, and your commitment to the book's success. "Often," says Hooper, "authors later realize you were right."

THE AUTHOR'S MOTIVES

Roessner ticks off a list of markers that you should look for to gauge an author's likely receptiveness to developmental editing: she has "writing chops"; she's a "known commodity"—that is, ideally you've worked with her previously; she has "fantastic raw material"; and she's interested in "getting out of her own head to reach a targeted audience." This last factor is key: most authors will *say* they're open to constructive feedback, but once they're being prepped for the open-heart surgery that is developmental editing, they have second thoughts.

If an author demonstrates lack of openness to development, you must make a judgment call about whether to pursue the matter further. Usually it's best to "avoid pleas of desperation," Roessner says. Edgar agrees that you have to know when to give up on a project—sometimes an author is so enthralled with her raw material that she cannot see the need to articulate a clear point of view. But he avers that he usually tries "to break down that barrier, rather than just throw up my hands."

With significant trade projects there's usually a third dance partner in the mix: the agent. In proposals presented by agents, it can sometimes be difficult to distinguish the agent's agenda from the author's. Agents bring a whole set of additional concerns to the process, such as whether a blockbuster movie on the author's topic is in production in Hollywood. Orchestrating three-way project development can be nerve racking for all, especially when you throw in the publisher's marketing and sales directors and other key stakeholders. Some agents will step aside once they've clinched the deal and earned their percentage of the advance on royalties, but others won't.

It's worth noting that some "highly invested" agents are themselves tal-ented editors who add value to the development process, often serving as the editor's ally by helping to manage the author's expectations. Either way, you do well to make a candid assessment of the agent's motives along with the author's before investing time in development.

THE PUBLISHER'S INVESTMENT

As an acquiring editor, you are steward of your employer's most valuable resource: your time. In trade publishing it is generally assumed that you will spend time developing nearly every book you sign, but in other parts of the industry you will probably need to use your judgment. Before deciding how much developmental effort to invest in a project, it's important to do a cost-benefit analysis. Think "quantitatively," Roessner says. She asks herself, *Do I think I can expand a book's sales potential enough to warrant the investment of time that development would require?* In some cases this means enlarging the book's audience from a narrower group of aficionados or specialists to a broader trade audience made up of those elusive creatures we publishers call "general-interest readers."

For a book to have trade potential, the topic must be "zeitgeisty," says Schneider. Edgar seconds this observation but also notes the importance of author cachet and timing. "We tend to hang a lot on platform now," he says, referring to whether the author has cultivated a public following in print, radio, television, and social media. "But that's not as important as credibility and addressing the right topic at the right time."

Some editors believe in spending a small amount of time on development even for books with limited sales potential as a way to cement an author-editor relationship. "The idea is to earn the loyalty of a promising author by engaging directly with her work," Roessner explains. "Then, hopefully, the author comes back to you with her big trade book." But she notes this approach is hard to sustain while meeting your signing goals and can become a point of contention in the publishing house.

All four of our editors ask a few key questions about everything that comes across their desks: Does this proposal articulate a clear argument? Does the table of contents support that argument? Does the author's writing style engage the reader? For most projects, this mild level of review, resulting in minor feedback, can be all that's needed and can free up time for the few projects on which they lavish deeper attention.

COACHING VERSUS MODELING

Pressed for time, acquiring editors provide their developmental feedback using a combination of two basic approaches: coaching and modeling. "I can't imagine doing only one or the other," Roessner says.

....

Coaching involves providing summary feedback about suggestions for improvement. Usually coaching begins with a written overview of the proposal's strengths and weaknesses, along with some specific suggestions for improvement. This initial step can be executed quickly because it makes no attempt to work out solutions in the text; and it can cement an early bond between the editor and an author anxiously awaiting feedback. "I skim a lot," Schneider says. "I try to get back to my authors in three or four days, to build momentum."

As the revision plan takes shape, coaching often moves from email to the telephone. A lot of context gets lost in written communication, Roessner says: "Brainstorming sessions can really help." She has had more than one "very intense whirlwind developmental romance," receiving and making phone calls at odd hours from airport gates and hotel lobbies.

Modeling allows the acquiring editor to demonstrate what she's looking for. Sometimes the rewriting is limited to the table of contents; other times it's used to demonstrate the desired writing style in the main text. Roessner "plays ghostwriter in Track Changes" in Word for a few sentences and then says, "Please do more of this."

Edgar coauthored several books before joining UC Press as an editor. His preferred mode is to give detailed feedback on individual chapters or clusters of chapters as they are drafted. He attributes his developmental ability to having learned this rhythm of collaboration in the scientific research setting, but he has had to adapt his process to the quicker pace of publishing. "Now I push the guidance upstream," he says—that is, before the full manuscript has been written. "I focus on providing input at the proposal stage, fleshing out an outline, and making sure the plan holds together before I invest any more time."

Throughout the process, remember to lavish praise on your author. Roessner recalls walking toward several authors chatting at a conference and overhearing them discussing—admiringly but apprehensively—her "tough love" style. She says she battles a tendency to skip acknowledging the strengths of a manuscript and "dive right into the problems," which can shake the confidence of authors, who think they're being asked to start over from scratch. "Tough love is fine," Roessner says, "but only if you don't forget to show them the love. Remind them that you wouldn't be spending all this time on their project if you didn't believe in it deeply." One simple rule: use change-tracking software to remark on nice phrasing and effective passages.

DEPLOYING EXTERNAL REVIEWS

In academic publishing, external reviews from experts in the author's field are required as part of the vetting process. But seeking other readers can be valuable in any sector of the industry. "Any author should try to get some feedback from the type of person he's envisioning as the end reader," Edgar says, "especially if his book is intended for a general audience."

External reviews can usefully augment the developmental process. They can alert you to the weak portions of a proposal or manuscript, validate your intuition that a project is worth pursuing, and bolster your revision plan with the author. Reviews can give your advice more credibility: "There is strength in numbers," Edgar says.

But reviews can also backfire. Precisely because reviewers are usually also experts in the author's field, they can grandstand for their own theories and methods or misinterpret the author's thesis in light of their prejudices. More dangerously, reviewers can succumb to reputational bias, fawning over proposals by authors who are influential in their fields but not necessarily gifted writers. "Some reviewers say, 'I would read anything this author wrote, even if it was on a napkin,'" Roessner warns. "But as editor, I have to veto that endorsement if I see that the writing needs work." Yet even wrongheaded reviews can be useful, because they give you an opportunity to demonstrate to the author that you're not blindly siding with your reviewers.

To harness the power of external reviews as a developmental tool, be sure to find reviewers that appreciate the discursive form in which the author is writing. If the text is a polemic, find reviewers who appreciate the role of polemics in public discourse. "Choose reviewers who are going to enhance your vision for the book," Hooper advises.

CONDUCTING MARKET RESEARCH

Sometimes there's nothing inherently deficient in a project, yet marketing analysis reveals the need for development. If there are other comparable books in the field, the acquiring editor must explore whether there's enough distinguishing the proposed work from its competitors. *How are we going to position this one?* Edgar asks himself. He cites the example of a guide to an emerging wine region: the authors initially proposed a first-person travelogue, but when a competing volume came out using that approach, they successfully switched to a reference format.

In textbook publishing the market research process can be baroque. The acquiring editor (or her assistant) may send out each chapter as it is drafted to a large number of instructors, who teach the chapter in their classes and provide feedback, which is then collated on an extensive grid. This empirical approach maximizes the potential for the text to be adopted, but it also results in the lowest common denominator in terms of pedagogical sophistication,

....

says Hooper. At UC Press, a publisher known for works of progressive cultural politics, "we tell our authors that they can have a point of view that may not appeal to creationists in Texas."

Roessner points out a beneficial side effect of this type of market research that is not developmental per se. "The marketing check is on a rolling basis" — that is, chapters are sent out to reviewers as they are drafted—"because you want to build your eventual market by having people invest in it early on," she says. "They become your early adopters."

But many works of nonfiction can be developed for the classroom without such labor-intensive research. "We do little SurveyMonkey things," Schneider says of herself and her assistant, referring to quick online surveys of course instructors. These surveys can elicit responses to the author's entire proposal, or they can gauge general interest in a proposed table of contents with a one-page project description. The surveys often ask three key questions: As outlined, would you consider using this book in one or more of the courses you teach? If yes, which courses? If no, can you recommend any changes to the author's approach?

Some books can become core texts—books around which an instructor builds her syllabus—simply by having the author map the content of known courses onto the book's structure. Other books, if kept short, can stimulate classroom discussion as supplemental reading.

One widespread concern about developing core and supplemental texts in the digital age is whether they are still relevant. In the early 2000s many publishers assumed that the first generation of students born during the internet era would prefer online learning environments in the classroom and began investing heavily in building out that new technology. But our four editors are finding that the death of the print textbook has been heralded prematurely. "Even digital natives prefer print for learning," says Hooper. "This is as true on the state campuses as at the elite universities." Edgar adds that "you have to plan for the eventuality that the audience preference may ultimately shift. And there are a lot of digital opportunities that you can get an early start on." These may include teaching students to mine Big Data online.

Like textbook publishing, professional publishing requires a large investment in developmental editing. Readers expect a series of professional handbooks to present its information in a consistent format, and the subject experts who serve as authors rarely have the skills to adapt their prose to series specifications. Thus these franchises often have in-house developmental editors.

In professional publishing a franchise may require intensive developmental coordination, says Roessner, who worked in this arena at Oxford

University Press. For instance, a series on cognitive behavioral therapy may require a treatment sequence for anxiety in children that includes a clinician's workbook, a homework guide for the child, a parent's guide, and a school psychologist component. Not all of these works would be produced on the same timeline, but all would need to have the same look and feel, requiring an integrated approach to developmental editing. Once a sequence like this has been established, "you replicate that little ecosystem for different topics," Roessner explains.

REVISING THE PROPOSAL

Once a project's developmental needs have been identified via marketing research and external review, the revision process begins. Usually the acquiring editor's first task is to work with the author to devise a "resonant" thesis, says Schneider. "You can't just cobble together your blog entries, no matter how many 'likes' they got," she says. "If you don't have a thesis, the reader asks, 'What is this book trying to do and why should I care about it?'" Even a biography needs a thesis, she points out: the reader wants to know what key insights she can take away from the subject's life.

An author can have such an overabundance of experience in the field, or have interviewed so many people, that she struggles to draw out a singular argument from her raw material. This is a common problem among anthropologists and qualitative sociologists, who rely heavily on case studies: the book cannot "just be a march through sob stories," Roessner says. An author needs to analyze her case studies: "it can feel like an impossible task to theorize that misery, but it's what the author has to do."

Other times the thesis is present but not sufficiently highlighted. "For some projects, all I do is supply a new title," says Hooper. This limited intervention can be critical to the book's success, positioning it correctly in the marketplace or forestalling criticism that the book overstates its case.

With a sharp thesis and piquant working title in hand, author and editor can get down to the business of reworking the table of contents. The chapters must be arranged so they build the central argument: some editors draft a new table of contents, while others prefer to broadly sketch an approach and let the author refine it. Either way, it is important for the editor to invite the author into the process so that she feels personally invested in the resulting plan.

Sometimes revising the TOC reveals gaps in the author's research that send her back into the field. This new research can be revelatory—Hooper notes one case that yielded an archival finding that became international

....

news. But sometimes additional research can get out of hand: another of his authors returned from the field with three times the amount of content and wanted to publish it in three volumes.

Authors' enthusiasm for their subject often results in overwriting. "People write too many chapters. For most books, I don't want more than five or six chapters," Schneider says, by which she means chapters of eight to ten thousand words. "Most subjects just aren't big enough for a longer book; you end up with padding." She finds that most of her developmental efforts involve cutting entire chapters or combining chapters and boiling them down to a reasonable length.

FINDING THE AUTHOR'S VOICE

An author's writing style, or voice, can be bound up in her manuscript's structural flaws. In first drafts, many authors have not sufficiently synthesized their raw material; in these cases, development involves "pushing toward describing the gist and greatly reducing the amount of direct quotation," Hooper says. In books with broad narratives involving many characters, the author may have trouble deciding which characters to foreground and might inadvertently allow a crowd of competing voices to drown out her own. The editor's job then is to "make the author's statement sing through the stories" of her subjects, Roessner says, "but not let the subjects just speak for themselves."

This drive toward synthesis must be calibrated to avoid dumbing down a sophisticated argument. Pushing specialists to write trade books can be risky: the author's technical voice may put off general-interest readers, while her attempt to simplify the argument may put off other specialists, prompting negative reviews in the media. That said, Hooper admits that he cannot always tell when synthesis has gone too far: a text that seems "dumbed down" to him may draw reviews from instructors who say it's still written over the heads of their students.

When time is limited for detailed line-by-line editing, focus on chapter openings and closings, Schneider says. These "have a responsibility to engage you, to show you how each chapter builds on the last."

Finally, when coaching an author to find the right tone for her manuscript's voice, furnish examples of published books that are written at a level that speaks effectively to her audience. These models should be realistic, written by others who share your author's degree of skill and experience. Your author needs "to aspire to being that person," Schneider explains. "Not Malcolm Gladwell."

Acquiring editors tend to prefer to do their own developmental editing. But sometimes an exciting project surfaces when the editor is up to her neck in previous obligations; in those situations she may consider outsourcing the development to a freelancer. This arrangement can have advantages: a freelancer may have time to generate three or four scenarios for an author and publisher to choose from, itemizing the level of investment involved in each. And many DEs have the ability—often handled as a separate, in-house function by textbook and professional reference publishers—to develop online components for books, coordinating them closely with the main text.

Of course, the success of outsourcing depends entirely on the skills of the freelancer. Edgar advises against allowing authors to pick their own DEs: these may be friends or relatives who don't have sufficient experience with book content, leaving a lot of mop-up work for you to do. Make an effort to identify a small pool of trusted DEs, and keep their contact information handy.

Another collaborator who can help with the developmental process is a series editor, the best of whom can bring to their series not only leads on promising projects but also a guiding vision to shape each project so it makes an original contribution. Schneider looks for these sterling attributes in a series editor: they are productive, deadline oriented, and collaborative, with a knack for networking and a strong organizational mind. In these partnerships the series editor usually represents the specialist audience's needs, while you champion the general-interest reader's point of view.

A book's production team, too, can make crucial contributions to project development. Edgar remembers one meeting in which he, a designer, and a production editor sat around a jumbled pile of photographs and constructed a sequence for a color insert that told the author's story visually in a compelling way. "What a worthwhile meeting!" he recalled. He has since made a practice of involving the designer and project editor in many of his books' illustration programs. Production editors also frequently help by rationalizing subheads in the text. "I can be looking at the manuscript from a pretty macro level, and they have the ability to dig into the details," he says. Illustrations, signposting—these elements may seem trivial in comparison to the work of reshaping an argument, but in actuality they highlight the work you've done on the argument.

Finally, a critical member of the acquiring editor's team is the editorial assistant. Schneider's assistant "keeps the trains running," she says, giving her time to focus on project development. "I want her to be the front line

....

with most authors. She does a lot of the logistical stuff like finding blurbs and working with authors to format the manuscript." Even so, with many contracts to negotiate, Schneider finds herself doing a lot of developmental editing on her own time.

When all is said and done, you'll be most effective as an acquiring editor when you cultivate a clear sense of your own readership. Knowing your target audience well can guide your choices about which projects to sign and which to invest in. This is not the same as being a "taste-maker," Roessner points out. "It's not about me: it's about putting the market first and foremost," she says.

A good developmental editor has humility toward both a book's audience and an author's intentions. "Nobody taught me how to be an acquisitions editor," Hooper says. "I felt so fake for a very long time." Part of his way of dealing with that anxiety was to tell himself, *I'm really just providing a first read.* But humility notwithstanding, the successful acquiring editor must ultimately trust his own editorial instincts, his own vision for a project's potential. That first reading, in which you stand in for the readers who will follow, can be crucial to sharpening the author's thesis, helping to build her argument, and clarifying her voice.

9 THIS NEEDS JUST A LITTLE WORK
ON LINE EDITING

. . . .

GEORGE WITTE

Very. Really. Actually. Vaguely. Badly (as in felt and written).

Truth be told. Without a doubt. Be that as it may. When all is said and done.

He was the one who. It was at this moment that. Five years ago had been when.

An entire manuscript in which she was / they were walking, was/were driving, was/were doing whatever she/they was/were doing.

Very unique.

Line editing is much more than nitpicking, but many writers and would-be editors perceive it as such. In fact, the line editor can restructure a novel or a work of nonfiction; ask crucial questions about plot points, assertions, conclusions, and other matters; meticulously clean up sentences and paragraphs and shape text so that a muddy manuscript gains clarity and flow; and, yes, search and destroy the clichés, imprecise adjectives, and passive verb constructions that might mar an otherwise strong book.

What do line editors do, and how do they learn? The answer to the latter question explains why the former is difficult to define. There is, in fact, no specific training path for professional editors of books. Most people who become editors are self-trained, some of them benefiting—as I did—from generous and knowledgeable mentoring, but many finding their own ways through trial and error, and developing different skill sets.

Editors all have one thing in common: we are helpless, passionate, hungry, lifelong readers, and we gravitate toward editing the books we most enjoy reading. Many of us began as critical readers in high school or college; with the guidance of smart teachers, we learned to read not just for pleasure. We learned to ask, *How did he surprise me with that revelation?* or *Why did she choose to tell the story in first person, and what did she gain or lose by that*

GEORGE WITTE has worked at St. Martin's Press for thirty-two years as an editor of fiction and nonfiction books, publisher of Picador USA, and for the past sixteen years editor in chief. He also is the author of three collections of poems: *The Apparitioners, Deniability,* and *Does She Have a Name?* He lives with his family in New Jersey.

choice? or even *Why am I bored although I'm supposed to like this book?* Many editors worked on school newspapers or college literary magazines, or as researchers for professors; some were aspiring writers and worked through draft after draft of material. Some studied areas that had nothing to do with literature: business, or science, or another discipline. And once in publishing, some were taught by skilled senior editors, then given manuscripts to edit, and through practice and repeated evaluation learned the trade.

While there are academic courses on line editing, most such courses focus on copyediting, a distinct procedure usually applied to a fully edited manuscript that has been accepted for publication. People who don't work in publishing often mistake copyediting for line editing, and with good reason; many copyeditors do the work that line editors should have done. The job of a copyeditor is to prepare a manuscript to be set in type; all professional copyeditors are trained to apply a set of printer's marks (or today, electronic codes) to the pages of a manuscript.

But good copyeditors often save an inattentive or poorly trained editor's proverbial bacon. They correct grammar and spelling but also can do significant work on tightening sentences and reshaping paragraphs that have gone astray. They query facts, register confusion when a manuscript is unclear, and police internal consistency in the work; and in some cases they aggressively root out clichés and awkward constructions. Most copyeditors, however, will not undertake a full, top-to-bottom edit of every line of every page, nor will they suggest significant structural changes to a book.

Those larger changes, if necessary, are the job of the line editor to identify and work with the author to address—because most large changes require not just editing but rewriting. That relationship with the author is the crucial difference between a line editor and a copyeditor. Copyeditors don't necessarily have direct contact with an author; their work is done on the manuscript itself, and the author addresses their work on the page. But the line editor typically is the acquiring editor of the book, and as such is the author's primary relationship in his or her working life: the source of money, the point of contact, the guide through the publishing process, the cheerleader, the writer's advocate, the person to cry to or, perhaps, to complain about, the lunch or drinks companion, sometimes the friend, and above all the most attentive and most honest reader of an author's work. The line editor is supposed to be a book's ideal reader, the one who asks all the questions and heads off all the problems in a book so that it is satisfying—rather than maddening, confusing, or just a little too dull to finish—to other readers.

Does that mean that there are different kinds of editing for different authors? Yes. And the line editor needs to learn what different authors need and will tolerate, rather than imposing a standard of editing that might damage the relationship with the author or even harm the author's ability to write. It's the author's book, not the editor's; the editor should be working to help the author write and revise the best book that he or she means to write. The editor should not impose a voice, a vision, a point of view, an agenda, or a too-aggressive critical approach that leaves no room for praise and disables the author's confidence and creativity. You want Roger Federer to play the match without looking at the coach's box for approval after every point.

Some writers will accept no editing whatsoever. In my experience, those authors are usually the least professional: people who will write only one book (a memoir, for example) or people who are successful in another field (most often business), where they are used to having their own way. And yes, there are some very grand authors who will brook no editing; they deliver the manuscript, the editor gently conveys it down to production, a light copyedit for printing purposes is applied, and the book is set in type. Without citing examples, I will say that authors who claim they need no editing, do.

Some writers will accept modest editing: corrections to grammar and spelling, minor marginal queries that address specifics and might help clarify certain questions, and perhaps suggestions to make key points more dramatic, more memorable, more telling within the context of the book.

Some writers don't merely accept but need and ask for significant editing: a line-by-line grind through a 160,000-word manuscript to get it down to 100,000 words, for example. Or exchanging many hundreds of passive verb constructions for active forms in order to enliven a flaccid manuscript. A line editor doing this kind of work might get through ten pages in two eye-straining hours, cutting sentences, shortening paragraphs, weaving stray threads, and trimming excess words.

Some writers don't need line editing as much as a sounding board for plot ideas, or general book direction, or maybe special attention to the beginnings and endings of chapters within the dramatic structure of the story being told.

When can an editor make the most difference to a given book?

The answer depends on the author, of course, but also on the book in question: fiction or nonfiction, literary or genre novel, how-to or history, "voice driven" or "plot driven," and dozens of other distinctions. There is no one-size-fits-all approach to editing, just as there is no single way to tell a story. That said, editors can most affect the quality and, perhaps, the sales of a book in a few general areas.

MICRO

On the level of diction, a careful editor can help an author identify when given words or habitual constructions are being overused. I recently finished editing a powerful debut novel which needed some work on the plot but also required close attention to the line-by-line writing because the author had the habit of leaning on certain words. *Dark*, for example, or *darkly*: dark clouds, dark shades, dark water, dark eyes, darkly thinking, darkly imagining, and so on. To my eye and ear, *dark* is an imprecise adjective; it's a young writer's fallback, and I've read many a short story or poem (and written a few myself) where that word is used to suggest a larger profundity imbuing whatever is described. So when editing this manuscript, I marked *dark*, *darkly*, *black*, and *blackly* over and over, along with other words that seemed to me inexact, or overused, or showy, or just plain bad. (On one occasion rain fell "wetly"—we cut that.) Other words that can fall before the pencil with no loss to quality and considerable gain to clarity and punch, when multiplied by five, ten, and more occasions over a book-length manuscript: *very*, *vague* or *vaguely*, *really*, *generally*, *mostly*, *nearly*, *pretty*, *pretty much*, *beautiful*, *ugly*, and other words that do no work. I have an aversion to clouds "scudding," since they seem to do so in nearly every poem and literary novel I read, but maybe that's just me.

Ditto clichés: even the best writers fall back on the old familiars, and a sharp editor can help freshen up a book by calling them out. If it reads like the wind, writes like an angel, flies like a bird, squeals like a pig (except in *Deliverance*, where James Dickey deliberately makes the cliché terrifying) . . . , the editor should groan like a door and cut accordingly.

MID-MICRO

On the level of sentences, an editor can help an author vary the length and structure of sentences in order to enhance a manuscript's dramatic flow. Most people think of drama as a function of plot and story, but there is drama inherent in the rhythm and movement of lines and sentences. I might be a bit more attuned to this dramatic potential than most; as a poet, I know that poems find momentum not by structuring events or fulfilling a reader's expectations but by deploying meter, rhyme, enjambment, and varying lengths of lines and phrases and sentences. Prose writers, especially young ones, often fall into habitual sentence structures that can have a cumulatively soporific effect. Subject-verb-predicate for paragraphs on end. Single-sentence paragraphs, meant to heighten a dramatic moment or frame an argument or announce a revelation, that become gimmicks through overuse. Sentences beginning with "And," intended to create momentum at the ends of paragraphs in order to propel the reader to the next, deployed so often that they lose effectiveness. Overly complex sentences with multiple dependent clauses that slow pace and obscure information, as often occurs in nonfiction books. In my experience, nonfiction books tend to need more sentence work than novels, perhaps because many nonfiction books are written by people who have less training in writing than the typical fiction author.

MACRO

On a more general level, an editor can dramatically improve a piece of writing by focusing on certain structural areas that most manuscripts have in common. Beginnings and endings, of the book and each individual chapter, are areas of particular focus.

Does a manuscript begin with a dramatic moment? Not all do, or should, but every manuscript needs to begin strongly enough so that the reader will want to turn the page and keep reading. That long dream sequence, or complicated flashback explaining reams of backstory (before the actual plot has begun), or pages of lovingly detailed landscape evocation that conclude with . . . well, not much? The line editor may ask an author to cut those passages entirely, or put them somewhere else, or (in the case of landscape) parcel out those details in smaller doses in the course of telling the story, and make them germane to its purpose rather than a static clump of description.

Does the manuscript end on the right note? It doesn't have to end with "a bang," and in fact that dramatic high point may come several pages before the end, but the end should feel like a conclusion, not a trailing off or a too-extended running of the credits. In particular, an editor might warn a novelist against what my mentor Tom McCormack called "serial resolution," where plotlines are wrapped up in a plodding series of consecutive scenes, rather than one scene that ties together the novel's central stories.

Paragraphs, too, have their own dramatic function, and editors work to ensure that paragraphs serve individually and collectively within a book's dramatic movement to keep the reader turning pages, advance the story being told, complicate or clarify issues as they are explored, and develop characters. When editing, if I find myself bored or confused, I pause to ask myself: *What did this paragraph just do? Did it do anything? If not, why not? Why was it a paragraph in the first place? What is supposed to be happening here, and where has the story or the point being made gone astray?* The reader should be getting something from every paragraph, and if a given book is lagging, it often means that paragraphs are taking up space without having a purpose.

In fiction, purposeless paragraphs often mean that time is spent getting people from one place to another when they simply need to be *there*. Or that backstory is told in undigested form, rather than informing the overall story and being revealed as characters grow and change through the entire narrative. Ditto long descriptive passages about landscape or interiors, the details of which are necessary but need to be doled out gradually. In nonfiction, purposeless paragraphs—and therefore behemoth books, often described as "exhaustive" by reviewers—usually derive from an author's unwillingness to cut researched material. It's there because the author can't bear to leave it out: it happened, it's true, there's this great stuff that nobody knows about, I have it on tape, wait, there's a photograph, it's *really* important, etc. The line editor needs to identify what must stay and what can be sacrificed.

Transitions—the beginnings and endings of chapters or sections—also are places where an editor can help an author improve a book. Many manuscripts arrive with too few chapters or lack section breaks within long chapters. In those cases, the editor's job is to help the author identify opportunities to start and end scenes, so that the reader feels a sense of shape and momentum. What is a given chapter meant to accomplish in the overall dramatic structure of the book? And how do the scenes within that chapter contribute to that purpose? If a chapter begins on an irresolute note—with no connection to the previous chapter's end and no sense of dramatic promise—then the line editor might suggest adding a sentence (or two) that establishes direction, or perhaps cutting an extraneous descriptive opening and focusing on a character's point of view. Or if a chapter ends by trailing off in a welter of details, the editor might suggest that the author find a cleaner cut: a way to close off the chapter and move to the next, rather than cluttering a transition point that should be more dramatic.

Example: I work with an author of genre fiction who sometimes concludes scenes and chapters with the characters taking their time in exiting the premises. Let's say two cops have just been chewed out by a supervisor. They leave his office and get some coffee in the squad room, one takes milk, the other doesn't, they go out the door, close it behind them, walk out to the parking lot, notice it's sunny outside, get in their patrol car, roll down the windows, and finally exchange a line of dialogue that flips off said supervisor. I would suggest ending the chapter in the supervisor's office, with his last words booting them out and into the next sequence, where the action picks up; or, if we need that clever line of flip-off dialogue, then cut quickly to the patrol car by writing "Two minutes later . . ." and get rid of all the stage business in between. We don't need to see routine to-and-fro taking up space and sapping momentum; we need to get to the next scene.

WAR STORIES

I've edited hundreds of books over a thirty-year career, fiction and nonfiction, across more categories than I can recall. Here are some examples of dos and don'ts that I hope will be instructive.

The very first book I acquired and edited was a novel by a woman who grew up in the South. She was a natural storyteller but an untrained writer. Her first novel was written in thick first-person dialect and recounted the story of a young white girl and an older black man who lived on the outskirts of her small town. Fresh out of graduate school and full of self-importance, fancying myself an authority on southern literature since I had studied with the leading scholar of the region, I wrote her a long editorial letter. I recommended lightening up the dialect (because, being from New Jersey, I knew all about how white and black folks in rural Georgia in the 1940s talked) and also suggested dozens of plot changes, dramatic twists, and a more upbeat ending.

A few weeks of silence followed my letter. One afternoon the phone rang, as phones did in those days before email chimed its perpetual arrival. It was my author, and she wanted to talk. For once, maybe because my mother had told me to respect my elders, I listened. She patiently explained why her characters spoke as they did, and said she couldn't lighten their dialect because then she couldn't hear them in her head. As for the plot changes, she said, "You know, George, I appreciate everything you have suggested, but . . . it just didn't happen that way." And then I knew: this book was her life, she was the narrator, and that was that. The novel was published, found its way into the world, and eventually became a successful made-for-TV movie. So did her second novel, which I also published—and didn't suggest changing a word. Sometimes an editor needs to leave well enough alone.

A very different challenge came from a businessman, a sales/marketing guy and an expert in his field, writing a how-to book for others seeking success. It was the kind of book a young editor acquires: a proposal by a novice author who promised—and delivered—a full-bore campaign that would sell his book and tap his client base. A year later the manuscript arrived in a massive box. He'd written it himself, at great length; the manuscript was seventy thousand words too long, loaded with extraneous material. It began with a potted autobiography, from grade school to high school to college, including summers, then a blow-by-blow account of his career, before getting to the heart of the book: the how-to-succeed techniques, which really were unusual and demonstrably effective.

The author wanted to come in and meet me for an editorial conversation. I girded myself, knowing this would be a tough one. He arrived with a strange light in his eyes, reminding me of Coleridge's Ancient Mariner, as if tormented by visions that no one else could or should perceive. I began as my wise boss had told me to approach such conversations, with praise for the book, how illuminating it was, how instructive and valuable it would be, and how much more so we would make it together with just a bit of work. When he realized that "just a bit" meant we needed to take it down by seventy thousand words, nearly all of it the autobiographical material, he began to cry. Really cry. I mean, weep and wail—as if he had lost a loved one. His shoulders heaved, he could hardly speak. Finally he sobbed out, "Do we really have to cut it?" I said yes, we did, but that we'd make it a bestseller by doing so. The tears abruptly stopped. "Do what you have to do, that's all I care about." I cut the seventy thousand words—an easy task, in fact, because most of them came in one clump—and we ended up with a pretty good self-help book that sold to international publishers in several languages and stayed in print for many years. *Nota bene*: It didn't best-sell. More tears. If you become an editor, never make that promise.

One of my most challenging edits was a very long biography of a writer I intensely admired. In this case, the writer in question had enjoyed a comfortable and not terribly interesting childhood but led a colorful adult life, in particular the ten to twelve years during which he was the best in his field, bar none. The last twenty-five years of his life and work were a period of long and mostly sad decline, with flashes of the old brilliance and some personal drama that bore telling.

The biography's author and I had agreed that we didn't want a doorstop book; in order to achieve that goal, we would highlight the best work and the most relevant stories from the man's life and would fast-forward through the weaker work and the everyday details. In this case, "everyday" meant just that: what the book's subject ate for breakfast, lunch, and dinner; dull conversations recounted in excruciating detail, to no purpose; the to-and-fro of a writer's life from teaching to conferences to awards ceremonies; books written, published, reviewed, and returned; and so on, and on, until the manuscript topped two hundred thousand words and thirteen hundred–plus pages, and weighed more than my leg.

I set about a meticulous and challenging edit. Biography and history can be difficult to cut, because every sentence is part of a chronology. I excised chunks of text and suggested compressing chapters from a year-to-year accounting into periods of time, especially when not much was happening. (The phrase "Three inconsequential years passed" would have saved everyone some time.) I also made myself trim at least three lines from every manuscript page, which reduced the whole by 125–50 pages. I minimized the scholarly analysis of obscure or less important writing—since this wasn't meant to be an academic book—and reduced what had become a prosecutorial recounting of the author's bad behavior to salient examples.

Nearly every one of the cuts somehow made its way back into the manuscript—in a different place, or rewritten, or added to the burgeoning notes section, or justified as crucial. In the end, as I said earlier, it's the author's book, and as an editor you can't impose your will on an author. The only whip you have is the word count in the book contract, and while some editors will insist that the author hew absolutely to that count under penalty of cancellation, it's hard to enforce that threat when an author has spent years on research and writing. In any event, the biography never became the lean model of its kind that it might have been. Sometimes you can only do so much.

Finally, every so often an editor reads a book that seems, well, perfect. When that happens, I find myself wondering: *Am I getting lazy? Not doing my job? Reading with complacent acquiescence rather than attention? Surely there must be something wrong with this thing!* Recently I had the pleasure—the honor—of acquiring a novel by an acclaimed literary author, one with a long career behind him and still ahead. On first read, the book seemed impeccable; second read too. I had nothing to say, and almost nothing to mark with my pencil. The author and I spoke by phone, and the most I could come up with was the simple suggestion that maybe the book could be a little longer and round out its story a bit more. What did that even mean? Beats me. I could hear Tom McCormack growling in my right ear, because he hated that kind of editor: the old-boy, indifferent but charming, gracefully-faking-it kind of fine fellow, a minor character from a Fitzgerald novel, utterly useless to all but the most talented writers.

Well, this was one of those writers; he heard me, understood that something was missing at the end, and went to work. A few weeks later the final draft arrived, rewritten at the end and arriving at exactly the right place. If I had come up with suggestions, details, plot points to be resolved, energetic interventions, and other tools in my kit, I might have ruined the book (or,

. . . .

perhaps, been ignored by my wise and experienced author). Lesson learned: talk to your authors, get to know them and understand how they work, and edit accordingly.

Can a line editor transform a book? In some cases, yes—Gordon Lish's work as an editor was transformative, albeit painfully, for certain authors, changing their voices and rendering their sentences down to the essence of what they had been. Maxwell Perkins did heroic work in carving coherent novels from Thomas Wolfe's massive rough drafts; more recently, Robert Weil did the same in editing Henry Roth. In less extreme examples, an editor's best work can be in helping the author develop over many years, book by book; the editor's role might combine line editing with guidance about story ideas that will enhance a given author's talent. There are many instances where an editor has helped a capable author grow into a bestseller, where editing and loyal support and productive collaboration over several books create the conditions for an author to find a large audience.

But most editor-author relationships have a different balance of power, and even with vigorous give-and-take over several drafts of a difficult process, the line editor can hope to improve a given manuscript just incrementally— perhaps lifting a C+ to a publishable B, or in the happiest cases taking an A- to an A.

Having done both, I'll say that the former helped me learn my craft—and taught me to respect those who practice it with more talent than I do. The best editing I've done has been on manuscripts in desperate need of it, where every page—and on some pages every line—requires the ministrations of the pencil. In such cases I'm fully immersed in the book for days, even weeks on end, and emerge squinting against the painful light of dawn. Sometimes that work has been worth the time (as measured by both the quality of the book and the sales); sometimes it hasn't, but even then I learn something new about editing and hope my author will do the same.

The A books come across one's desk just a few times over a career. Whether you're a writer, a reader, or an editor helping one to find the other, those are the books you live for.

10 TOWARD ACCURACY, CLARITY, AND CONSISTENCY
WHAT COPYEDITORS DO

· ·

CAROL FISHER SALLER

WHAT COPYEDITING IS

Anyone who looks critically at someone else's writing—as a job, as a favor, or just to meddle—is probably about to copyedit, which means scrutinizing every inch of that document for grammar, spelling, punctuation, capitalization, and good expression. Professional copyeditors do this for publishers, corporations, nonprofits, small businesses, web startups, law firms, and so on, whether on staff or freelance. But anyone who evaluates or tweaks the writing of someone else may be said to copyedit, and that includes teachers, administrative assistants, interns, writing partners, bosses, moms and dads, and perhaps (since you're reading this) you.

Some copyeditors do much more than copyedit: they develop projects, write or rewrite, or do production work. Many copyeditors email and talk on the phone with writers; they hire and supervise assistants and freelance editors. Freelance copyediting amounts to running a small business, which entails bookkeeping, marketing, writing estimates, and chasing down payments from clients.

THE COPYEDITOR IN THE BOOK PUBLISHING PROCESS

Publishers come in all shapes and sizes, and their procedures vary to fit the end product: newspapers, magazines, websites, financial reports, coloring books. Copyeditors, too, have many different job descriptions. In one organization they do nothing but copyedit; in another, they might wear a few more hats. Some copyeditors move on to become managing editors and production editors, sometimes while continuing to copyedit as well. And the various titles given to in-house editors are fluid and overlapping.

CAROL FISHER SALLER is the longtime editor of the *Chicago Manual of Style*'s online Q&A and was chief copyeditor for the 16th edition of the *Manual*. She also writes the Editor's Corner feature for the *CMOS Shop Talk* blog and is the author of *The Subversive Copy Editor: Advice from Chicago (or, How to Negotiate Good Relationships with Your Writers, Your Colleagues, and Yourself)* as well as the young adult novel *Eddie's War*. She is online at @SubvCopyEd and http://www.subversivecopyeditor.com.

In book publishing, however, a copyeditor typically is given an assignment by a managing editor (sometimes called production editor,[1] assigning editor, or supervising editor). The managing editor has probably already evaluated the manuscript (a term still more widely used in the industry than *typescript*) for the amount of editing needed and has set the editing schedule and deadline. Managing editors assess material by skimming through it and reading any accompanying notes or files, and they set a schedule and choose a copyeditor based on the complexity of the work and the requested publication date. They might also do an initial cleanup of the document, apply typesetting codes or styles, negotiate the fee (if the copyeditor is not on staff), write up instructions and deadlines for the copyeditor, and let the writer know what to expect as the project moves into copyediting.

While the copyeditor is working, the managing editor monitors progress, advises or updates when necessary, and keeps the author up to date (unless the copyeditor has taken over with that). After copyediting, the manager looks over the work, checks the manuscript against design specifications, and completes any paperwork required for sending the project to production. Managing editors typically work with several or even many copyeditors simultaneously, whether in-house or freelance. They also keep departmental statistics (budget, workloads, attendance, etc.), hire and pay freelancers, and liaise with other departments. Managing editors sometimes copyedit as well.

In addition to editing, copyeditors are sometimes asked to take on publishing tasks normally done by managers. The copyeditor might

- check that all illustrations are present and ready for production
- check permissions and credits for illustrations
- apply for ISBNs and Library of Congress Cataloging-in-Publication data
- compare a document to a graphic design to make sure the design is complete
- arrange for proofreading
- convey corrections to the typesetter and check the revisions
- arrange for indexing
- check marketing and catalog copy

1. *Production editor* is also sometimes used for a manager in a production department who does not copyedit at all but gets bids from typesetters and printers and paper vendors, sets typesetting and printing schedules, and monitors the quality of the physical product.

WHY COPYEDIT?

Publishers who hire copyeditors obviously believe they are worth the expense. That's because editing amounts to the quality-control phase of a product. No publisher (or hospital, investment company, university, or department store) wants its books (or newsletters, quarterly reports, donor appeals, or online shopping cart) to have typos and grammar goofs. Sloppy publications cast doubt on a venture's legitimacy and on the author's intelligence, judgment, and resources.

For the same reason, writers trying to sell their work do well to have it copyedited before submitting (though this doesn't preclude the need for further copyediting down the line). Although a professional-looking document can't hide inferior content, the reverse is often true: an editor faced with a mountain of submissions may reject good work that is poorly presented before reading far enough to find what's good about it.

THE COPYEDITOR AT WORK

The actual task of copyediting, no matter what project or client is involved, means sitting with a document in front of you with the goal of improving its writing and presentation. It might be helpful to consider copyediting as five categories of things to monitor, starting with the essential tasks and then moving on to some that are more optional.

Spelling, Grammar, and Style

Checking even the simplest document for grammar, spelling, and style requires knowledge, restraint, and editorial judgment. If a first-grader writes "I am 6, I have a dog Spot," does that pass your test? How about if your boss writes "Hopefully, each accountant will submit their summary on time" or a poet writes of "a quiver filled with eros"? In copyediting, the right answer is often a surprising "That depends."

Each publisher follows its own guidelines, and some contexts may permit divergence from formal English. To the surprise of many self-proclaimed experts, not even punctuation is set in stone. In a dictionary, a word may be spelled two equally correct ways. Rules that govern "style" (such as when to capitalize, hyphenate, spell out, or abbreviate) are quite variable and often negotiable. Grammar and usage rules tend to be more lasting and more universally followed than style rules, but even they evolve (when did you last hear someone use *thee* or *thou* or *doth*?), and even up-to-date formal grammar would be out of place in many contexts.

The reason there are so many different style manuals and dictionaries is

. . . .

that different kinds of writing call for different rules. For instance, the conventional style for book, magazine, and movie titles is italics (*Out of the Dust, Dirty Dancing, Barron's*), but newspapers traditionally eschew italics, so the Associated Press Stylebook puts book and movie titles in quotation marks ("Out of the Dust," "Dirty Dancing") and leaves magazine titles with merely caps (Barron's). Scholarly journals that feature science articles with lots of statistics tend to adopt science-oriented stylebooks (such as *Scientific Style and Format*) that advocate using numerals to express numbers, as opposed to more humanities-oriented guides like *The Chicago Manual of Style* that advise spelling out numbers in the text.

Here are a few examples of styles that vary depending on which guide you follow (at the time of this writing). Notice differences in capitalization, italics, quotation marks, numerals and abbreviations versus spelled-out words, and the presence or absence of hyphens, commas, and periods:

Chicago Manual of Style	*Associated Press Stylebook*
eighty-five cents	85 cents
Senator Barbara Mikulski (D-MD)	Sen. Barbara Mikulski (D-Md.)
bread, milk, and cheese	bread, milk and cheese
cofounder	co-founder
BA, PhD	B.A., Ph.D.
Gone with the Wind (book)	"Gone With the Wind" (book)

Unlike style guidelines, grammar and usage rules tend to be fairly standard. Writers, however, are not always proficient. Here are a few examples of grammar and usage issues a copyeditor must keep an eye on:

- agreement (subject-verb, pronoun-antecedent, etc.)
- verb tenses, moods, and voices (*ran* or *had run*? *was* or *were*?)
- pronoun cases (*I* or *me*? *who* or *whom*?)
- articles (*a* or *an*?)
- position of adverbs and adjectives
- dangling modifiers (*after working out, the pie was gone*)
- preposition and conjunction issues (*like* or *as*? *or* or *nor*? *contrast to* or *contrast with*?)
- parallel sentence structure

When you think of the many, many style manuals besides Chicago and AP, plus myriad dictionaries, you begin to see what a copyeditor faces when styling a manuscript. And you can easily understand how one source of trouble

....

between writers and copyeditors is the mistaken belief that there is a single "correct" way to render a piece of writing.

Given all the choices, editors must cope by aiming to attain appropriateness and consistency in spelling, grammar, and style within a given document. This kind of editing is sometimes called line editing, and it may overlap with the close textual editing that, in many houses, acquiring editors do before the manuscript passes to the copyediting stage. Professional copyeditors follow a designated style manual and dictionary, and they record any editing decisions that depart from those guidelines on a style sheet, which they might later share with the author or (even later) with a proofreader or typesetter. A single style sheet might also be developed for a series of related projects. A successful style sheet might evolve into a company style manual. (The now-famous thousand-page *Chicago Manual of Style* got its start in exactly that way at the University of Chicago Press.)

Rigid consistency in following a style manual, however, is rarely a worthy goal, and an obsession with it can get in the way of thoughtful and economical editing. Good writing allows for reasonable variation—and sometimes requires it. Copyeditors must develop editorial judgment, and it takes time and practice to acquire knowledge of the various options, keep that knowledge up to date, and learn how to apply it with flexibility.

Accuracy

A sentence can be flawless in spelling, grammar, and style, and yet be untrue. Detailed fact-checking is not automatically a part of copyediting (something that should be clarified at the start of a project), but routine editing tasks such as confirming the spelling of names and places and historical events can overlap with fact-checking. Copyeditors are expected to flag suspicious statements for the author to check. They point out flaws in logic and outright contradictions. They inspect the data in tables for logic and readability; they might check the display and "grammar" of equations; they confirm simple calculations. They also flag potential libel and plagiarism if they spot it.

Even copyeditors of fiction must check for accuracy, although in nonrealistic fiction this may primarily amount to keeping track of internal consistencies. A style sheet for a mystery novel or fantasy can become complex, as it must include a timeline of events down to the time of day, character traits (everything from eye color to political affiliation), and any number of arbitrary distinctions and invented places and histories.

Editing for accuracy also involves a great deal of cross-checking within a manuscript: the table of contents against chapter heads and subheads, captions against illustrations, note citations against bibliography, abbreviations against a list, and any other elements that cross-reference another part of the document, such as figure numbers.

In some fields, inaccuracy could become a matter of life and death. Medical and legal texts, for example, require special care and are usually handled by editors with special training and access to specialized reference works.

Structure

Checking the structure of a manuscript involves looking at its organization somewhat mechanically to ensure that headings and subheadings are correctly formatted (bold, italic, caps, etc.) or labeled (A, B, 1.2, 1.2.1, or whatever) and that all elements other than straight text are identified or coded (title, author, epigraph, bulleted list, etc.) well enough to make their relationship to each other clear for the designer, typesetter, and eventual reader. For materials that will be typeset, this used to mean putting labels in the margin with a blue pencil (A for an A head, CT for a chapter title, EXT for a block quote); these days, typesetting codes specified by the publisher or client are usually applied electronically. The editor either types them in or applies styles from a menu.

Logic

One of the tricks a copyeditor must learn is how to switch constantly from little-picture to big-picture issues. Many rookies read everything at least twice: once for structure and logic, and once for mechanical editing (spelling, punctuation, grammar, and expression).

Bad logic shows up in non sequiturs, inconsistencies, exaggerations, misrepresentations, repetition, and other gaffes that result from fuzzy thinking. Editors look for these problems at the sentence level and at the argument level, and they address them either by querying the author or by rewriting, depending on their instructions and on how confident they are that they understand the author's intentions and can convey them accurately in the right tone.

Elegance

Finally, copyeditors monitor the appropriateness and consistency of a writer's voice. They point out or tweak unwarranted changes in tone or complexity. They keep an eye on prose rhythms, word choice, syntax, transitions, and everything that contributes to graceful writing. This is copyediting at a high level—a level that many projects don't allow time and money for, but one that editors can aspire to and find joy in.

WHAT COPYEDITING ISN'T

Proofreading

Proofreading is the reading of typeset copy ("proof ") that was already copyedited (usually by someone else) before it was typeset. The object of proofreading is to check that copy was set correctly, not to evaluate or edit the content—although proofreaders who spot what appear to be copyediting errors should flag them. In the old days, proofreading required two people: one to read the edited copy aloud and another to listen and check the proof. More typically today, a proofreader is given the edited copy for reference but is not expected to read the proofs closely against it. A "cold" or "blind" reading without benefit of the copy is not uncommon.

The word *proofreading* may also refer more casually to any final, last-check reading of copy, even if it's not being typeset. Copyeditors sometimes accept proofreading jobs on the side or proofread their own work or the work of others as part of a copyediting job. Among nonspecialists, proofreading and copyediting are often conflated or confused, which makes it important for both editors and hirers to state expectations clearly at the beginning of a project.

Creative Writing

Bad writers make bad copyeditors, but the inverse is not necessarily true. The opportunity to improve someone else's prose is not an invitation to make it one's own. Copyediting means stifling one's own voice in favor of the writer's and honoring the type and purpose of the document.

Rewriting

A copyeditor's "improvements" should not be excessive. If a text truly needs rewriting, the copyeditor should go back to the author or assigning editor to either redefine the assignment or reassign it to a developmental editor.

Doing Lunch

There is no glamour in copyediting. There are times when a copyeditor's contribution is so great that it would seem to merit coauthor status, but that is rare; anonymity is the norm, though the copyeditor might be mentioned in the author's acknowledgments. Anyone considering a career in copyediting who has illusions of martinis with writers, expense accounts, and jetting to

. . . .

New York or Frankfurt is in the wrong chapter of this book. It's important to examine your temperament and leanings when considering a copyediting career: if it strikes you as an exciting alternative to the monastery or tuna factory, you're on the right track.

BECOMING A COPYEDITOR

Anyone can claim to be a copyeditor, and the field abounds with incompetents. But according to the Editorial Freelancers Association's annual surveys, the main source of editing jobs for freelancers is word-of-mouth referrals from clients—which means it literally pays to be good. Many hirers require applicants to take an editing test. But few copyeditors have formal training—after all, you can't get a degree in it. So how to learn? There are several traditional paths.

If you are literate and lucky, on the strength of your aptitude you might land an entry-level job where you can learn copyediting by trial and error and by close supervision by a mentor. This was a common scenario before the availability of editing classes and certificates. Today such classes are everywhere, and if you find that you need to learn one or more of the major styles (Chicago, MLA, AP, etc.) in order to get work, a class might be your best bet.

If that's not a possibility, there are plenty of online resources at hand: distance-learning courses, electronic emailing lists and forums, chat rooms, blogs, and social media offer information, advice, and community. The websites of the Editorial Freelancers Association and the American Copy Editors Society are good places to start.

There's also plenty you can do on your own. While you're wading into the world of copyediting, start reading the manual of the style you want to learn first. If you want to edit books, read *The Chicago Manual of Style*. If you want to work for a newspaper or magazine, read the *The Associated Press Stylebook*. Read *The Bluebook* to learn legal editing, the *AMA Manual of Style* for medical editing, or the Council of Science Editors' *Scientific Style and Format* for work in the sciences. Browsing a style manual will tell you almost instantly whether you really want to be a copyeditor, so pay attention to your gut reaction. If your eyes glaze over, it might not be for you.

But if your heart whispers *I love this stuff* and you decide to pursue work as a copyeditor, here are some ways to proceed.

Learning and Practicing
Proofreading is a good way to immerse yourself in a given style without having to have a thorough knowledge of it. Proofreaders are usually told what

manual or style sheet was followed during editing. If you are proofreading against copy that shows the editing marks, you can learn a great deal by studying the editor's corrections and suggestions and the author's responses. If you can afford it, do a few projects for free and consider it an investment in your training and future. Almost any organization that depends on volunteers might welcome an offer to proofread its publicity, grant proposals, or reports. If you do a good job, ask your contact to recommend you for paid jobs.

Meanwhile, study a style manual, take a class, and test yourself with on-line quizzes—all to prepare yourself to apply for a copyediting job. Volunteer copyediting offers the same opportunities as volunteer proofreading, so consider doing that. Copyedit someone's dissertation or novel or family memoir. Apply for internships, paid and unpaid, where you will benefit from on-the-job mentoring. Accumulate feedback and references.

Taking the Typographic Oath

The first rule for editors, sometimes called the Typographic Oath, is *Do no harm*. Editors do harm in two basic ways: they edit where it isn't needed, and they fail to edit where it is needed. New editors err overwhelmingly in the first way. They wade in, determined to slash away, confident they know what the author does not, and they introduce all manner of errors and blemishes on copy that was just fine to begin with. Two ways to avoid doing harm:

- Never change someone's copy unless you can cite to yourself the justification from a style manual, dictionary, or other *up-to-date* authoritative source. (Grammar you learned in high school doesn't count.)
- Never challenge a writer's spelling or expression without looking it up first or knowing that you have looked it up before.

Over my years at the University of Chicago Press, I have supervised many of the brightest possible young editors, and not one of them could resist breaking those two rules repeatedly, and to some humiliation, in the first year of their apprenticeship, if not longer. New editors, even impressively educated ones, haven't necessarily been exposed to the jargon, antiquated expressions, and allusions that veteran readers are familiar with. I'm not ashamed to admit that I have many deep pockets of ignorance, but my trust that most authors know what they're talking about (added to the ease of typing an unfamiliar phrase into Google) continues to save me from embarrassing myself and wasting everyone's time with stupid queries.

Building a Career

Given the potluck nature of getting your first copyediting job, added to the way word-of-mouth referrals tend to lead to work of the same type, there's a danger of becoming specialized without intending to, stuck in a field you wouldn't have chosen for yourself. With that in mind, aim to find proofreading or copyediting work that reflects your own interests, passions, or skills. If you start by volunteering or applying for unpaid internships, you can more easily choose the general direction you wish to go.

Specializing can benefit you in several ways. You will acquire expertise faster than if you were spreading your learning out over many different kinds of editing; you will make connections that lead to more work of the same kind; and you will build a résumé faster.

Staying Current

Once you're up and running as a copyeditor, remember that language trends and styles change. The tools of editing change even faster. To best serve readers and give value to clients, continue to educate yourself. Online articles and social media provide an excellent, economical way to do this. Follow language writers and authoritative editors on Twitter and at their blogs, and their posts will give you an idea of what's currently being debated or invented. If you paste the URLs of your favorite sites into an aggregator like Feedly or Netvibes, anytime you have a few minutes you can go there for a list of the sites that have updated since you last checked. Scan the headlines and excerpts, and click through to any that look interesting. It's like reading a newspaper that focuses entirely on your business.

By following your interests and continuing to educate yourself, you can build a copyediting career—in book publishing or elsewhere—thoughtfully and with purpose.

PART THREE

Publication

. . . .

BRINGING THE BOOK
TO THE READER

11 THE FLIP SIDE OF THE PIZZA
THE EDITOR AS MANAGER

. . . .

MICHAEL PIETSCH

Long ago, soon after I reported for work as an assistant at the venerable Charles Scribner's Sons, a friend gave me a copy of a recently published biography. *Max Perkins: Editor of Genius* was the story of the legendary Scribner employee who published luminaries including Ernest Hemingway, F. Scott Fitzgerald, and Thomas Wolfe. Scribner's offices were behind the ornate façade of a landmarked building on Fifth Avenue, just a block from Saks and three from the statue of Atlas in front of Rockefeller Center. The idea of publishing that had drawn me to this $9,000-a-year position was embodied in that biography and that building: books and publishing were at the center of the universe, and the heart of the business was recognizing and nurturing literary talent.

When I finally managed to read *Max Perkins* (an editorial assistant's outside-the-office reading life consisted, then as now, almost entirely of unpublished manuscripts, not finished books), I learned that Perkins's genius went far beyond recognizing the literary qualities that might cause a writer's work to win prizes and fame. It had a broad base: he worked with writers of many kinds, including writers of romance, comedy, humor, cookery, and various kinds of nonfiction. His ability to recognize books that would satisfy many reading tastes was matched with an ability to muster support and attention for those books within the company and out in the world. He also worked extraordinarily hard, was not at all a literary snob, and understood the importance of bestsellers—books that made money in the present moment, not in some distant golden future.

Books that Perkins acquired were still Scribner's financial foundation

MICHAEL PIETSCH is CEO of Hachette Book Group and has worked as an editor for decades. He's had the great fortune to work with superb writers including the novelists Mark Childress, Michael Connelly, David James Duncan, Michael Koryta, Mark Leyner, Rick Moody, Walter Mosley, James Patterson, George Pelecanos, Anita Shreve, Donna Tartt, David Foster Wallace, and Stephen Wright, and the nonfiction writers John Feinstein, Peter Guralnick, Keith Richards, Stacy Schiff, and David Sedaris. A career highlight was editing a posthumous memoir by Ernest Hemingway, *The Dangerous Summer*. Twitter: @wordfellow.

when I worked there in the early 1980s, a half-century after many of them were published. Those long-selling books, I learned, had also been bestsellers when they were new. At college I had absorbed a romantic notion that great books were usually unrecognized when first published. This was indeed the case with some iconic works, such as *Moby-Dick* and Faulkner's early novels. But as I looked around, with eyes opened by *Max Perkins*, I saw that the opposite was truer: *The Catcher in the Rye, To Kill a Mockingbird,* and most of the books on the "classics" syllabus had been significant bestsellers when new. Hemingway and Fitzgerald had been bestsellers, media sensations, and literary celebrities from the publication of their first novels.

Scribner is still a great publishing house, now a successful division of Simon & Schuster. But when I worked there, new bestsellers were rare birds. Perkins's desk was still on the premises, but his skills seemed to have left the building. In the ranks of filing cabinets that housed old author correspondence, I pulled open drawer after drawer, looking to understand why so many good writers the company had published into the 1960s and 70s were no longer there. Many a folder gave up the same story: disappointing sales, better offers elsewhere, unsatisfied concerns. "Someone in royalties has a brain like the flip side of a pizza," read the last letter to the editor in one file. "Fix this."

I looked around the industry for models of success and saw relatively few editors in their fifties or sixties. There were plenty of younger ones, and some who had successfully moved into management, but not many who had made long-lasting careers as editors. I met editors who had once been employed by publishers but no longer were—many now worked as freelancers, performing the same kind of editorial work they always had, digging into manuscripts with authors, sharpening, trimming, querying, cajoling. But they were no longer being paid by publishing companies to acquire books. I became concerned, for self-interested reasons, with understanding what made editors valuable over the long term.

What I came to realize, through observation and experience, is that our business values the broad set of Perkins's skills—diligence, diversification, financial acumen, project management, enthusiasm-spreading—as much as it does his literary genius. Of course, the ability to recognize books that will move and please large numbers of readers is the editor's first essential skill, and the ability to work well with writers to help them improve their books is the second. I don't mean to downplay those skills, which are the sine qua non of a successful editor; some of the greatest joy I've experienced in my career has been in acquiring books and working with writers on their manuscripts. Other essays in this collection delve into the alchemy of those roles.

. . . .

But seeing the books you've worked on *sell*—that's when the joy of being an editor really takes root, because you've helped the writer achieve his goal of connecting with readers. Editors who are successful over a long term are often those who are able to add to their editorial judgment and text-editing skills the capabilities that help make the book a success for their employer: skills as a financial analyst, a negotiator, a communicator, a relationship builder, a marketer, a long-term planner, a portfolio builder. In short, management skills. If there ever was an editorial ivory tower in which publishing careers were sustained only by literary judgment, it has long since been repurposed. The old Scribner building now houses a Sephora store.

My own career has taken me from assistant to editor, editor in chief, publisher, and now CEO of Hachette Book Group, a publisher of books for general readers whose divisions include Little, Brown and Company, Grand Central Publishing, Little, Brown Books for Young Readers, Perseus Books, and numerous other imprints. In this capacity, I have the responsibility to ensure the company's financial success, establish its strategy, oversee its staffing and its operations, and represent the company broadly to authors, literary agents, retailers, and the public.

From the vantage point of this broader role, I have come to see editorial work in a different light from when I started. When I began, I assumed that the editor's essential job was to help authors make their manuscripts all they wanted them to be. Now that intimate, careful, nourishing work of editing feels like a privilege that editors earn by doing all the other important work that writers need done to bring their books into the world effectively. Most writers value editing. But almost all have a circle of trusted readers from whom they receive valued feedback. For the editor to become part of that circle of advisers, even to be privileged as the primary voice, she must also be the person who represents to the author all that the publisher can and should be doing for the author and his book.

And what is that "all"? The editor, from her employer's point of view, is an investor, entrusted with risking the company's money in contracts with writers, with the intention of making a profit from those investments. The contract establishes that the author's responsibility is to finish and deliver a specified work of a certain length by an agreed delivery date, and usually to participate in the marketing of the book. The publishing company's responsibilities include, usually, paying an advance against future royalty earnings from the not-yet-published title; working with the writer to ensure that the book is of the quality that the author and the company desire; copyediting the work to bring it to an agreed standard; designing the book's interior and exterior appearance; printing the book, if a print book is agreed upon, and warehousing it; making it available for sale in print and digital forms; distributing it to retailers and listing it in catalogs and databases that make it findable by individuals and retailers; marketing the book to entice potential readers; licensing the work in whole and for excerpts; reporting to the author regularly about sales and royalty earnings from these activities; and paying the author royalties if earnings from sales exceed the amount advanced.

In all this, the editor stands at the fulcrum between the author and the publishing firm. She is responsible to the publishing company for the profitability of the investment she has advocated, and responsible to the writer for the publishing company's performance of its obligations. The writer has usually spent many months or even many years creating the work that is entrusted, via the editor, to the publishing company; the writer sees the editor as the product manager for his book, responsible in spirit if not in fact for everything that the house does on the book's behalf.

Since the editor is responsible to the author in this way, it has always felt essential to me that she comprehend the entire business operation. The better the editor understands the whole of a publishing company's many functions, the better she can help make sure that the book's publication goes well, head off foreseeable problems, prepare the author's expectations, answer questions, and ideally oversee a successful publication that leads to a happy long-term business relationship. At the same time, the more the editor understands how the books she acquires fit within the company's entire enterprise—the more she thinks like a manager—the better she'll be able to influence the success of the books she's taken on and shape a successful career.

And, perhaps most important, an editor who does her job well on these many fronts is helping the writer she has invested in earn a living. Authors often work project by project, in a financially uncertain environment very different from the editor's salaried position. When they feel that the editor is their business partner as well as their partner in making their manuscript all it can be, the bond can be very deep.

Below are some of a publishing company's basic management areas, and some thoughts on how editors can usefully interact with each.

FINANCE

Any editor's employment is a financial investment by her company. Editors who have long careers are those who year after year bring in new books that make a profit for the house. Ultimately, it's as simple and as hard as that.

....

Editors should know the basic economics of publishing inside and out, and understand what elements of a book's P&L they can influence to promote the profitability of each book. (Perkins studied economics in college.) What formats is a book likely to sell in, and what is the best price for the book in those formats? How much of the book's cost is paper? If it could be shortened by a signature, what could that mean to its bottom line? Does this title require extraordinary marketing costs, and how effective are those marketing investments? Is there a strong possibility of licensing rights, and what could those rights be worth? What is the relationship between the advance against royalties and profitability? What is the unearned advance risk for a particular book? Does my portfolio of books include different levels and kinds of risk?

Editors usually publish a range of books, and they need to manage their lists carefully. Publishers understand that many books make little or even no profit, but an editor should be able to show plausible signs that those writers who do not make money are on a path to doing so with future books. Some investments are expected to pay off immediately, some are for the long term. Editors need to be clear about this with the people whose money they're investing, and make sure the risk level of each project is tuned appropriately. The editor should attend to her portfolio with serious attention to delivery dates, publication timetables, and other factors that affect how each book will come into the world. An effective editor should bear in mind the company's fiscal year and budget timetable, and manage her own list with those in mind.

Most publishers of any size have a business manager or CFO. In smaller houses, big responsibilities may be held by a small number of people. Whatever the structure, the editor does well to know the people who hold these key positions and to take every opportunity to learn from them. One of the felicities of my career was a first job at David R. Godine, Publisher, a small, privately held company in Boston, where the entire central work of publishing was accomplished by a dozen people. Seeing all that performed by a few hearties gave me an early understanding of how the parts of the business interlock, and my first taste of the camaraderie and sense of mission publishing people often share.

The finance group oversees the work of paying and getting paid. Long after the editor oversees the launch of a new book, an author's regular communication will be with the royalty department that sends periodic accounts of sales, returns, earnings against advances, and ideally a check for royalties earned on copies sold. The author's (or agent's) questions about the information on those statements are likely to come to the editor, and it is essential that she know what's on them, including what various terms and categories mean, and have relationships with the royalty team to facilitate untangling and correcting any errors.

SALES

Inattention to the sales department's needs—for cover images, selling materials, manuscripts, reliable schedules, pricing, publicity commitments, and other essentials—is a common and dangerous error for an editor. The sales team solicits orders and promotions for new titles, gets backlist books reordered and marketed, and maintains fresh and positive relationships with the many retailers who get books to readers. The editor needs to know sales colleagues well and understand what it takes for them to get the orders, placements, and promotions essential to success in the channels and accounts they oversee. Careful editors will work hard to learn the profiles of different retailers and what it will take for the books they've acquired to succeed in them. Really savvy ones get to know some key buyers themselves and are able to work with sales reps to build up anticipation for books with high potential in a particular account.

PRODUCTION AND OPERATIONS

Getting books copyedited, typeset, manufactured, warehoused, shipped to retailers across the country and around the world, created in digital form appropriate to the requirements of different etailers, with appropriate metadata for online discoverability, on a schedule that makes books available for sale at the same time that publicity and marketing events occur—all this takes a sophisticated group of interlocking organizations, collectively known as the supply chain, whose function and continual improvement is enormously complex. When these operations systems and processes go smoothly, editors often take them for granted. Getting to know them well helps editors serve authors more effectively and answer the kinds of questions they are likely to ask: How long does it take from when a reprint is commissioned to when a book arrives in stores? Is it possible to change the teaser chapters at the end of backlist e-books in order to promote a forthcoming book? Why do some etailers and not others have live links to my other books at the end of my newest one? Or, less benignly, why isn't my book available for sale from important retailers at precisely the moment that a major publicity event encourages sales?

Knowledge of the basics of bookmaking and text design is among the editor's significant responsibilities. Working with the author on how best to embody his manuscript in a book can be both consequential and delightful.

....

Whether to use endnotes or footnotes, how paper weight, color, and opacity affect the reader's experience, the cost of design flourishes like ragged edges or topstains and whether they're likely to return their cost in sales—the editor is expected to know all this and more. Such decisions have significant effects on the book's profitability as well as on the reader's experience and the author's happiness. An off-standard trim size may be right for conveying something about a book's central idea, but it may also mean a longer reprint time and a higher manufacturing cost—all variables that will need to be discussed with the author and the production team before decisions are made.

Working with production staff on scheduling, quantities, and costs should be basic for every editor. Digital production capabilities change constantly, and it's well worth exploring with digital production staff the possibilities for enriching e-books with additional features.

Larger publishers employ production editors, whose job it is to make sure all the pieces of a book are in hand and of appropriate quality. They work with copyeditors, proofreaders, designers, illustrators, indexers, and others to assemble all of a book's parts and make sure they all work effectively together. These experts know well which editors deliver manuscripts to them on time and in good order, and which dump partial bits into their inboxes and expect them to figure it all out and put it all together. An editor who gets to know her company's production editors will likely find they are able to bring flexibility and additional resources when one of her books needs them.

MARKETING

Marketing and publicity should be areas of strength for every editor. In deciding what projects to recommend for acquisition, an editor needs to have a vision not just for the book's intrinsic qualities but also for how the book can become known, and an understanding of the resources it will take to achieve that. This requires a realistic knowledge of the company's marketing tools, staff, and budgets, and a capability for getting the marketing team to share the editor's vision. Marketing techniques change constantly, and it's important for the editor not just to be up to date on them but to know how effectively a given author will be able to promote his work.

The editor should be a key voice in planning the marketing campaign for a book, coming up with ideas, contributing to the plan, and bringing the author's experiences, connections, expertise, and expectations into the discussion early on. This includes ideas about visual presentation, selling lines, and copy—all the ways a book will be summarized compellingly to different constituencies. As representative to the author of what the publisher is doing on behalf of each book, the editor must be able to influence and communicate about the company's efforts on the author's behalf.

It's particularly important to be able to articulate to the author clearly and truthfully the efficacy of those efforts. Too often the power and force of the publishing company's sales and publicity capabilities are taken for granted. Every retailer that is persuaded to stock the book, every display and promotion a book is chosen for, every review solicited and gotten, every online, radio, TV, and print outlet presented with the book needs to be communicated to the author. Publishers put huge effort into creating effective relationships with retailers and media outlets, through which they are able to influence them to give their attention to the publisher's books. These relationships are among the most important marketing tools the publisher has, for books of every kind, and people on the editorial side—including authors—often fail to appreciate their complexity and value. Beyond all this influence marketing, publishers invest heavily in mailing lists and direct consumer outreach—not to mention the traditional publicity tours, online marketing, social media campaigns, and advertising that are more readily visible. Creating a campaign appropriate in direction, scale, timing, content, and tone for every book a publisher brings out—often hundreds a year—is intricate and demanding work.

The editor's job in contributing to the campaign and sharing it with the author is essential to the relationship. In the absence of evidence to the contrary, authors often assume that little is being done for their book, when in fact much work is being done at all levels of the company. In addition to these core efforts undertaken for every book, news of more elaborate and detailed online, publicity, social media, and advertising campaigns should be passed along abundantly and enthusiastically. The more the editor communicates about each marketing achievement, the more the author will appreciate the nuance and difficulty of getting any single book noticed and sold out of the hundreds of thousands published each year.

It's worth saying a little about jacket making. Creating cover art for a book is one of the most important things a publisher does. It's an oddity of the business: a work made out of words must be reduced to a picture for the purpose of conveying what it is. This symbology is wildly complex and ever changing—and the editor needs to be able to talk equally effectively with the author about what kind of face he would like his baby to have and with the marketing and art departments about the shorthand a jacket conveys: both what kind of book it is and how the image should differentiate this one from its ilk. Jacket designers are creators, like authors, and smart editors learn how to appreciate their efforts genuinely even as they ask them for a revision or new approach. In a world where every writer has access to image banks and design tools, their role in decisions about jacket art grows ever stronger, and it is important for editors to start the jacket process by drawing out the author on the kind of images he thinks might work for his book.

LEADERSHIP

Publishing is done by groups, and every book is its own little (or sometimes big) business. Although the editor will usually work with a different constellation of production, publicity, marketing, design, and other collaborators on each book, she needs to be the de facto leader of each of those teams. These colleagues all have their own managers, workloads, priorities, and long-term plans. The editor needs to earn their trust by being organized, setting clear goals, understanding team members' differing priorities and viewpoints, and being positive in spirit. The editor who can communicate a clear vision of a book's unique qualities, why the company has invested in it, who its readers might be, how the company might reach those readers, and how big a seller it might be if everything goes right lightens the load of colleagues in every department. Communication is essential, as well as realism. Acknowledging mistakes and misdirections when they happen helps too. In cases of disagreement, knowing when to appeal to higher authorities, and doing so transparently, will help keep the team moving forward effectively and with trust intact. Most of all, the team wants to feel that the editor knows what she's doing and where she's heading, that her books are part of a larger plan of publishing that will lead to all of them thriving together in the future.

Editors are sometimes seen by their colleagues as prima donnas, paid well to arrive at the office just in time to go out for a long, expensive lunch. They may be thought to care little about the workloads or scheduling needs of those in other departments. The fact that the editor may be routinely working past midnight reading and editing manuscripts, and that lunch and dinner meetings are essential for attracting submissions, spreading the word about the publishing company, and maintaining author relationships, may not be widely appreciated. The more editors learn about their colleagues' work, the less they will be seen in this negative way, the more likely they will be to share the spotlight when there is a success, and the smoother they will find their path on future projects. Taking the time to understand the pressures and priorities affecting the people they interact with in other departments will allow editors to internalize their needs and be able to collaborate effectively when problems arise. How does the publicity director allocate projects among publicists? How many cover mechanicals is the production manager working on every week, and what does it mean for her workload when one of yours is delayed because your cover copy is late? Ideally the editor will get to know these things and treat those who work elsewhere in the company as the full partners in publishing that they are.

COMMUNICATIONS

Publishing is a communication business, and at the join between the author and the company, the editor's most important job may be communicating fully and accurately in both directions. Silence is dangerous and easy to misread; the editor who thinks that the author knows she and her colleagues are working hard on the author's book makes a very dangerous assumption. One of the bestselling authors I've ever worked with, someone with whom we believed the house communicated fully and transparently, once told me that during the publication of each of his books he felt like he was on the outside of a dark-glass building, barely able to make out the shapes of people moving inside. If this author felt benighted about publication processes, just imagine how other writers feel.

That author's statement was the occasion for a company-wide transparency project, during which we mapped out every step of a book's life and what communication, if any, accompanied it. We added a large number of standard communication points for every book and wrote a "what to expect when you're being published" booklet that we now send to every author upon signing a contract. But these are only initial steps. The editor needs to communicate fully and constantly to the author and agent, and equally fully and constantly to colleagues working on the book and to managers. This constant communication allows everyone to know what to expect, allows anticipation of problems, and helps those working on a book feel they are truly colleagues, not hired hands meted out information on a need-to-know basis.

Communicating is easy when things are going well. Few communications are easier than the call to the author with news that his book is a bestseller, or has won a prize, or has a positive review in an important publication. Communicating about disappointing results, or confusing ones, is less satisfying but probably more important. Our world has much more ambiguity and disappointment than triumph. The job the editor does of setting expectations and staying in touch constantly during the lead-up to publication will ease communications once the book has come out. An author who has been involved in the marketing planning for his book, who has heard regularly from his editor throughout the prepublication process, and who learns regularly and truthfully about what is happening once the book is off press is more likely to return for future publications than one who feels in the dark, kept out, or confused about it all.

STRATEGY

The editor needs to think constantly about the future and about how she is shaping an editorial program that will thrive in that future. A first step is understanding the strategic goals of the company she is a part of. Are the books she's acquiring in areas that the company is expanding in or cutting back on? Are they titles suited to an increasingly online marketplace? Should the editor be expanding the range of books she acquires or concentrating on a smaller area of expertise? Do the editor's books line up well with the company's investments in marketing? With its international profile? Most important, are they profitable and a growing part of the company's overall profits? Are they reliable—does the success of one book lead to increased sales of the author's backlist, or is each book starting over from scratch?

The author, too, wants the editor to be a partner in a long-term plan, in which hopefully the present book is leading to another that will sell even better and will help ensure the author a secure future. Writing is a solitary business in which long-term prospects can be hard to discern. An editor who is trusted by a writer in developing a long-term plan has done a very good job of collaborating and communicating, creating the kind of partnership that is the ideal in publishing.

The joy of the editor's work can be enormous. Being trusted by a writer to comment on his work, even influence or change it, before it goes out to the public is intimate and gratifying. Having a hand in bringing good books to readers effectively and helping writers earn a living from their creations—it's engaging, important, rewarding work. But the frustrations are enormous too. Ours is a big and busy country, and it's hard to get attention for any one out of the hundreds of thousands of books published every year—not to mention all the other entertainments competing for readers' dollars and time. There are few more deflating experiences than seeing a very good book that an editor has selected, invested the company's money in, sweated with the author on revising, and worked with colleagues on designing, manufacturing, and launching get little public attention and insignificant sales. Yet it happens over and over, year after year, at every publishing company. It always has and always will. In a talent-based business, selling products whose audience is usually unknowable in advance, most of which fall short of their creator's hopes, there will always be a rich loam of disappointment in which negative perceptions readily take root.

The best way an editor can limit those unhappy experiences, and project the best aspects of the work publishers do, is to understand that having a good book is just the beginning. To get that good book heard and seen and sold requires mastering the many details of the publishing process. Doing so will give every book the editor works on the best chance of success. Even in cases where success is limited, a full measure of communication can leave the author feeling that he was truly a partner with his editor and publisher in trying to find a readership for his book. This full-spectrum approach can give the editor the rich pleasure of collaborating with writers on their work, and enjoying a flourishing career, for many rewarding years.

12 START SPREADING THE NEWS

THE EDITOR AS EVANGELIST

. . . .

CALVERT D. MORGAN JR.

In my younger and more vulnerable years, my publishing mentor gave me some advice that I've been turning over in my mind ever since.

An editor, he said, *must be the associate publisher of his own books.*

This left me with many questions. Such as:

Have you mistaken me for someone who knows what he's doing?
Does this mean I'm getting promoted?
And most of all: what's an associate publisher?

Today, older and wiser and still somewhat vulnerable, I know far better what my mentor meant. But I would use a different phrase:

An editor must be a person of faith.

Not in the churchgoing sense, of course. What I mean is that an editor must believe in his books, with a conviction that's as pure, unshakable, and infectious as the zeal of an evangelist. This faith is what carries us through the everyday transactional world of trade publishing—what inspires us to believe that something as subtle and idiosyncratic as a long, unbroken parade of words can become a subject of passion for our colleagues, for the bookselling community, for reviewers, and finally for readers everywhere.

Our job, as editors, is to inspire that passion in others. It's a delicate business, like tending and stoking a campfire.

That's where the faith comes in.

Here's how it's supposed to work:

You receive a submission from a literary agent. The quality of the writing is apparent from the first sentence; the story is so compelling that the pages

CALVERT D. MORGAN JR. is vice president and executive editor at Riverhead Books, an imprint of Penguin Random House, and also the board chair of the Center for Fiction. He has been an editor and publisher in New York since 1988, most recently as executive editor at Harper and editorial director at Harper Perennial, two imprints of HarperCollins Publishers. He has worked with authors including Jess Walter, Roxane Gay, Lidia Yuknavitch, Lauren Redniss, Molly Crabapple, Elizabeth Tallent, Kate Zambreno, Blake Butler, Tom Piazza, Porochista Khakpour, Stanley Crouch, and James Herriot. A graduate of Yale University, he lives in Pelham, NY.

race by; the ending leaves you breathless. The next morning, reeling from your all-night read, you dash into your publisher's office and announce, *I've found it! The book I've dreamed of, the book America has been waiting for, that big bestseller we need!* The publisher leaps at the news, sends you off to buy the book at any price, then calls a meeting to toast the acquisition and start brainstorming ideas with the publishing team that reports to her.

The way it really works? That's usually less romantic. Yes, if you're an established editor, you still have the pleasure—several times a year, if you're lucky—of falling desperately in love with a book, in a way that's more than ordinary, and coming in the next morning flush with excitement and ready to snap up the rights.

What happens next, though, is the start of a trickier process: a moment when you draw upon all your reactions to the project—rational and emotional, business minded and literary—and, in a few minutes of largely improvised monologue, try to convince your publisher that this is a book you've got to publish.

These reasons are often abjectly personal:

Her sentences are so breathtaking, I kept stopping to read them to my wife.

But they're just as often commercial:

Look at the best-seller list. This is the kind of book that's really working these days.

And they're most often convincing when they capture the book's actual power:

You just care about these characters. You're dying to find out what happens in the end. And when it's over you see the world in a whole new way.

By the time you're through, you've invented a kind of story of your own: a conversion narrative. *I have seen the light. Come with me, I'll show you.* And if you're lucky, this is the story you'll return to over and over as you share your newfound treasure with others.

Publishers, of course, have heard it all before. This is not a bad thing; a wary skepticism is at the core of their gatekeeper job. They know that editors have weaknesses (*You know how these Macedonian epics cry out to me!*) and blind spots (*Oh, the length didn't really bother me. It's under a thousand pages. And, my God, those descriptions!*). They know that some editors have better batting averages than others and that some let their zeal to acquire overwhelm their judgment, especially when it comes to money. A good publisher will test even the most passionate conversion narrative with questions, like the church elders in *Seinfeld* testing George Costanza on his unlikely interest in Latvian

Orthodoxy. (*Is there one aspect of the faith you find particularly attractive?* one elder asked. *The hats?* hapless George replied.)

Most editors are better than that. They're perceptive and articulate about new work, knowledgeable about similar books in the field, and convincing in their arguments. Sometimes, the publisher responds by authorizing an offer on the spot. More often she asks to read the material herself or asks the editor to get other reads—from fellow editors, from other departments—and re-group in a few days, either informally or at the next editorial (or "pub board") meeting. When the project is nonfiction, this is simple due diligence; sales and marketing and publicity will all have useful takes on a project's potential in the prevailing marketplace. When it's a novel, estimating sales potential can be far more subjective, and while an enthusiastic response from all quar-ters can be a huge help, the final decision on whether to acquire a book—and how much to pay for it—may have less to do with sales feedback than with the editor's passion and the publisher's willingness to endorse it.

With luck, the other readers—and the publisher—will see the book as an opportunity, encouraging the editor to pursue the project; such early sup-porters can become an editor's important long-term allies. "These colleagues are likely to remember the project fondly, speak up in meetings to mention that they liked the material, and feel (rightly) that they played a part in the acquisitions process," notes Marian Lizzi, the editorial director of Tarcher Perigee. "This type of early support can be much more influential than the kind you try to get going later in the process."

Every now and then an editor is able to acquire a book almost immediately through a preemptive offer; more often, competition is strong enough that the literary agent holds an auction for the rights. Nearly every book is sold to the highest bidder—and yet good agents notice not just the dollar signs but the quality of an editor's response, which can speak volumes about how the eventual publication will go. "I've often found that the first editor who calls to tell me that he or she loves my book is the one who gets it," says agent Alice Tasman of the Jean V. Naggar Literary Agency—not least because the most enthusiastic editor often makes the most aggressive offer. "I'm lit up and dancing in my seat when I take on a project. I want the editor to be, too."

Once the deal is made, word of the project starts to spread through the industry as excited colleagues extend congratulations and thwarted editors at other houses grouse over their desk salads while they sift through their inbox for something new. The editor celebrates the deal with the modest little ritual of composing a haikulike announcement for PublishersMarketplace.com, the main industry news blog; especially exciting deals are sometimes called in as scoops to *Publishers Weekly*. These days, all three parties—author, agent, and editor—might also announce the deal on social media; if the book isn't finished when it's sold, the author might spend the ensuing months chronicling its completion online with the diligence of an expectant parent, posting a photo of the words THE END on the final page, then Snapchatting the fateful click that sends the final draft to the editor.

When it comes to spreading word of a book in-house, though, this kind of early online buzz is just a rumble in the distance. The real work begins roughly nine to twelve months before the book goes on sale, during the run-up to the launch meeting: the official start of the publishing cycle, when each editor presents a season's worth of titles to the sales force, the marketing and publicity departments, the people who handle translation and other subsidiary rights, the art department, and other key players. The size of this meeting may vary with the size of the house, but unless yours is truly a mom-and-pop operation, the moment will come when you're called upon to brief your colleagues on your upcoming books.

A few weeks before launch, editors are prompted to circulate sample reading materials for their books. If you're lucky enough to have the final, edited manuscript by that point, you can always make the whole thing available, although many readers won't have time to finish more than a twenty-page sample. You might call a couple of early supporters in other departments, or even a couple of well-chosen friendly faces, and give them a little pre-launch pep talk:

You remember that novel I bought last fall? I just wanted to let you know that the final manuscript's just in, and it's amazing.

Or

You remember how much you loved The Last Sadie Hawkins Dance *by Paulina Friendly? Well, I've got this new novel that I think is just like that, but with a bit of Fran Sorensen's* Howling at Thirty *or maybe Elspeth Ninny's* Breathing Rights.

Either way:

Can I send you a copy to read? I can't wait to hear what you think.

And it's true, you can't. And if your colleagues love the book as you do, what you really hope is that they'll speak up at the launch meeting. Because each book's two- to five-minute slice of that marathon meeting is the moment that sets the tone for its entire publication. Your launch presentation will be (no pressure!) the most important airing the book will get in-house, the moment when you deliver an expanded and polished version of your initial conversion story, hoping to win the publishing team over and leave them wanting more. You go into that room hoping that your presentation will be as convincing and memorable as any that day—and that a few friendly voices will second the motion.

Every editor approaches launch meeting differently. Some prepare exhaustively, typing up presentations as carefully crafted as the books themselves. Others wing it, gambling on the energy and sense of immediate connection that can come with a spontaneous presentation. The dangers of winging it are obvious: everyone who's ever attended launch has sat white-knuckled as a colleague loses his train of thought, rambling over the seven-minute mark, waxing on about plot points the room will never retain, groping blindly for a finish. On the other hand, even a well-written scripted presentation can fall flat, lulling readers into hypnotic slumber.

I learned early that the best approach for me is usually to spend some time beforehand writing each presentation out, which helps me to crystallize and organize my thoughts, but giving myself the leeway to stray from the script if the mood feels right. But many of the best presenters I've ever seen are those who work without a net, who know just what they want to say and manage to say it with care, conviction, and—that underappreciated quality—*delight*. I once watched a widely beloved colleague of mine—an infectiously enthusiastic champion of fiction who (to no one's surprise) has since been given her own imprint—present a debut novel at launch meeting. She started her presentation in the editor's traditional perch, seated at the end of a long, long conference table, working without notes, describing the book with the excitement of a party host introducing the guest of honor. As she built up a head of steam, the force of her enthusiasm seemed to draw her up and out of her chair, farther and farther forward, until I was convinced she was about to float over the table and drop a copy in the sales director's lap. Her presentation was the song everyone left the room singing.

That kind of spontaneous passion can work wonders at launch meeting—especially for fiction, where the goal is to convey the joy of discovering a great new voice. With nonfiction the goals are often more down to earth, and savvy editors adjust their tactics accordingly. A written presentation—or at least a detailed set of notes—can be indispensable, as your most important task is usually to dazzle the room with concrete, objective *information*: the author's qualifications and platform, statistics about the size of the market, comparisons with other books in the field. For Marian Lizzi, the goal is to get the publication team feeling *invested*: "to leave people wanting to pick up the manuscript, talk about it, and dig in to the challenge of trying to make it work." She makes a point of being "transparent about why I bought the book and what sets it apart—being as specific as possible." And she makes an effort to anticipate potential pitfalls. "Is there an obvious objection or challenge? I'll always mention it and try to address it."

That last point—being straight with the publishing team—can't be overemphasized. Editors are continually forced to balance credibility and salesmanship, and while a zingy pitch might catch the eye of a few people in-house, too much hype can backfire. For instance, one of an editor's core skills is being able to cite appropriate "comp titles": comparable, or competitive, books whose sales track might shed light on a new project's potential. But a tendency to choose the dreaded "outsize comp"—the category-killing hit whose success is one of a kind—is the quickest way for editors to undercut their reputation for good judgment. "These become clichés of the day," Lizzi points out. "Every editor wants to have the next runaway phenomenon (*The Girl on the Train, Lean In, The Life-Changing Magic of Tidying Up*)"—but even an ingenious imitation can rarely match the blockbuster performance of a true original. Instead editors should look for "specific, realistic, and focused examples that are actually useful for the sales team. Comp titles are tools you're offering them, not hype you're using *on* them." Over the long term, she says, "choosing your comps wisely will serve you well, establishing you as an editor who understands the market in a particular category and not someone who oversells again and again."

And after all, not every project you publish—not every book worth buying—requires a full-court press. For every potential bestseller, we all publish plenty of other books that have value but may need only a well-crafted launch and a few judicious nudges to achieve the kind of success they deserve. The more carefully you choose your battles, the more energy, and credibility, you'll have for the projects that deserve it.

After the thrill of launch has gone, what happens next?

This is when the editor's role splits into two different tracks—call them scripted and unscripted. The scripted track involves managing several processes—seeing the manuscript through production, helping the art department generate a great jacket design, finalizing promotional copy—and they're largely a matter of making sure nothing goes wrong.

When it comes to building buzz in-house, the real work is on the unscripted side. In the weeks after launch, the various departments—sales, marketing, publicity, subsidiary rights—regroup privately to review the entire list, set their goals, assign their teams, and prepare their plans and campaigns. In theory, this is a natural and rational process, steered sagely by the publisher and marketing director, and reflects a fair and objective assessment of each book's true potential. When you're an editor, though, it can be a harrowing time, because now your book is suddenly competing for priority with every other title on the list. And the publishing team's decisions, which are subject to unavoidable pressures (involving time, money, and less tangible considerations), are ultimately presented as faits accomplis and tend to be difficult to reverse.

This is when my mentor's old advice—*be your own associate publisher*—kicks in.

In this all-important period, your unofficial but crucial role as an editor is to keep your book on the minds of the publishing team—to keep that sense of momentum building as they formulate their plans and to use any new piece of evidence you can to get the parties involved to see the book in a bigger way. Long before those plans are presented to the company at sales conference a few months later, you want to make sure that the book you love is being treated as an opportunity, a priority, a potential bestseller.

If I'm not in those conversations, you may wonder, *how can I influence them?* On this point, standard practice varies widely. Some editors like to cast a wide net, subjecting people in every department to the same pitch, walking the halls to hand-deliver galleys to everyone they see. But not every publisher encourages informal contact between editors and sales staff, or marketing managers, or publicists; at some houses, editors are expected to pass the baton to the rest of the publishing team right after launch. One young editor I know, a genuine enthusiast with a knack for championing her books, got a surprised reaction during a job interview when she talked about her strategies for promoting her books, in-house and beyond. "It's great that you do all that," said the associate publisher interviewing her. "But isn't that someone else's job?"

Not always. Faith may be powerful, but hard work helps the mind rest easy.

In the critical weeks after launch, the most important thing you can do is to keep an open dialogue with your allies—the early adopters who have supported the book since acquisition. Atop this list are your publisher and probably an associate publisher or marketing director, who have final say over all the key decisions, from how many advance reading copies will be printed to when the book will go on sale. If they believe in a book as strongly as you do, it's a good idea to touch base soon after launch, to share your own promotional thoughts (such as ideas for potential blurbers or bookstore mailings) and ask for help and advice on reaching your goals. For young or bashful editors the idea of asking for special attention may be intimidating, but when a truly promising book is competing for priority on a large list, a sincere personal appeal can make a lasting impression—and help nudge a book from midlist sleeper to potential lead title.

And the publishers aren't the only players who can make a difference. "Behind every good publication is a village of support," says Meredith Kaffel Simonoff, an agent with DeFiore & Company. "The most effective editors know how to mobilize their own troops through the careful selection of trusted in-house readers." This is why it helps to develop real relationships with key people in the company—to ask them about their work, what they love to read, even a little bit about their personal lives. A good editor, Simonoff says, will try to think of "specific reasons why a book should appeal to different members of his or her team: *This book is set in western Pennsylvania—aren't you from western Pennsylvania?*" Asking these team members for feedback, and for their own promotional ideas, also fosters a sense of shared ownership in the project. "The more a sales rep, marketing person, and publisher feel that they've personally contributed to the positioning and energy of a publication, the better that publication will be."

Another key ally is the author's literary agent. Some agents are more collaborative than others, but I always prefer working with those who stay involved long after the deal is made—brainstorming about strategy, conspiring on the blurb campaign, passing on news of encouraging developments in the author's broader career. "Every good effort put forth by the agent and author can lead to a chain of reactions in-house—and vice versa," says Simonoff. One game-changing way to focus attention on a project, she notes, is to suggest that the author come in to meet with the publishing team, "early enough in the process to make a difference"—ideally, before marketing plans have been set in stone. Scheduling an author meeting is a great way to get key players to read at least some of the book, and nothing brings a book to life like hearing the author speak firsthand about the experiences that inspired the book or his goals in writing it. Even just hearing an author promise to promote his work can embolden a publicist or marketing director—especially if the author is charming and his eagerness is backed up by promotional ideas that seem smart and realistic. Besides people reading the book itself, I've never seen anything transform a publication effort more thoroughly than a good author meeting.

Yet it's worth remembering that every house is different, and what one house values as an editor's friendly-persuasion campaign may puzzle or even annoy a different team. "You have to figure out the machine you're working

....

in" and adjust your approach accordingly, says Maya Ziv, an executive editor at Dutton. As an assistant at HarperCollins, she watched carefully as her bosses navigated the system—sending early galleys with personal notes to the Barnes & Noble sales rep or accompanying their authors to book clubs once the book was on sale to keep the conversation going. "Today I would tell any assistant, 'Keep your eyes and ears open for what you see working, and learn how to do it yourself.'" Once she started acquiring her own titles, she found that her overtures to the sales department were welcomed. "I asked, 'Could I write letters to the editors at Amazon and tell them how much I love the book?' And the Amazon rep said, 'Yes! That's a great idea!'"

The key to working successfully with your publishing team, Ziv says, is to be "pleasantly in their face." Building trust with other departments helps you stay close to the conversation as a book makes its way through the system. Once she got a call from a friend in sales asking for a bound manuscript of an upcoming book—a first novel she'd acquired for a modest advance—to pass to a major account buyer. "Oh, have you read it?" she said. "Oh, my God, I loved it!" the rep cried. If it hadn't felt natural for that rep to call the editor directly, Ziv would never have known that the novel was winning fans in the sales department.

So what comes of all this? How do editors know if a pitch has connected with their colleagues? Publishers today differ in how they reveal their decisions about marketing plans: Some review them with editors at a planning meeting a month or two after launch, others not until the later, more formal sales conference; some simply post them in their internal marketing database. Good news is generally easy to identify: a strong quantity of advance reading copies, an aggressive announced first printing, creative marketing plans, a tour that goes beyond the author's hometown. Of course not every match sparks a flame, and sometimes an editor's most tireless effort fails to arouse much interest. "What no editor wants to face is the moment when you realize that no one's getting back to you," says Ziv.

Yet a passionate editor keeps the faith and keeps looking for new openings—mindful that a book can catch fire at any time. The editor's cheerleading role is just as important in the months between sales conference and publication, when the field reps and publicists are actively pitching each book, and an important piece of news can be just the ammunition they need to up their numbers on a given title. This is where social media can play a hugely important role: many editors maintain a steady dialogue with a network of like-minded booksellers, book reviewers, publishing colleagues, and readers, and their tastes, opinions, and real-time intel can be invaluable. Using social media in a professional context requires care and self-awareness—it's not always easy to engage others with your favorite projects without becoming tiresomely promotional—but the effort can pay off in unexpected ways.

If you notice a book reviewer who gets involved in lots of tech-based conversations on Twitter, for instance, a quick tip to your publicist can help ensure that your upcoming book on the future of broadband gets into the right hands. Find out that your favorite New Orleans bookstore manager loves southern gothic fiction, and you can drop her a message mentioning your upcoming novel about Marie LaVeau—while alerting your Louisiana sales rep to flag the book for special mention at that store. Even after publication, a good editor is always looking for ways to fan the flames, online and off—sending copies out to industry colleagues, Facebooking photos from the launch party, making sure that big, influential reviews are circulated in-house as quickly as possible. As with every other stage in the process, the key is to keep information flowing but to do so with a smile, a light touch, and a nod of gratitude.

With luck, your months of attention, care, and hard work will pay off—whether that means turning a first novel into a breakout bestseller or simply helping a little-engine-that-could find a solid readership. Whatever the outcome, advocacy on behalf of great books is never a waste of time. A passionate in-house campaign is the best expression of your own first encounter with the project, of that moment when you found yourself thinking, *I love this. And others will, too. This I believe.* When an editor commits to a project, dozens of people on the publisher's team are energized to enlist hundreds of new potential allies around the country. In the best cases, their enthusiasm spreads joyfully and fast to eager booksellers, welcoming reviewers, and grateful readers. And even when a book's initial publication is quiet, an editor's advocacy still does something extraordinary: it helps thousands of people discover the work of a single human mind.

In this attention-depleted world, that's more than an act of faith. It's a miracle.

13 THE HALF-OPEN DOOR

INDEPENDENT PUBLISHING AND COMMUNITY

....

JEFF SHOTTS

> *Every person is a half-open door*
> *leading to a room for everyone.*
> —Tomas Tranströmer, *"The Half-Finished Heaven"*

Independent publishers are a refuge for great writers and great books. They are a testing ground for what literature is, what it can be, and how it will endure. An independent publisher exists on its own terms outside of a larger corporate structure, and it is autonomous in its publishing decisions, from what to publish to how to publish it. All publishing was once more or less independent publishing, into the nineteenth and twentieth centuries, until the corporatization of the last fifty years restructured larger publishing houses into something else, something bigger. Sometimes this leads to the conclusion that independent publishers are small—some are, while others have dozens of employees and publish many dozens of books—but the impact of these publishers is enormous. When we first imagine what a publishing house might be, we likely imagine an independent one: a publisher with a mission to publish great books for the love of great books.

But who can say what we imagine anymore? Our culture has in many ways complicated our vision of what publishers and editors do. The larger, dominant industry model has moved faster and farther away from the original, independent model of book publishing. Many of the traditional literary houses have been consolidated and conglomerated so that these publishers are nearly unrecognizable, if not indistinguishable. Even the industry refers to them simply and anonymously as the Big Five, the defining image being

JEFF SHOTTS is executive editor at Graywolf Press, an independent literary publisher, where for twenty years he has acquired and edited poetry, essays, literary criticism, and other nonfiction titles. He has worked with many award-winning writers, including Elizabeth Alexander, Mary Jo Bang, Eula Biss, Mark Doty, Nick Flynn, Leslie Jamison, D. A. Powell, Claudia Rankine, Vijay Seshadri, Tracy K. Smith, Susan Stewart, Mary Szybist, Natasha Trethewey, and Kevin Young. Shotts received the 2017 Editor's Award from Poets & Writers. He lives in Minneapolis, Minnesota, and on Twitter he's @JeffShotts1.

that they are but two things: large and few. They are together, in fact, so large and so few that they make up nearly 80 percent of the entire book-publishing industry.

There is now, as a result, a vast commercial enterprise around book publishing, where annual profits are valued above cultural currency, books are spoken of in terms of "units," and readers are sorted by algorithm into categories by which they can be told with increasing accuracy just what it is they want. Commercial values have conflated quantity with quality, and commercial publishers are forced to create the appearance of quality, if there is none, in service of quantity. High advances and movie deals make the news, as do celebrity authors and their book parties and television appearances.

While many add all of this up and forecast the demise of literary culture, in fact the opposite is true. Astonishingly, the result of all of this has been a vibrancy for independent publishing, made possible in part by what commercial publishing has had to give up in order to remain commercial—namely, literature. Large conglomerate publishers are forced to compete with each other and even within themselves for books driven by higher and higher advances, larger and larger marketing campaigns, and wilder and wilder risks with hope that something, *anything*, might eventually make them a massive profit. This has meant these publishers have by and large turned ever further away from the works they consider unprofitable but that make up much of the literature of our time: poetry, essays, criticism, experimental fiction, short fiction, works in translation, and those uncategorizable books that challenge genre altogether. These are vast and fertile grounds that commercial publishing has largely ceded to independent publishers. It's remarkable that while publishing as an industry has undergone massive change in recent years, the centrality of the independent publisher to our enduring literature has not. The commercial climate threatens independent publishing, to be sure; it also makes independent publishing more literary, more necessary, and more alive.

Just as twentieth-century literature depended on the vision of independent houses, New Directions and Grove foremost among them, contemporary literature depends, and will depend, on independent publishers with a mission to take risks on challenging books and create communities around them. Many of these are small nonprofit publishers headquartered outside of New York, such as Coffee House, Copper Canyon, Dalkey Archive, McSweeney's, Milkweed, Sarabande, and several other publishers of distinction, including Graywolf Press, where I have worked as an editor for twenty years.

I went into editing for Graywolf because I looked at the books on my

....

shelves, amassed as a reader and as a student of literature, and the ones that mattered most to me, then and now, were published by independent publishers: works by Samuel Beckett, Jorge Luis Borges, Anne Carson, Lucille Clifton, Allen Ginsberg, Harryette Mullen, Frank O'Hara, and many, many more, from Sherman Alexie to Howard Zinn. These were the books that risked authentic voices, real emotions, challenging language, and innovative form; they were, at their cores, both works of art and works of social justice. I wanted to work as an editor to support books like these, because I believed that those kinds of books had made me, saved me, and that they could make and save others, and that they could even, a precious few of them perhaps, endure enough to penetrate the wider culture and change forever the ways we engage with ourselves and with the world. I suspect that many editors start with those ideals but that it's often hard to keep them.

Working for an independent publisher not only allows for those ideals but demands them. Those demands may shift from book to book, but as a guiding principle, it's a rare and marvelous gift, as well as a formidable challenge, for a publishing house to select its books based on literary quality and social impact. At Graywolf, we go into editorial meetings ready to discuss manuscripts under serious consideration first in terms of their artistry, singularity of voice, inventive approaches to important subjects, and innovations with language, genre, and style. And then we discuss them in terms of their potential to reach and serve readers both broadly and in specific communities, including those that are too often overlooked, and we consider the ways these literary works might contribute to important cultural conversations. These are the criteria we are concerned with first and foremost when selecting what books to publish. Determining their sales and marketing potential will come into the discussion, certainly, but later in our deliberations. The mission of the press provides the basis for these decisions, and we are led by a vision for social impact above commercial enterprise.

It cannot be exaggerated how rare and how valuable it is for an editor to have the freedom to take on books based on their literary quality and their capability for social change. I read for language, for the sentence, the line, the phrase, the perfectly selected word. I read for a voice challenging the reader about what it means to be human, to be alive now. I read for elegance of form, sophistication of syntax, music and rhythm. I read for subject matter that addresses issues of social importance such as violence, war, gender inequality, health, race, climate change, new family making, poverty, illness, and, broadly, how we encounter each other. I read for a wildness just barely contained, or for an exquisitely controlled lyricism, or for an overall shapeliness that seems so unlikely that I have to read the whole work again to believe it all somehow holds together. I read with communities of people in mind who might need a book to address them, celebrate them, or challenge them, or inspire them, or join them, or even just see them. I read to see how writers are guiding literature now and for the future, and how writers are risking new language, new subjects, new forms, new feats of daring, or how writers are making innovative new works out of very traditional shapes, forms, and subjects. And I read for my own ongoing need to see and to be changed.

To read this way requires editors to think counter to much of the rest of publishing culture. It requires an empathy that allows the aims of the writer to supersede those of the editor or publisher, all in service to the work and to the author and ultimately to the reader. This means trusting writers and readers and the work itself—sometimes over a very long time: an editor is building books, building lists, and building careers. To do so requires a very long view. Many editors at larger houses leave, get fired, or move to other publishers again and again, and often so quickly, such that the view is always necessarily short.

Literary editing requires a patience that most commercial publishers cannot afford, a patience that our culture increasingly has no patience for. Yet I believe that patience is the most valuable asset of the editor in finding, editing, and promoting the work of the most talented writers. This is true for the development of every season's offerings, and for many books and the ongoing careers of many authors. I want to describe the cases of Eula Biss and Claudia Rankine as important writers whose careers thus far are just two examples of how an independent publisher can uniquely and successfully publish literary works of real social impact and support them over time.

Biss and Rankine are brilliant writers for the ways they confront big subjects with challenging, multifaceted forms. In both cases, but in different ways, their works employ the language and structures of poetry toward new modes of essay or nonfiction or multigenre work. Their books don't fit neatly into established categories, and in some cases, bookstores were hard pressed on where best to shelve them. Along with an experimental disposition, Biss and Rankine share a commitment to writing about social justice issues—fear, race, health, violence, gender inequality, the broken history of this country. How they are writing about these subjects is as essential as what they are writing about—which might be as good a description as I can offer of what Graywolf books do.

Both were writers that had caught my attention as a reader well before

I had the honor to work with them as an editor. I first read Biss's writing in *Harper's* magazine in 2002, and wrote her what was essentially a fan letter and asked if she had more. She wrote back and said that she did, and we began a lively correspondence that lasted five years before Biss had an essay collection that even started to look like her groundbreaking work *Notes from No Man's Land*, which Graywolf published in 2009. Before that, I had first heard Rankine read her work while I was a graduate student, and her voice stayed with me viscerally, such that when I took over editing Graywolf's poetry, she was a writer I dreamed of inviting onto the list. In 2002 she sent a draft of *Don't Let Me Be Lonely: An American Lyric*, which invented a new genre—part poetry, part lyric essay, and part visual images—a meditation on post-9/11 America and our overmedicated, hyper-televised society. Graywolf published the book in 2004, during the heat of that year's presidential election.

These are books that didn't debut on the best-sellers list or receive immediate major media attention, but they absolutely found significant readerships over time—and continue to do so. *Notes from No Man's Land* and *Don't Let Me Be Lonely* provided opportunities for Graywolf to push these books toward very passionate booksellers, teachers, and readers who instigated extraordinary word-of-mouth, on-the-ground movements behind these titles as important discussions about American culture and as touchstones for new modes of essay and poetry. We recognized we had profoundly intelligent speakers in Biss and Rankine, and each of them conducted readings and conversations small and large in bookstores, classrooms, and conferences on writing, and worked with Graywolf publicists to amplify that word of mouth. In 2004 and into 2005 and beyond, *Don't Let Me Be Lonely* had become a regular text on many campuses, had earned Rankine a prestigious fellowship with the Academy of American Poets and established her as a major voice in innovative writing. Across its year of publication in 2009, *Notes from No Man's Land* picked up extraordinary momentum, and eventually more visible reviews and media, and received the National Book Critics Circle Award in criticism. Both books remain among Graywolf's bestselling titles, carried over time by academic promotions and classroom adoptions, and our ongoing efforts to position the book with major campus-wide programs and with community organizations and book clubs.

The success of these books fortunately led to extraordinary subsequent works, both published by Graywolf in 2014—Biss's *On Immunity: An Inoculation*, a remarkable and empathic exploration of vaccination and cultural fears, and Rankine's *Citizen: An American Lyric*, an astonishing collage of poetry, prose, and visual artwork, and a gut-wrenching work about America and race.

These books did not come fast on the heels of their previous successes. For Biss, there were five years between projects; for Rankine, there was a decade. Both required a great deal of time, as these were labor-intensive projects requiring meticulous research and curatorial organization as well as the writing itself. Given that both of these books-in-progress were confronting major issues garnering a great deal of attention in the media, and given that both writers had earned sterling reputations and significant followings, I have little doubt that they could have landed much larger advances at larger publishers. But both writers wanted the same team that had published their previous books, both wanted a process that involved them from the beginning with the contents, design, copy, and promotion of their books, and Biss has said how important it is for her as a nonfiction writer confronting major cultural issues and controversies to publish with an independent publisher free from corporate entanglements, or even the perception of those entanglements. We went to work.

For both *On Immunity* and *Citizen*, Graywolf set up carefully tailored promotion campaigns, leveraging the support for previous books, but especially bringing the books to targeted media and organizations specific to vaccination and health, on one hand, and racial injustice and visual artwork, on the other. The promotion of these books was less in the service of book sales and more in the ambition of our mission to bring them into large-scale public conversation. Both were extremely successful right away, landed on the *New York Times* Best Sellers list, and received extraordinary accolades: *On Immunity* was named a Top Ten Book of the Year by the *New York Times Book Review*, and *Citizen* received many literary awards, including the National Book Critics Circle Award in poetry. But we recognized too that publishing these books came with a social responsibility of our own. We donated numerous copies of both books to organizations and readers who needed them—for *On Immunity*, parenting groups, medical clinics, and doctors' offices, and for *Citizen*, YWCA chapters, African American libraries and community organizations, and Black Lives Matter and law enforcement and civic groups after so many police shootings of black Americans.

I offer the examples of Biss and Rankine to illustrate how long it can, perhaps should, take for literary works and careers to grow and thrive, over many years and over multiple books. What smaller, independent, and often nonprofit publishers can't provide in terms of high advances or expensive marketing resources, they can make up with the generosity of time. The time involved in developing books is an extraordinary commodity to serious writers, who should not be rushed. They should be encouraged to write the best book, not the most lucrative one, which are not the same thing. Nor should the promotion of books be rushed, nor done by assembly line, but instead each book should be conducted into the world as the unique creative work that it is, which requires time, research, and the development of an individualized campaign—almost always on a limited budget—to reach a book's potential and plural audiences. An important resolve for these books' ongoing success is to never stop publishing them, to continue to bring them to new audiences, to keep seeking out their potential readers, even as they move onto the backlist. Finally, as with *On Immunity* and *Citizen*, each book's success should not be measured by sales alone but by its impact on readers, on people in particular places and in particular communities—all of us—who might not know what they need to hear.

Of course very few books will win a major prize or land the huge review or sell beyond all expectations or change the terms of cultural conversation. Biss's and Rankine's books are really the exceptions. It is hard, then, not to think more often of those many more authors and their careers and those many more books that are still on their way, still in process, still being written, encouraged, and coaxed out, and how the work begins all over again for every writer—and his or her editors—for every book. With a smaller list of annual titles—thirty, say, instead of three hundred—independent publishers are able to treat each book individually in their acquisition, editing, design, marketing, and promotion, and each writer as an original, unique talent. There's nothing at all small about that.

At the opening of this piece is the epigraph from Nobel Prize–winning poet Tomas Tranströmer: "Every person is a half-open door / leading to a room for everyone." These words hang above my editing desk as a statement I try to remember when thinking about each writer, each submission that comes in, and the potential for each one to reach many. The editor is in service to the writer; the editor and the writer are in service to the book; the book is in service to an entire community.

That community begins with the writer alone but then includes the writer's trusted friends, and then perhaps an agent or magazine and online editors, and then a book editor who gets excited. And then the community includes a copyeditor, a type designer, a proofreader, a cover artist, printers, a publicist who thrills at this writer's work, and gathers interest from media, reviewers, critics, and interviewers. And then the community includes sales reps who fan out, and booksellers become invested, and then event coordinators, librarians, distributors, and on and on until the book then reaches readers, who in turn bring the book to their book club and post about it on social media and talk about it with their friends. And then it reaches a writer, inspiring her, challenging her to write something new. It's an astonishment to recognize that an entire network has been activated. Every book is a community event. It's the publisher's job to keep the door at least half open.

PART FOUR

From Mystery to Memoir

....

CATEGORIES AND CASE STUDIES

14 LISTENING TO THE MUSIC
EDITING LITERARY FICTION
. . . .
ERIKA GOLDMAN

> *"Beauty is truth, truth beauty,"—that is all*
> *Ye know on earth, and all ye need to know.*
> *—John Keats, "Ode on a Grecian Urn"*

Editing involves a mixture of taste, acuity, craft, passion, and persistence. It's a subjective process that can feel intuitive but draws on an editor's experience—both literary and lived. Being an editor is a lifelong apprenticeship: the books you read, the jobs you have, influence your approach to any given text. Yet in a sense I'm the same editor I was at the beginning of my career, an idealistic former literature student who took pleasure in books whose form and content I understood to be symbiotic, indivisible. What I mean by "literary" writing, both fiction and nonfiction, is writing as an art that uses language as sort of musical instrument to produce meaning through narrative.

The publishing industry has evolved a great deal since I first got into it; it was already a different beast from that of my mentors' early careers.[1] Publishing in the twenty-first century, with the advent of the internet and its enormous impact on book distribution, is as volatile as it has ever been. No one can predict what it will look like ten years from now.

ERIKA GOLDMAN is publisher and editorial director of Bellevue Literary Press (BLP), a nonprofit mission-driven publisher that has been publishing literary fiction and nonfiction at the intersection of the arts and the sciences since 2007. BLP's books have received major literary prizes: *The Sojourn* by Andrew Krivak was a 2011 National Book Award finalist and 2012 winner of the first annual Chautauqua Prize and Dayton Literary Peace Prize; *The Jump Artist* by Austin Ratner won the 2011 Sami Rohr Prize for Jewish Literature; and the *New York Times* bestseller *Tinkers*, by Paul Harding, received the 2010 Pulitzer Prize.

1. Two excellent histories of the twentieth-century publishing business: Jason Epstein's *Book Business* (New York: W. W. Norton, 2001); Andre Schiffrin's *The Business of Books: How the International Conglomerates Took Over Publishing and Changed the Way We Read* (New York: Verso, 2000).

My initiation into publishing, straight out of college, was as the editorial assistant to Richard Marek, who had just founded an eponymous imprint at St. Martin's Press. Marek had left G. P. Putnam's Sons following the loss of an author, Robert Ludlum, to Random House. He experienced Ludlum's defection as a grave betrayal—he had, after all, transformed Ludlum from an unknown into a bestselling author, and they had been close friends for years. As painful as this chapter was for him, Dick made it known to me so that I would learn never to make the mistake of letting down my guard with an author to the extent that he had. I must never forget that this was a business.

St. Martin's was known at the time for publishing large numbers of inexpensively acquired British imports in relatively short runs—mostly mysteries and Regency romances. Among these imports were James Herriot's bestselling books that had been adapted into a popular BBC-TV series called *All Creatures Great and Small* and had made St. Martin's a fortune. SMP's chairman, Thomas McCormack, was renowned for his frugality, but he fostered the careers of many people who have held prominent positions in the field. He gave Dick relative autonomy—the ability to decide on his own acquisitions up to a certain, significant dollar amount—which meant that we were excused from the sometimes-contentious St. Martin's editorial meetings.

Sometime during my first week working for Dick, he handed me two books, Robert Ludlum's commercial mega-success *The Bourne Identity* and John Yount's modestly selling literary gem *Hardcastle*, and asked that I take both home and read them. His point was that in order to have a thriving career as an editor, you had to publish popular books that would carry the literary love children on your list. I devoured *Hardcastle*, but the Ludlum seemed like a comic strip to me (Pow! Bam!) and I couldn't get through it. I should have known then and there that I wasn't cut out to be an editor of commercial fiction, but for as long as I worked for Dick, I studied his editorial techniques and acquisitions, and within the first two years I acquired a thriller of my own.

Dick was tolerant of my English-major taste; he abetted it by introducing me to Richard Yates's *Revolutionary Road* and assigning me a summer's worth of research at the Mid-Manhattan Library, during which I pulled together the essays for James Baldwin's collection *The Price of the Ticket*, work that "Jimmy" (as Dick called him) didn't have the patience to do. This was the early 1980s, before computers and word processors. (I was a lousy typist and ashamed of the evidence of this left in the filed carbon copies of the editorial letters that had been dictated to me. I soon learned to slip off to xerox the corrected originals instead.)

. . . .

Additional hours at the Xerox machine were spent copying the manuscripts that Dick had edited; this was how I learned what line editing was—and where, why, and how much a good editor should intervene in an author's text. Dick Marek may have had a paperback of a Henry James novel in his raincoat pocket for subway reading, but he knew how to edit for plot.

When I left the job after three years, it was not because I was unhappy there but because I felt I'd been well launched. Besides, Dick had admonished me, for the sake of my own development, not to spend more than a few years at this first job. (There was relative stability in the business then; to hold onto a position at any level for that long today is a triumph!) After this auspicious beginning, during which I had been encouraged to cultivate my taste and hone my skills while absorbing the realities of the business world, I spent many frustrating, less-than-happy years trying to be a successful "professional" at jobs where my personal interests didn't necessarily dovetail with those of the people who ran the institutions I depended on for my livelihood. In the years to come, I would alternately bless and curse Richard Marek for allowing me to believe that I could remain true to my values and myself and have a publishing career.

It wasn't always terrible—along the way I enjoyed the collegiality, intellectual stimulation, and friendship of a variety of dyed-in-the-wool "book people." But the business was consolidating. Historic publishing houses were bought out and reduced to the status of imprints of large corporations that made enormous profits in trades that had nothing to do with books. Editors were rewarded for how much they spent to acquire "big books," not the craft of editing. Often these books would not earn out their huge advances or sell anywhere near what the original profit-and-loss calculations, devised to justify the terms of their acquisition, had predicted they would. And the more literary or "midlist" acquisitions were now required to carry their own weight.

I am resolutely, and unrepentantly, a midlist editor. To publishing professionals, *midlist* is code for books that may be substantive, artistic—prestigious, even—but of limited sales. We're just about extinct in commercial publishing. This is not to say that there aren't brilliant literary editors in the mainstream; of course there are. But you might as well pin a scarlet A onto your Oxford cloth shirt as describe yourself as a midlist editor. The culture and economics of contemporary corporate for-profit publishing won't stand for it. This is why so many literary writers have found their way to independent small-press publishers.

As publisher and cofounder, with Jerome Lowenstein, MD, of Bellevue Literary Press, I have had the privilege of managing a nonprofit press devoted to serious literary fiction and nonfiction "at the intersection of the arts and sciences," as our mission statement puts it. I have the freedom to follow my editorial bliss as long as the books I choose fall within that mandate. My staff and I must devote a good deal of time to fundraising in order to have the means to run our small operation. This is because many of the worthy books we publish don't sell in great enough quantities to offset the cost of their production, staff time, and marketing even though we may sell them in numbers that are comparable to, if not greater than, what larger houses will sell of analogous titles (yes, some still slip through). We focus appreciable marketing attention on each one of the few books we publish per season, and book publishing, in spite of all the technological innovations of our electronic age, remains a hugely labor-intensive and inefficient process.

It isn't easy to raise money for literary publishing. Along the way, you must make the case for the value of the book, since the long-form narrative is under siege from, among other things, the distractions of the internet and social media. As a result of the stock market crash of 2008 and the withdrawal of a major individual donor, we came perilously close to shutting down our operations, when in April 2010 a first novel that we had published, *Tinkers* by Paul Harding, won the Pulitzer Prize in Fiction. It has since, to date, sold well over half a million copies and kept us afloat.

A Pulitzer Prize isn't a business plan. It hasn't assured our financial stability, nor is it a guarantee of future success. It *has* provided us with an extraordinary opportunity to bring *Tinkers* to the attention of readers and elevated it to the status of a contemporary classic. It has also put our small press on the cultural map.

During the first flurry of post-prize publicity, I was asked by a well-known, long-standing editor of an august house how I knew what I had with *Tinkers*. After all, it had been passed over by top mainstream editors. One of them had even suggested to the author that it would never sell because it was too "slow."

How did I know? Perhaps I had misunderstood the question. I couldn't have known that the book would win a Pulitzer Prize. Nor could I have predicted how it would sell. Before winning the Pulitzer it had sold ten thousand copies, which would have been a strong showing for a first novel even for a commercial publisher. What I did know was how I felt about it and, by extension, how other readers might. Of that there was no doubt: by the time I had made it through the first few paragraphs, the beauty of the prose had reduced me to tears.

········

Manuscripts come to us in a number of ways: directly from the writer "over the transom" (though our electronic submission system or the mail), via literary agents, or with referrals from writers or other publishers. *Tinkers* had been passed on to me by a generous and thoughtful publisher named Jonathan Rabinowitz of Turtle Point Press, who, over dinner, had asked whether I'd be interested in taking a look at a novel that he'd received and greatly admired but felt wasn't right for him. In our small literary-press world, if you're not convinced that a book is right for you, there's absolutely no point in taking it on, since it's passion, not profit, that drives the acquisition process.

An editor of a literary text must be its protector and advocate at every step along the way to publication. If your vision of a work is divergent from that of its author, this can sometimes, though not necessarily, put you at odds. Before embarking with a writer on the adventure of publishing her or his book, if possible, I contact the writer by phone. In the course of my call with Paul Harding, I described to him my response to his book and sought to confirm that I had read the book that he had intended to write. As I remember it, we had a long talk—it may even have gone on for an hour or two. While I don't recall what I learned about Paul then versus what I came to know of him later, we initiated a relationship of mutual trust that has served us well ever since.

For me, the first meeting with an author is as much about exchanging basic information about the press, our process, and the market as it is about discussing the author's expectations and ascertaining that we are generally in alignment. This is very important, as the relationship of editor and author over a text is an intimate one that requires mutual sympathy to be effective. Ideally, if the phone meeting goes well, we celebrate our decision to work together over a meal. Even if the era of the three-martini lunch is gone forever, direct contact between author and editor in a convivial setting involving food can go a long way toward forging a strong and effective connection that will withstand the fraught experience of bringing a book from manuscript to market.

By the time *Tinkers* came to me, its author had taken it through an extensive rewriting process and it required very little editorial intervention. To quote Paul, "plot is the precipitate of character." I discovered characters that were richly alive, even in their death throes. My conceptual edits were light and consensual: the excision of a chapter and a shift in concrete detail on a plot point. While I don't hesitate to line edit and have done extensive line work on many manuscripts over the years, when the author is stylistically sure-footed I refrain as much as possible from asserting my presence in a text.

I've heard Paul say that he thinks of *Tinkers* as "unlineated poetry." It needed no line editing; line by line, it is a multifaceted jewel.

Any editorial critique, before being adopted by an author, should ring true to her or him. While an editor might gently nudge an author to make changes, this should always be in the spirit of bringing the book to its fullest realization in a way that is consistent with the author's conception. This is the case for both fiction and nonfiction. While I will always express my opinions (with necessary care and diplomacy), I will never insist that an author follow my advice. In fact, if I feel that she or he is being too agreeable I become un-comfortable. Though this ought to go without saying, an editor should never forget that a book belongs to its author—at least until it has been released to its readership, after which an author no longer has control of how it will be received and understood.

This means that I won't sign up a book unless I feel that should an au-thor reject my editorial suggestions (unless specified in advance by contract, which is rare) I will still be proud to publish it. The implication here, then, is that I've got a complete manuscript at the outset, so that I know what I'm dealing with.

I don't know how frequently editors go to contract on partial manuscripts of literary fiction; this is rarely the case for me, even when I know a writer's work well. Commercial publishers that offer large advances are more likely to take this risk than I, if they are anxious to secure a book in a competitive situa-tion. Another case where editors may sign up a work of literary fiction without having first read it in its entirety is if they acquire it from a language that they don't read in order to publish it in translation, in which case, presumably, they're relying on the recommendation of a third-party reader. Much as I love to publish literature in translation, I try to avoid this scenario, since it may lead to an unpleasant surprise. This limits me to works written originally in the languages that I read, English or French, unless a full translation has al-ready been made into either of these languages.

Editors of literary fiction—like all editors—are likely to be involved in the marketing and promotion of their books, and it is prudent to discuss mar-keting plans with an author early on. Believing as I do in the adage "Fore-warned is forearmed," I make clear the difficulty of getting attention for any book—let alone a literary one—and the frequent disparity between a book's intrinsic quality and its sales. Paul Harding and I had this conversation, and many others, along the way. There's only so much that a publisher can do to attract publicity for a book, and wherever possible the author should be a willing participant in the process. Paul had been a touring rock-and-roll drummer, so he understood publicity and marketing as performance and was well aware of the vagaries of the marketplace. He was game to do what was necessary to get attention for the book and recognized that opportunities were likely to be rare.

We dedicate a lot of energy to launching each one of our books, but the results of our efforts can vary widely. The experience of editing *Tinkers*—if we understand "editing" to include engagement in the full process of bringing the book to readers, including book design, production, marketing, and publicity—turned out to be exceptional. The book came to us with the endorsements of three highly regarded literary writers: Marilynne Robinson, Barry Unsworth, and Elizabeth McCracken. We were lucky to have found a cover designer whose photograph represented our (and the author's) vision of the emotional atmosphere of the book and to have chosen a format that was attractive to people. I'm convinced that the combination of blurbs and book design got people to pick up and open *Tinkers*, and when they started reading, many wanted to read further.

I'd always heard of the importance of "word of mouth," but this was the first time I've directly observed the phenomenon. Mostly we editors toil away in isolation and rarely have the opportunity to hear from readers of the books we love. For *Tinkers* there was an extraordinary outpouring, beginning with our first "outside" reader, the then co-editorial director of *Publishers Weekly*, Michael Coffey. Within a day or two of my handing the bound page proofs to him over lunch, as he read through the book, he wrote me a series of notes of praise for the writing, comparing Paul to other modern writers whom he admired. At sales conference, having read the bound proofs we provided before the meeting, our sales rep for the San Francisco area, Lise Solomon, declared that she was intent on making *Tinkers* a bestseller and she and her colleagues inspired two booksellers to commission special limited-edition versions for their subscription book clubs. Postpublication but pre-Pulitzer, the book received over twenty-five excellent reviews in major newspapers and other media, won the PEN / Robert W. Bingham Prize, and was nominated for other notable awards.

A young bookstore events manager, Michele Filgate, broadcast her love for the book to readers early, often—and decisively when she signaled it to Rebecca Sinkler during New Hampshire Writers' Day, without knowing that Sinkler was the chair of the fiction jury for the Pulitzer Prize that year. When Sinkler returned home that evening, she mentioned the book to her husband, who downloaded it to his Kindle, read it, and recommended that she take a look at it. It became her choice, and then that of the full committee, for the Pulitzer Prize.

Any link of that chain might have broken and what *New York Times* critic Motoko Rich deemed "perhaps the most dramatic literary Cinderella story of recent memory"[2] would never have been written. To once again quote Paul Harding: "Go, Art!"

2. Motoko Rich, "Mr. Cinderella: From Rejection Notes to the Pulitzer," *New York Times*, April 18, 2010.

15 DUKES, DEATHS, AND DRAGONS
EDITING GENRE FICTION

. . . .

DIANA GILL

What is genre? Merriam-Webster defines it as "a category of artistic, musical, or literary composition characterized by a particular style, form, or content." Genres of fiction include mystery, science fiction, romance, fantasy, westerns, erotica, and horror. Genre fiction can be commercial, it can be literary—and it can be both.

The one thing a genre novel must do? Entertain. It can provoke, amuse, terrify, delight, intrigue, and enchant all in in turn, but it cannot be boring. As entertainment, genre fiction competes against TV, movies, music, naps, games, cat videos, and the entire internet, anything and everything humanity can conceive to procrastinate or relax, and so above all, it must be compelling. It can illuminate, provoke thought, or call for action, but must do so while still keeping the reader engaged—for genre fiction, boredom is the true deadly sin.

What do the Harry Potter, Twilight, and Fifty Shades of Grey series have in common besides being gigantic, genre-changing blockbusters in both print and film? First, very strong storytelling (which is very difficult to teach and is not the same as writing ability) that pulled millions and millions of readers into these works and made them empathize and identify with the main characters. Second, through that character identification all three series fulfill, for their respective audiences, the universal human desire to feel special: Harry's letter to Hogwarts makes him not only not a Muggle but actually a very special wizard; Bella Swann is chosen by the most intriguing boy in school; and only Anastasia can redeem the tortured hero Christian . . . The audience's strong ability to identify with the main character in all three of these series drove millions and millions in sales.

DIANA GILL is an executive editor at Tor/Forge/Tor Teen. Prior to Tor she was at Ace/Roc and HarperCollins, where she ran Harper Voyager for twelve years. Some of the many bestselling and award-winning authors she has worked with include Charlaine Harris, Kim Harrison, Richard Kadrey, Mark Lawrence, Zen Cho, Genevieve Cogman, Alastair Reynolds, and Brom. She also teaches at New York University and is a University of Chicago alumna. Twitter: @dianagill. Instagram: dianacgill.

Thanks to its potency as entertainment, genre fiction is a large and extremely profitable part of the marketplace, comprising more than half the publishing industry's sales in digital form and a large percentage of print books as well. For example, romance sales in 2015 were more than 29 percent of the fiction market, according to Nielsen Bookscan. Combined with mystery/thriller and science fiction and fantasy, they made up more than a third of the entire market and more than half of the adult fiction marketplace sales for the year. Beyond that, most of the big media properties in film, TV, and computer games of the last decade-plus are derived from genre fiction, as shown by the immense successes of the *Lord of the Rings* movies, *Sherlock*, *Game of Thrones*, *True Blood*, *Gone Girl*, *The Hunger Games*, the many retellings of Jane Austen, and more.

Despite the rapidly changing marketplace, genre fiction remains an extremely profitable sector of the industry, and if you can establish yourself as a first-rate genre editor, you're likely to have a successful career.

ACQUIRING GENRE FICTION

You cannot acquire projects in a genre if you do not know, and love, that genre.

I have loved genre fiction since I was very little and would be frankly abysmal as a mainstream literary editor. Every genre editor has a specialty, and preferences within the genre (psychological suspense à la Gillian Flynn versus action thrillers like Lee Child, historical versus contemporary romance, fantasy versus science fiction, etc.), but you will edit all types of subgenres within your genre, so expanding your tastes by reading widely throughout the genres, not just your favorite, will make you stronger and better at both acquisitions and editing. Reading romances will show you character tension and dialogue, whereas mysteries and thrillers demonstrate foreshadowing and how to create spine-tingling suspense. Science fiction and fantasy will help you recognize great world building. At times the genres can merge and create new categories, such as when romance and fantasy spawned urban fantasy and paranormal romance. The more you know about every genre, the better you'll become at editing any one.

When acquiring genre fiction, just as when reading it, you want the stories you absolutely cannot put down—the ones you read until midnight on your cell phone (guilty as charged), the ones you can't stop thinking about. You want to fall in love with the story and not clamber back out until the very bitter end, blinking muzzily at the time / date / missed train stop / burnt toast / patient family.

. . . .

After all, if you as an editor are being paid to read a submission and do not love it (or cannot point to a viable market for it, given the nature of commercial publishing as a business), how can you convince the rest of the house to love it, much less persuade a reader to spend his money to buy it? Editors are the constant in-house champions for their titles and authors, and if you do not adore a story at the start of the process, you will certainly not love it after a year to two years of working with and on it.

Knowing the market and honing an acquiring eye take years of practice, like the old saw about Carnegie Hall, but to get started, here is a useful exercise: take five to ten bestselling commercial fiction novels across genres and read the first paragraph, then the first page of each one. You'll see that regardless of genre—mystery/thriller, romance, or epic fantasy—every single one of these bestsellers hooks your interest. There's something there that makes you want to keep reading, and that's what you look for in submissions as well. On a more detailed, craft level, look at the first couple of lines of ten or so genre classics, and you'll see the same thing, even more concisely.

Keep an open mind as well: often submissions might sound preposterous, but you truly never know . . . One submission I received sounded so small and "niche" (editor jargon for a book with a narrowly defined audience), with a seemingly preposterous title—*The Nymphos of Rocky Flats*—that I was certain it couldn't work. But I picked up the manuscript and laughed out loud at the first sentence, and then throughout the entire story, and ended up publishing five books with the author. Every editor has found a submission she thought she would hate and ended up falling in love with it, so it pays to be willing to read a submission, just in case.

So you love a book—what's next? The first task is to use the genre and subgenre of the book to determine the market and potential audience for the book. Things to consider: How crowded or mature is the market for this genre (i.e., is there room for a new breakout book)? Where does it look like it will be next year? The year after? Is it selling like crazy right now, meaning it might be overcrowded when this title comes out a year or two from now? What about three years down the line, for the sequel? Or is it an area that is starting to bubble—perhaps with self-published titles—but has room for great new voices?

Similarly, consider the competition, both in and out of house: Does the imprint or house have other books already signed that might be too similar? Would this compete with an existing project? Does another house have one that is very similar, or has someone else published a big "buzz book" along the same lines the last year or so, and how did it do? If analogous books—"comp titles" in industry jargon—did not publish to expectations, or if an imprint has published several similar stories over several years without success, it may be hard to launch this project. Every editor has had to pass on projects he or she loves because the market was too difficult, or because it was a niche or small enough project that it would be extremely tricky to publish successfully, or because the readers were simply no longer interested.

More considerations: Will readers follow these characters—are they engaging? Where does this story fit within the genre? A commercial genre story should be familiar enough that genre readers can recognize and find it, while still fresh and innovative enough that it does not feel tired. Also, this submission should ideally offer the possibility for more novels, whether a classic fantasy trilogy, a long-running detective series, or a linked band of heroes for romance. Stand-alone novels can and do work well in genre fiction—particularly if they are more literary, though that can carry its own set of challenges for publicity and sales—but the overall market and audience are very strongly weighted toward series or linked novels.[1]

To take one example, Kim Harrison's *Dead Witch Walking*, which began the number-one *New York Times* bestselling Hollows series, caught my eye because for more than a year I had been looking for a supernatural series with humor. Harrison's character, tone, and setting all were a great fit for the just-starting-to-boom urban fantasy market while her work stood out for the unique world building and voice.

EDITING: NOT JUST PRETTY PROSE

The basic mechanics and goals of editing are the same across the genres and disciplines: the end goal is to make the text as clear, engaging, and correct as possible. That said, there are some key considerations in editing genre fiction that do not apply when editing nonfiction, academic works, or literary fiction—most notably genre conventions, the importance of world building, and the primacy of series.

Each genre has its own general "rules," or at least expectations that certain conventions will be kept within the genre novel. Horror novels, by definition, should unsettle and scare the reader, whether through psychological

---

1. Horror is distinct in that its works are often as much stand-alones as series, in part because horror can and does move fluidly into other genres (even romance, such as urban fantasy / paranormal romance, where traditionally terrorizing creatures like vampires and werewolves became romantic).

suspense or the "buckets of blood'" spilled in splatterpunk novels back in the 1980s. Cozy mysteries shouldn't have serial killers and gruesomely graphic dismemberments (but baked goods, libraries, and pets often appeal), while if a dragon appears in a science fiction novel, the explanation must be rooted in science. And so forth. Genre editors must know these conventions—which ones must be kept and which can be broken—and keep in mind how this particular story should be new and fresh without violating the implicit trust of the genre readership. If you're editing a mystery and the murder is not solved by the end of the book, the audience will not be satisfied, while romance readers expect a HEA (Happy Ever After) where the couple end up together, even if they no longer actually ride off into the sunset.

These conventions inform the shape but not the sole function of the story, so to be a good genre editor you must be widely read within the field, both to recognize Star Trek episodes with the serial numbers filed off, as it were, and to see how the story you're reading takes a familiar trope or beloved classic and uses that inspiration in an innovative new story. John Scalzi's *Old Man's War* reinvigorated the science fiction field when it was published in 2005, in part because it harked back to the classic military science fiction of Robert E. Heinlein's *Starship Troopers*, but also because it was a new, fun, and extremely accessible take on military science fiction and more, appealing both to existing fans who loved Heinlein and to new readers who had not read the classics. *Old Man's War* is still immensely popular, one of the best gateway science fiction novels to introduce new readers to the genre.

World building—creating place and atmosphere—is another key factor in genre fiction. Whether a London gambling hell in Regency England like that in Sarah McLean's superb Scoundrels historical romance series, a small town perfect for cozy mysteries, the back streets of a city rife with the supernatural, a world that becomes a character in its own right like George R. R. Martin's Westeros, or a far-flung planet, world building is an integral part of most genres, setting the stage for the reader to enter an exciting new world. It's not surprising that there's a strong correlation between readers who love historical fiction and those who read genre fiction—in both, a vivid sense of place and time is key to establishing the story.

The writer's world must feel real to the readers, and thus the author must do a lot of research and a lot of thinking about that world to make it credible and evocative. World building must serve the story: you never want the readers to get bored with pages and pages of details, or encounter a setting that requires so much suspension of disbelief that it becomes laughable. Genre editors work with their authors to avoid showing the dreaded "iceberg"—while the author needs to know huge amounts of detail about her setting for it to be credible, readers only need to see the very tip of the iceberg. Of course every genre takes license—there are enough dukes in historical romances to populate an entire metropolis, versus the very small number that exist in real life and history; in reality every inhabitant of Cabot Cove would have left the minute Jessica Fletcher appeared, and (unfortunately) there isn't a secret Platform 9¾ at King's Cross—but when the author uses details convincingly, the reader will accept, and savor, the story-world.

Ultimately, an editor is first and foremost a reader: an informed one with an extra set of tools, but still a reader. First reactions are important. Does the world building ground and support the story or overwhelm it? Does the story move at the right pace, neither too fast nor too slow? The setting and conceit should be intriguing or evocative but not distract from the heroine and hero and their difficulties. For example, Ann Leckie's *Ancillary Justice* won the Hugo, Nebula, and Arthur C. Clarke Awards all in the same year. Using only female pronouns for all the characters regardless of gender was novel for the genre and sparked discussion across the field, but the story also worked extremely well in its own right.

Once the world building and setting are solid, a strong voice, characters, and story are all extremely important in genre fiction. Unlike literary fiction, where novels usually stand alone, genre fiction is typically published in series, some of which go on for decades—consider Sue Grafton's Kinsey Millhone series, which started with *A Is for Alibi* in 1982 and is now nearing the end of the alphabet twenty-plus books later. Even romance novels, which traditionally featured one single hero and heroine, have evolved into linked series featuring families, Special Forces squads, vampire clans, or motorcycle clubs (just to name a few), so that the books are connected and favorite characters can reappear later on. This means the characters must be engaging—you can hate them or you can love them, but the minute you get bored and don't care, the story is over.

Some long-running genre series are basically stand-alone stories with a recurring central character, but even there the character needs to slowly evolve or progress to keep the reader entertained. For example, in Lee Child's excellent Jack Reacher series the basic elements of Reacher's personality and general story elements remain constant for each adventure, but the reader slowly learns more about Reacher's mysterious past as the series progresses. That combination of always-exceptional thriller action and an intriguing, enigmatic character has made Child one of the most successful genre

....

authors, perhaps even "the strongest brand in publishing."[2] In other series where the novels are direct sequels, the editor must watch for the continuity of both story and world, along with how the characters (and again, sometimes the setting) evolve and grow throughout the novels.

The one true constant in publishing is change, and editors must be extremely flexible: both watching the larger picture of the field/market, thinking years in advance given publication schedules, and at the same time keeping close watch on the small details like the letterspacing on a cover, clues to the murder, or key points about a character or world. The editor must know where a given story fits both within the history of the genre and within the changing marketplace. This is especially true in romance, where the trends move extremely quickly and what might have worked a year ago may be extremely difficult to publish now (witness the shift from historical romance to paranormal romance, and from urban fantasy to contemporary erotica after Fifty Shades). Genre editors must keep abreast of what's hot now versus "so last year," but given the twelve-month-or-more timeline of traditional publishing must also try and gauge whether a trend is peaking. (Alas, we cannot predict the next trend, though are always asked and wish we could—if only to play the market and retire happily in some idyllic locale). Similarly, genre editors must pay keen attention movies and TV, video games, YouTube sensations and other elements of pop culture, as any of these can spark new areas for fiction and be a barometer for genre popularity.

Acquiring and editing a genre novel follows much the same process inhouse as acquiring a mainstream novel or a nonfiction work, with a few key differences. One of the most important things with genre novels is a strong voice and story: you need and want to be swept away and fall in love with some part of the book (character, voice, story, or ideally all three). I remember reading a submission and being so caught up in the story and characters that I didn't realize until halfway through the entire manuscript that it was in present tense, which I absolutely hate. That manuscript, Richard Kadrey's *Sandman Slim*, became both a bestselling and a critically acclaimed series for me.

CASE STUDY: *SORCERER TO THE CROWN*, ZEN CHO

Zen Cho's novel *Sorcerer to the Crown* came in with everything to check off on an editor's wish list: a fabulous query letter, a debut author with some

2. David Vinjamuri, "The Strongest Brand in Publishing," *Forbes*, March 4, 2014, http://www.forbes.com/sites/davidvinjamuri/2014/03/04/the-strongest-brand-in -publishing-is/.

great short-story credentials and award nominations, and a great premise about English magicians facing all sorts of challenges, including prejudiced colleagues, plus an absolutely enchanting story with room and ideas for two potential sequels.

In terms of the market, the story appealed to the fans of Naomi Novik's bestselling Temeraire series, which is an alternate history set in the Napoleonic era, with dragons, and to the many readers who made Susannah Clarke's *Jonathan Strange and Mr. Norrell* a bestseller. The Regency London setting and hint of romance also offered crossover appeal to romance readers. And the book explores racial and feminist issues, which I knew would attract support in the indie bookstore community.

Here I had a fabulous story I loved, and the setting and themes of the book gave us a clear audience to target, in a genre that was popular but not overcrowded: All this made it a very strong candidate for us to pursue, even within an auction.

Once I bought the trilogy for Ace Books, our science fiction / fantasy imprint, the next step was the editing. Overall the manuscript was in very good shape, as the author and agent had already revised it, further revisions were still needed. I worked with the author on sharpening the opening chapters so that the story started more quickly, showing the hero's predicament rather than telling it in numerous conversations, as well as tightening the story and pacing throughout the manuscript. We also cut the heroine's introductory chapter, which was more preamble and in the past, so that her actual introduction in the present/main storyline had more impact. Then we worked on her goals and motivations throughout the story, to more fully develop her character and ground her plot. The narrative space we gained was used to more fully develop the main relationship. The hero's motives and issues were more fully developed within the story arc as well. And of course there were detailed story and character notes and queries throughout. Some genre books require detailed line editing, some do not—this edit was more on the level of story/concept/characters/pacing than line-by-line revision, as the writing was very strong to start.

We announced the acquisition, as usual, with a press release to the industry and genre community. As soon as the release went out, it was clear we had something special, as authors of all types offered to read the manuscript for prepublication blurbs (this is, shall we say, *not* usually the case, as most high-profile authors are deluged with requests constantly). From there we began the reader outreach online and at conventions—a cover reveal at a key account, galley giveaways at conventions, talking to key booksellers while

....

publicity pitched for reviews, and so forth. We ended up with nine blurbs from a wide range of authors, along with great reviews, including a starred review in *Publishers Weekly*. *Sorcerer* was one of PW's Top Picks for Fall 2015, with a lot of reader/author buzz surrounding the debut. Since then the book has been shortlisted for awards and won Best Newcomer in the British Fantasy Awards.

BEYOND THE RED PENCIL

Once the manuscript is acquired and edited, genre editors have another role that nongenre editors generally don't: engaging with the genre audiences both in person and online.

Genre audiences are incredibly involved, vocal, and voracious, forming online and offline communities and holding genre-specific conventions across the country. The closest analogue for literary fiction or nonfiction authors is location-specific book festivals, but there the speakers and topics range widely, versus "cons" where one genre—and sometimes one author, like Leakycon for Harry Potter—are the focus. The myriad genre-specific conventions include RT (Romantic Times) and RWA (Romance Writers of America) for romance; Bouchercon and Malice Domestic for mysteries (Malice Domestic is specifically for the subgenre "cozies," like those exemplified by Agatha Christie's Miss Marple); Thrillercon for thrillers; Worldcon, Dragon Con, & comic-cons for science fiction/fantasy; and more for horror and sf/f in general. The con behemoths like San Diego Comic Con International and New York Comic Con draw over 160,000 attendees—not including professionals and exhibitors—by focusing on comics, movies, and pop culture for the "geek" crowd. Genre editors, marketers, and publicists frequent one or more of these conventions each year for industry awards, promoting and meeting authors and agents, hand-selling titles and authors at publisher booths, and interacting with the many fans who attend. These attendees are some of the most devoted genre readers, and early buzz for a novel at conventions can do a lot to start building an author's career. Conventions also are a place to meet authors—those you are already working with, authors at other houses, and the genre fans who might very well become your next authors.

Fan conversations go on far beyond convention halls, of course, all year round. Online and social media are also vital to genre publishing—science fiction fans were online before any other genre buffs; romance readers are now some of the largest fan/genre communities on the internet; and mystery fans love Facebook and Goodreads. This means that genre editors, more than editors in other disciplines, must increasingly be online, whether interacting with authors and readers; networking with agents and bloggers; promoting books and authors on Twitter, Facebook, Instagram, Tumblr, and beyond; participating in Goodreads or "street teams," where fans of a particular genre or genre author spread the word about new books and authors; or simply keeping up with the industry news. Bloggers are another key constituency for genre publishers—where literary fiction and nonfiction depend on print reviews, genre fiction finds stronger currency in online reviews, and there are a number of extremely influential bloggers who can sway genre readers.

The importance of making connections with devoted readers is one more reason why the best genre editors are themselves genre fans. Whether it's knowing the canon of science fiction authors or knowing whom to schmooze at RWA, your passion for the field can be one of your biggest assets. Read and love your genre (whatever that may be), and then don't limit yourself to reading only what you work on—read genres outside your own as well. Genre is about possibilities—explore them and have fun!

16 MARGINALIA

ON EDITING GENERAL NONFICTION

· ·

MATT WEILAND

What a lousy name "general nonfiction" has! "*Non*fiction"—as if it were a negative thing, a thing defined only by what it's not. And "general"—so shapeless, so undistinguished; it sounds suspiciously like scrap metal or bulk mail. For so glorious a thing, "general nonfiction" may sound dull and uninspiring, but I take it as a mantra and rallying cry, and have come to feel that—generally speaking, of course—readers of general nonfiction are everywhere, if only we would recognize them. To my mind it's simple, really: a reader of general nonfiction is just one who is not *necessarily* already interested in the subject at hand. It's up to the writer to entice that reader to take an interest in the people and places the writer describes, to understand and care about the ideas or issues the writer tackles, to share some measure of the writer's fire for his or her subject.

Helping a writer form this connection with the reader—that is, to edit a manuscript—means telling the writer as candidly and directly as I can where those bonds are forming and where they are not. To this end, I've long been a heavy commenter in the margins of draft manuscripts. My focus is usually on structure and form: the trajectory of a book, its shape, the way it develops and progresses and resolves and (one hopes) satisfies. I must sound like the wide-eyed reader I suppose I am, forever scrawling NO WAY! or HOT DAMN or YEE-HAW, FLYING HERE in the margins. Or, given how common a problem repetition can be in a book-length manuscript, I sometimes jot a comment that a waiter at an Italian sub shop in south Brooklyn, on hearing me repeat my order, once growled at me: *Yeah—you said dat already.*

But all my marginal comments are aimed at helping the writer achieve the

MATT WEILAND is a vice president and senior editor at W. W. Norton. He has worked at Ecco Books, Granta Books, and Columbia University Press, as well as on *The Paris Review*, *Granta*, and the *Baffler*. He also served as project director for the documentary radio unit American RadioWorks. Weiland is the coeditor, with Sean Wilsey, of the bestselling *State by State: A Panoramic Portrait of America*, and his writing has appeared in the *New York Times Book Review*, the *Washington Post*, *New York Magazine*, *Bookforum*, Slate, and elsewhere. Originally from Minneapolis, he lives in Brooklyn with his wife and son. Twitter: @mattweiland.

qualities of a good and lasting work of general nonfiction I value most—drive, richness, economy, clarity, and an especially elusive quality I've come to call *curve*, meaning good shape.

I might as well admit that the marginal comment I make most frequently is this: *I'm bored here.* Sorry! But as John Berryman wrote, life, friends, is boring—and capturing it on the page, in any form, risks being more so. Even the finest writer may find it difficult to know precisely where a manuscript sags and where a reader's interest flags. My task, as I see it, is to help the writer identify and fix such issues.

Now, one reader's dew-dappled-hyacinth-lolling-in-the-breeze may be another reader's helicopter-getting-blown-up; who can say definitively what subject matter is most intrinsically interesting? So I'm not speaking of the content, exactly. In telling a writer where in a manuscript my mind wanders, I mean that the *way* he or she is telling the story or making the case leaves a reader feeling stuck and wanting to say, as Madam Oretta says to the knight who mangles his storytelling in Boccaccio's *Decameron*, "Sir, this horse of yours has too hard a trot; please be so good as to set me down."

Great prose has *drive*; it sweeps the reader along. I can still remember the exasperation in the voice of my tough but beloved high school English teacher as she looked over a broken jalopy of a piece I'd written and said just about the most exciting thing a revered teacher could say to a sixteen-year-old student: "But I want you to take me *with* you!" For prose to do that, it must be *persuasive*. Anyone who has told a story, true or otherwise, at a bar or a dinner table knows that giving your audience a sense of narrative progression is crucial. In conversation we get a wide range of feedback to indicate whether the story we're telling or the argument we're making is connecting—a listener may shrug or lift a brow in doubt or look around in boredom. Seeing these things, we may shift how we tell the story, fill in details, adjust the texture of our storytelling to reengage the listener's attention. My job as an editor is to make that shrug on the page.

For many readers general nonfiction is a kind of advanced education, a way of learning about a new subject, idea, or group of people in a manageable dose with a companionable guide and without the expense or commitment or lousy food required of formal schooling. Often the writers best suited to creating such works are exceptionally knowledgeable about the subject at hand or just winningly and inspiringly obsessed. I revere that kind of passion and expertise, and relish the books that come out of it. Yet such writers sometimes only sketch details that they've long since absorbed but that are new or unfamiliar to the reader.

To address this problem, I often make enthusiastic checkmarks in the margins of manuscripts but add: TOO FAST! I am trying to implore writers to be as generous as possible to their readers, to assume the best of their capacity for learning, and therefore to *slow down* and explain or describe more. I work with a lot of journalists, whom I admire for their devotion to the craft of reporting. In newspapers, magazines, radio, television, or online, they are masters of describing what they see and hear. And yet I often find myself reminding them that they can stretch out and describe everything at much greater length and in more detail in a book.

An irony of "general" nonfiction is that it often works best when it is most specific. The *New York Times* reporter John Branch's first book, *Boy on Ice*, was based on his front-page series of pieces about the heartbreaking early death of the hockey player Derek Boogaard. The book told the very human story of a life lived and lost in the glare of sporting fame. Branch is a dynamite reporter and writer—he is a winner of the Pulitzer Prize for feature writing, after all. But I think the book really found its shape as Branch added more descriptive passages about the prairies of Saskatchewan and the hockey towns in which Boogaard had grown up. These background details gave the book depth and texture and gave the reader enough knowledge to appreciate the full tragedy of Boogaard's demise.

Another example is *The Death and Life of the Great Lakes*, a debut book by the Milwaukee *Journal-Sentinel* reporter Dan Egan, a two-time Pulitzer Prize finalist, on the ecological catastrophe looming over the Great Lakes. In the course of editing successive drafts of the book, a powerful blend of character-driven reportage and explanatory science writing, I often found myself fascinated by some fact that Egan mentioned only in passing. Take phosphates, a key but complex source of pollution in the Great Lakes before the Clean Water Act a generation ago, and again a huge source of pollution today. I asked Egan to explain more, and—typically—he disappeared into a well of deep reporting for a few weeks and came back with an extraordinary account of the discovery of phosphorus and the ways humans have interacted with it over the centuries, which made the whole book richer.

Great works of general nonfiction *get into the details*—they use all that glorious space to explore beyond what author and reader may already know. I doubt I'd have said that the history of phosphorus was what general nonfiction readers were clamoring for. But in the hands of writers like Branch and Egan, such details allow books to reverberate and to live on in a way even the best newspaper and magazine articles may not. Think of such exemplary contemporary books as Eric Schlosser's *Fast Food Nation*, Adrian Nicole LeBlanc's *Random Family*, or Sheri Fink's *Five Days at Memorial*: all of them characterized by (among other things) an extraordinary level of reported detail. With models like these in mind, the questions I ask are: *Does it satisfy a reader's full curiosity? Is it generous to the best reader you can imagine, and yet appealing to those who might not otherwise consider themselves interested in the subject? Does it treat the subject with the richness it deserves?*

One of the hardest things for even the best writers to see in their own writing is the difference between the pretty good and the great. Inevitably, draft manuscripts include material that just doesn't feel essential, that—however interesting—drags the narrative to a halt. So I frequently put a squiggly line in the margins and write those dread words *TOO SLOW*.

I know, I know—I just made the case for slowing down. But it's vital to clear away extraneous good stuff to allow the great to stand tall and thrive. What I've long taken as the best advice for writing a book comes from Miles Davis, and it may be apocryphal. But the story goes that someone asked him, in the period when he was writing extraordinarily spare and powerful compositions, how he did it. Davis said this: "It's easy. I always listen for what I can best leave out." As I read a manuscript, I'm often looking for ways it can move faster, that it can be tighter. Sometimes this can mean cutting a line or a passage that was the kernel for the whole book. As playwright Sarah Ruhl put it in *100 Essays I Don't Have Time to Write*, "What seems like the most necessary thing in your play might be the least necessary thing." And sometimes it can mean cutting an excess of examples or vignettes, which writers often pile on to prove a point. As vivid as these may be, the point is usually stronger when just one of them is used. *Pick your best punch*, I tell the writer, *in order to avoid having your fists crowd each other out.*

Of course, suggestions for cuts can be perilous. A couple of years ago an agent called me and said, "I've got a great proposal for a book—I'm not sure what it is, but it roars." It was a memoir of life on the road by a long-haul truck driver named Finn Murphy, and reading the sample material that night, I thought two things: *First, he's totally right—Murphy has a sound on the page that rings in my ears; and second, I know exactly what it is: it's the book Anthony Bourdain might have written had he become a trucker instead of a cook.* We duly signed it up, and I had a ball working with Murphy. But somewhere in the editing it I told him I felt the extensive material about his middle years, when his life took a wrong turn and he took a long break from trucking, should be cut. Much as I enjoyed his account, it seemed to me to break the spell of the book. He cheerfully said he saw my point, and out it went.

We published Murphy's book, *The Long Haul,* to strong sales and rapturous reviews. Oh, the thrill of seeing it greeted by a rave from the daily book critic Jennifer Senior of the *New York Times*! She hailed his knack for telling astonishing stories and called the book "almost shamefully enjoyable." But she also said this: "Midway through *The Long Haul*, he does something disconcerting and entirely unexpected: He gives up driving. . . . And he never says why. Now, I'm not saying this omission is on par with the 18½ missing minutes of conversation between Richard Nixon and H. R. Haldeman. But it does seem like a literary crime of some sort."

Reader, that criminal was me.

As long as I'm confessing how rude and coldhearted I am on the page, I might as well reveal that in editing a book I also aim to be as ignorant as possible. In an effort to help the writer know precisely where her point is not coming through clearly and convincingly, I write LOST ME HERE in the margin.

I try to help the writer resist the temptation to prove his or her mastery of the subject and to embrace the fact that there are always other writers (and readers) who know more about it. A book is not an exam; the writer's task is not to demonstrate that he is the one and only expert in whatever he's writing about.

I also remind the writer that clarity is king. "There is nothing that requires more precision, and purity of expression, than to write in a familiar style," as the great English essayist William Hazlitt put it nearly two hundred years ago. "To write as anyone would speak in common conversation who had a thorough command and choice of words, or who could discourse with *ease*, *force*, and *perspicuity* . . ." To me these are the cardinal virtues of strong, convincing English prose. (Hazlitt's last term, meaning "clarity," is now, alas, an antique word.)

Sometimes I scrawl HUH? in the margins to indicate that I'm not sure the writer is being fair to those who might disagree with her or is not representing other views fairly or fully enough. In such cases I encourage her to do this thought exercise: *What would a reader (or reviewer) who doesn't sympathize with your position say?* The point is to give the writer a chance to inoculate herself against obvious criticism—and thereby make the book stronger.

I also encourage the *writer* to reveal her own ignorance, even about the subject she is writing about. I think of two classic works of general nonfiction that left a deep mark on me, both—as it happens—about building a house: Tracy Kidder's *House* and Michael Pollan's *A Place of My Own*. Each imparts an enormous amount of information about carpentry, house building, and architecture generally—but in each, the author allows the reader to learn along with him by presenting himself as on a kind of quest to understand his subject.

In 2015 I published a debut work of general nonfiction in this distinguished line: *Hammer Head: The Making of a Carpenter* by Nina MacLaughlin, in which she told of leaving her job at a newspaper to become a professional carpenter. The book was hailed by one perceptive reviewer as being "like if Annie Dillard had her own show on HGTV." MacLaughlin excelled at capturing the details of her experience, explaining her work and the ways in which becoming a tradesperson changed how she looked at the world (and how the world looked back at her). But the book really took flight in revision, when she winningly adjusted the early chapters to reflect the degree to which she didn't yet know what she was doing.

A great work of general nonfiction is a living, breathing thing. Like anything alive, it may have gangly bits, knots, asymmetries. But to keep a reader's attention and have maximum effect, it's got to have good shape, *curve*, and my most profound task is helping the writer find it. Curve often depends, I find, on the shape and sequence of the chapters themselves, the degree to which they contribute to the arc of the book and yield a sense of narrative progression. On early drafts I may ask about a chapter: *What is its point? What problem does it pose and how does it address it? Where does it take us?*

Achieving this sense of curve is hard and can prove frustrating to author and editor. It often requires not marginal comments but deep conversations on the nature of the book itself. I relish these, and if I've been of any use to the writers I work with, it's often because I've tried to wander just as deep into a dark wood as they have. In these conversations an editor, I believe, has to be willing to be wrong—to suggest the wrong thing, to ask the wrong question—in the service of finding the right solution.

Assuming the raw material (of story, character, scene, and style) is good, the questions I may raise about structure are often borrowed from other art forms: *Is the bass too heavy in this part? Why is there so much yellow in the corner of the painting?* I often find it useful to switch metaphors—postpunk to kitchen-sink drama; soccer to impressionism—to find whatever helps the writer understand what the experience of reading the manuscript is like for someone else, and adjust it as necessary to achieve maximum force. There is no cynicism in acknowledging that great works of general nonfiction manipulate the reader this way. As in chess, a particular move—the shape of a chapter—is often made to set up the next one or the subsequent ones.

My best lesson on achieving curve came in the 1990s, when I had a small hand in working on several of Studs Terkel's timeless works of oral history, some of the finest works of general nonfiction I know. A little later I started working with Craig Taylor, who I believe is the nearest thing to an heir to Terkel. Taylor's bestselling book *Londoners*, which he spent six years reporting, was based on his in-depth interviews with more than two hundred people. But his draft manuscript was some 1.1 million words—at least five or six ordinary books of ordinary length—and unsequenced. As we sought together to carve out the one great book within it, to find its best shape, we spent months arranging and rearranging index cards listing each piece. Ultimately we relied on Terkel's model in thinking of the book as collage, or better still as bebop, with scenes and characters riffing off each other and building to various climaxes even as the book as a whole developed. That intense back-and-forth conversation about the book's shape (and cutting almost 90 percent of the material) yielded what the *New York Times Book Review* hailed as "a rich and exuberant kaleidoscopic portrait" of the city and "a master-class in self-effacing journalism."

To take another example: In 2015 I published Mary Norris's *Between You & Me*, a bestselling book about language filled with colorful details from Norris's nearly thirty-five years in the celebrated copy department of the *New Yorker*. As I read the draft material, I'd buttonhole my colleagues in the hallways to say, *You have GOT to read this*. But while there were many laugh-out-loud moments and loads of useful language tips, the book lacked curve. At one point in the editing process, Norris wrote me to apologize (*unnecessarily!*) for falling behind schedule, and added this: "Also wondering if it should be this hard." Of course I tried to reassure her, but I also tried to prod her into writing in a slightly different mode:

It *should* be this hard, yes—it often is. That's nothing to be afraid of or worried about! But a lot depends on your ability to *think like a chapter*—i.e., to craft chapters that have narrative propulsion; that carry a reader through a series of questions or things the narrator wants to explore. . . . There has to be story, has to be a reason we're following you, and reading of your experiences.

Typically, Norris took my small, vague effort to prod her to reach new heights and soared with it. ("Gotcha," she wrote back. "Feeling edited! There should be an emoticon for that.") She began to send remarkable accounts of her family and life both within and beyond the corridors of the *New Yorker*, including her contemporary travels to such places as a pencil-sharpener museum and Noah Webster's birthplace—and to seamlessly weave these in with her sterling advice regarding grammar and usage. As she did so, the book really took shape. Her celebrated chapter "The Problem of Heesh," for example, about the thorny problem of using *he* or *she* or *they* without implying a particular gender, came together when she told the moving story of having a transgender sibling and its effect on her own view of personal pronouns. She nailed it! And I was thrilled to tell her so, dipping into the Italian which we'd both studied haphazardly over the years. To which Norris, in her inimitable style, replied:

So glad to have hit the mark.
P.S. *Ermafrodito* is masculine, by the way.

Ultimately, like a toolmaker or a tailor, I aim to be useful to the author but invisible to the reader. The marginal comments I make are best forgotten. Whether the writers I work with follow my editorial suggestions or not, what I hope they remember is the spirit in which they're made—an enduring commitment to a writer's ideas and style, a passion for making them public, and a diehard belief that there are plenty of good readers for great general nonfiction on any subject.

17 *ONCE UPON A TIME* LASTS FOREVER
EDITING BOOKS FOR CHILDREN

· ·

NANCY SISCOE

THE WHY

When I tell people that I edit children's books for a living, their first response is usually "That sounds like fun." And often it is.

It can also be heartbreaking—when a book I adore doesn't find an audience. And heart-swelling—when a child tells me a book I've edited has made her love reading.

From a creative standpoint, it is immensely satisfying. It is my job to help authors craft the best possible expressions of their stories. It's also my job to find the right words to explain to the rest of the world how brilliant those stories are. The days when I feel I've done those things well are truly rewarding.

But, as with any job, being an editor is also frustrating (when I lose out on a book I desperately wanted), boring (meetings, paperwork, more meetings), and relentless (there is always something more I could do, should have done, need to do to help the books succeed).

Really, *fun* doesn't even scratch the surface of it.

I edit children's books because I love them. I loved them as a child and never stopped loving them. I edit children's books because I think kids deserve the *best* we have to offer. Because the books I read as a child thrilled me and expanded my world and live on inside me. Because I want to help create the books that will delight and inspire the next generation of readers.

The books we read as children have an indelible impact. Most people can remember their first favorites in great detail. They are like cherished friends—first loves. But try to recall the plot of a book you read two or three years ago . . . Children's books *last*. Who wouldn't want to be part of that?

In my first week on the job as an associate editor, my new boss gave me a

NANCY SISCOE is a senior executive editor with Knopf Books for Young Readers, where she's worked for the past twenty years. Nancy's list includes *New York Times* bestsellers and award-winning titles from picture books to YA. Authors she works with include Carl Hiaasen, Jerry Spinelli, Philip Pullman, Cynthia Voigt, Wendelin Van Draanen, and Julia Sarcone-Roach. She is on Facebook, on Twitter at @siscoe_nancy, and on Instagram at nsiscoe.

copy of Isaac Bashevis Singer's comments upon being awarded the National Book Award for Children's Literature. I've kept it in my "inspiration" file ever since, as it never fails to reorient me if I'm in danger of losing sight of the audience.

> There are five hundred reasons why I began to write for children, but to save time I will mention only ten of them. Number 1: Children read books, not reviews. They don't give a hoot about the critics. Number 2: They don't read to find their identity. Number 3: They don't read to free themselves of guilt, to quench their thirst for rebellion, or to get rid of alienation. Number 4: They have no use for psychology. Number 5: They detest sociology. 6: They don't try to understand Kafka or *Finnegans Wake*. 7: They still believe in God, the family, angels, devils, witches, goblins, logic, clarity, punctuation, and other such obsolete stuff. 8: They love interesting stories, not commentary, guides, or footnotes. 9: When a book is boring, they yawn openly, without any shame or fear of authority. 10: They don't expect their beloved writer to redeem humanity. Young as they are, they know that it is not in his power. Only the adults have such childish illusions.

THE WHAT

It's the audience, of course, that distinguishes children's books from adult books. And so editing them requires that you keep in mind the intended readers and what they want in a story. What a toddler wants is obviously not the same as what a ten-year-old wants, so there are different formats and categories of books to suit different audiences. In broad strokes, they are as follows:

- *Board books.* Sturdy books for babies and toddlers. They are designed for small hands (and emerging teeth). The simplest are about early concepts—colors, numbers, object identification, new words. The more complex tell short stories or are reprinted versions of young picture books. Classic examples: *I Am a Bunny* by Ole Risom, illustrated by Richard Scarry; *Moo Baa La La La* by Sandra Boynton; *Black & White* by Tana Hoban.
- *Picture books.* Larger-format, fully illustrated books, usually thirty-two pages long, for toddlers through school-aged kids. At the younger end, there is little text and the pictures do the lion's share of the storytelling. At the older end, the stories can be quite complex and the interaction between the text and artwork gets more nuanced. Picture books are deceptively simple, compact treasures. Classic examples:

Where the Wild Things Are by Maurice Sendak; *Don't Let the Pigeon Drive the Bus* by Mo Willems; *The Snowy Day* by Ezra Jack Keats.

- *Leveled readers.* Specifically designed for kids just learning to read. The word choices and sentence structures are simple, and the artwork offers clues to help readers decode the text. Classic examples: *The Cat in the Hat* by Dr. Seuss; *Frog and Toad Are Friends* by Arnold Lobel; *Fox on Wheels* by Edward Marshall, illustrated by James Marshall.
- *Chapter books.* For newly independent readers, generally seven to ten years old. These short novels (say 75 to 125 pages) with illustrations bridge the gap between picture books, readers, and longer novels. Series are extremely popular with this age group. Classic examples: the Magic Tree House books by Mary Pope Osborne, the Ivy & Bean books by Annie Barrows, *The Stories Julian Tells* by Ann Cameron.
- *Middle grade.* For independent readers, generally ages eight to fourteen. There's a huge range within this category, from simple to mind-blowingly complex, with an explosion of genres—fantasy, historical fiction, adventure. Classic examples: *Charlotte's Web* by E. B. White; *The Golden Compass* by Philip Pullman; *Bud, Not Buddy* by Christopher Paul Curtis.
- *Young adult.* For older, more sophisticated readers, generally ages fourteen and up. There's overlap with adult books in this category, and many books can (and do) sit comfortably in both worlds. YA books tend to have teen protagonists, coming-of-age themes, and an expanding view of the world. Classic examples: *The Absolutely True Diary of a Part-Time Indian* by Sherman Alexie, *Speak* by Laurie Halse Anderson, *The Hunger Games* by Suzanne Collins.

THE HOW

The books are created for children, but an editor must also be mindful that they are usually purchased by adults. Parents, grandparents, teachers, and librarians choose most of the books that younger children read. These gatekeepers are so influential that it's not uncommon for books to be created specifically for them. Most gatekeepers play a benevolent and beneficial role. On the dark side are would-be censors who want to ban certain children's titles from schools or libraries.

Of course editors are gatekeepers too, of a sort. I say no to more than 90 percent of the manuscripts that cross my desk. The most emphatic nos: No moralizing, no finger-wagging, no thinly veiled adult agendas. Kids can spot a good-for-you book in a heartbeat. Eye-rolling starts young.

Philip Pullman says it best: "We don't need lists of rights and wrongs, tables of dos and don'ts, we need books, time, and silence. *Thou shalt not* is soon forgotten, but *Once upon a time* lasts forever."

Another piece I keep in my inspiration file is an article by the renowned editor Richard Jackson. Jackson describes the essential questions an editor learns to ask when reading any new piece of writing for young readers: "Does this story convince me? Do I care what happens to these people? Is the voice authentic? Has a young person's nature somehow caused the action? Have I read this before?" I try to keep all of those considerations and questions in mind when I'm deciding whether to take on a new book.

And beyond that, I'm thinking about what the author's next book might be, and the next. I always hope a long-term relationship will grow. Every editor has her own approach, and every author needs something a little bit different, so I try to gauge whether the author and I will make a good team. An agent acts as a matchmaker in that sense—sending the right writer to the right editor.

The vast majority of manuscripts do come to me through agents. Sometimes a project will come from a friend of a writer I already work with, or I'll find a new talent at a conference or suggest that someone not currently writing for children might want to try it. But mostly I'm reading submissions from agents and hoping for that spark of joy that comes with finding something *new*.

Of course the competition for that new voice is intense. Heated auctions are common. And so after weeks of convincing yourself a book is wonderful, and persuading the rest of your team to be excited about it too, and running profit-and-loss estimates, and getting approvals to make an offer, and putting your best offer together, after all that, you can *still* lose out to someone else. So deflating.

On the flip side, winning a book at auction is exhilarating!

It's not the acquiring I love most, though; it's the editing. The time the author and I spend working together, trying to make the story sing. Here's a look at how that process works for some different types of books.

Picture Books
I've heard it said that there are two types of readers—those who read to understand their world and those who read to escape. As I'm a largely escapist reader myself, this resonates. But for the youngest readers, pretty much all books are about understanding their world.

To a baby *everything* is new, and so the youngest books are all about recognition. This is you, these are the things around you—your family, your room, your house, your yard, your neighborhood. Understanding ripples outward, with the child always at the center.

For me things start to get really interesting when a child is old enough to add emotion into the mix. That's when you can start telling *stories*. The stories are still focused on understanding the world and the people in it—but oh, the great variety that encompasses. This is the realm of most picture books.

The perfect picture book is often defined as one where neither the text nor the art would make sense on its own. There are notable exceptions, of course—wordless picture books can be wonderful, and some texts can easily double as poetry. But it's most often true: a picture book consists of words and pictures working together to tell a story.

A picture book is also largely defined by the format. Just thirty-two pages. Those pages can be bigger or smaller. Crammed with art and text or left open and airy. But the length is pretty standard—determined by the way the books are printed, in sixteen-page signatures. You can add sixteen more for a forty-eight page book, but that often feels too long and is expensive to boot.

With a set number of pages, the pacing of a picture book becomes crucial. You want roughly the same amount of text on each spread so that the pages get turned at a consistent rate. And anyone who's sat with a child on her lap knows kids like the pages to turn fairly quickly.

First drafts are often too long. There's too much story and not enough space. And so the author and I begin the process of winnowing down. We're forced to decide what's truly essential to the story and what's taking up unwarranted space.

I often begin by making a map—a view of the book in miniature, all on one page. You block out the pages needed for a title page and a copyright page. How the story begins and ends is often clear, so you rough those in, and then you have a view of the space remaining to get from here to there.

Here's an example: Dan Yaccarino and I were working on a picture book called *Billy and Goat at the State Fair*. Billy and his pet goat are best friends, even though they have different temperaments—Billy likes to smell the flowers, and Goat likes to eat them. When the state fair rolls around, Goat is dying to go. Billy doesn't like the crowds and noise, but he does think Goat deserves to be in the best goat competition, so off they go. First thing, Goat takes off to explore the fair, and Billy chases after him. When he catches him at last, Billy realizes the fair is pretty exciting—as long as he's with his pal. They end up missing the best goat competition completely, but neither minds, for they've spent a great day together.

Dan is both an author and an illustrator, so the first draft I saw included sketches of the art he had in mind. There were brilliantly funny pictures of Billy and Goat at the fair riding roller coasters and log plumes. Dashing through displays of flowers and pies. Playing games of chance and eating corn dogs. They were all fabulous! And lots of them got cut. After reading the first draft again and again, we realized that the attractions of the fair were overpowering the story. We had oodles of middle and not so much beginning and end.

So we allowed more space at the beginning to get to know our two friends. (Even picture books need character development.) We needed space to show Goat's excitement for the fair and Billy's apprehension. We knew we needed space at the end for the rush back (too late!) to the goat competition, and a final page for the resolution. With all that blocked in, we saw what space remained for the fair. In roughly the middle of that section we needed to focus on the place where Billy catches up with Goat, finally takes a look around him, and decides the fair is more exciting than scary. This emotional pivot is crucial to the story and needed some time to feel genuine. We added another page there.

Bit by bit the space available for showing the rides and displays got smaller, but the *story* got clearer and stronger. It sounds easy in retrospect, but the process is painful, with lots of false steps and erasures before things finally feel right. Once we had the map of the story set, Dan could go back and revise the text and refine the pictures.

Key to the pacing and rhythm of a picture book are the page turns. Eric Rohmann is a master of the page turn (among many other things!) and taught me much about their potential while we were working on *A Kitten Tale.* Each turn of the page is this little moment of suspense. The pregnant pause between cause . . . and effect. Between action and reaction. Using these pauses well can add lots of drama to a story. The trajectory of a book is often determined by feeling it is absolutely crucial to turn the page . . . *there.*

In the case where the author and illustrator are not the same person, it's the editor, along with the art director, who has the delight of choosing what kind of illustrations will best suit the story. Pairing a text with an artist is a bit like matchmaking—ideally the two together will add up to more than the sum of their parts.

Usually a picture book begins with the text. Occasionally I've done books where the art exists and I'm trying to craft a story that holds it together—tricky. It's more often the case that I'll be searching for a text that will be a good vehicle for an illustrator I've been hoping to work with.

. . . .

Spotting a text that tells enough of a story to spark the imagination but also leaves room for an artist to add to and complete the story is a skill acquired over many years. Usually you begin with too much text.

One book where the text was, I thought, admirably brief was *An Annoying ABC* by Barbara Bottner and illustrated by Michael Emberley. It began: "Adelaide annoyed Bailey. Bailey blamed Clyde. Clyde cried." On it went—a tale of woe through an alphabet of kids. Barbara and I imagined all the kids together in a preschool classroom with events escalating to an all-out disaster by the time we get to Zelda, who turns her wrath back on Adelaide, who eventually . . . apologizes. It was funny and clever—and left a huge job for the illustrator.

It fell to Michael Emberley to figure out just what Adelaide did to annoy Bailey, and why Bailey then blamed Clyde. Each annoying action had to lead logically to the next. It was a twenty-six-link chain of events that all had to unfold Rube Goldberg–like to the desired end. All hail Michael, who made just brilliant choices and pictures.

In books for the younger end of the picture book audience, the art and text work together to tell the same story. But as the audience gets older and more sophisticated, text and art can sometimes contradict each other to great comic effect. Julia Sarcone-Roach's *The Bear Ate Your Sandwich* is a good example. An unseen narrator tells the story of a bear who falls asleep in the back of a truck and wakes to find himself in a "new kind of forest." But the pictures show the bear in the heart of a city. The text describes good trees for scratching (telephone poles), squishy mud underfoot (wet cement), and a cool pool for bathing (a fountain in a park). While in the park, the bear, understandably hungry, spots "your beautiful and delicious sandwich, all alone." After his snack the bear hightails it back to the forest, but the story has a final surprise. The unseen narrator is revealed to be a dog—spinning the whole shaggy-dog tale for a skeptical girl.

Do six-year-olds understand the concept of an unreliable narrator? Yes, they do! And their parents appreciate the joke as well. It is kind to remember that picture books are frequently read to a child by a tired adult at bedtime and to try to make the experience fun for that parent as well.

The best way to ensure a happy reading experience is to read the book aloud yourself. Note the places you stumble, where a sentence goes on too long, where the words don't quite flow. I'll read sections aloud as the book gets revised, and then one last time before it goes to the printer.

At their best, picture books are a point of connection between adult and child—offering a shared love, an inside joke, or the origin of a family saying.

As I edit, I imagine these things happening and plant a few seeds. "Let the wild rumpus start!"

Novels

Once children can read, the possibilities open up exponentially. They can decide for themselves what kind of stories they want. They understand enough about the world to escape it if they choose, and so in addition to realistic fiction you start to see fantasy, mystery, historical fiction, adventure, horror, and more.

I imagine the editing process for a novel for children is much the same as for a novel for adults. But everyone has their own variations on the theme, so here's what I normally do.

I read the book from start to finish. Just read, with no pencil in hand. Ideally in one long gulp. *Then* I start taking notes. What did I love? What didn't make sense? Where did things lag? Where did they move too quickly? What themes are emerging? Are they clear enough? Too overt?

After I've jotted down all my first impressions, I put the book away and give myself some time to think about what's on the page now and about the story I sense the author wants to tell. I think about what needs to happen to move from one to the other.

Then I read the book again more slowly, outlining each chapter as I go. I'll start writing notes to the author in the margins—asking questions, pointing out inconsistencies, noting wonderful turns of phrase and all the places that make me laugh or cry. If it's a book where timing matters, I'll keep a running timeline of events as well. From there I usually make a more concise map, one that shows where the major events of the story fall so I can see if they are well spaced or all bunched together. I can also see if there are long stretches where nothing essential is happening. With those insights, I go back through the pages again, adding more notes in the margins, suggesting where things might be condensed, offering alternate wordings.

Before I begin an editorial letter to the author, I return to my first impressions. Have they held up after repeated readings? Have new questions arisen? New ideas for where to go from here? I try to articulate in the letter all those big-picture thoughts about the story—what's working well, what might be emphasized more, and what could perhaps go.

So what specific considerations go into a novel for middle graders?

Carl Hiaasen asked me this before he began his first kids' book, *Hoot*, and what I told him cuts to the heart of it: never talk down to your reader.

. . . .

Kids may lack information, but they don't lack intelligence. Yes, you may need to offer some context that an adult reader would be expected to know already. But never for a minute assume that you are smarter than your reader. Kids can smell condescension and they'll stop listening. They get enough lectures—you're telling a story. Put a kid at the center of the action, view the world through their eyes, and let the story flow from there.

That's another point that's worth stressing—a kid should be at the center of the action.

This came up in the first book I worked on with sports writer John Feinstein. John had written a terrific story about two kid reporters who get a chance to cover the Final Four basketball tournament and discover that someone is trying blackmail a player into throwing the final game. The book was exciting and offered a rare behind the scenes glimpse of a major sporting event. But the first draft veered off course a bit at the end.

In the big denouement, the kids figured out what was going on, but then adult characters swooped in and saved the day. Realistic? Maybe. Satisfying to a kid reader? Not so much. The kid characters need to be the prime actors. They need to solve the puzzle and get *themselves* out of trouble and save the day. John came up with a brilliant alternate scenario that let the kids be the heroes.

I spend a lot of time thinking about the pace of a novel. Kids tend to be impatient readers, so I'm always looking for ways to move things along faster. (Of course it could also be that *I* am an impatient reader. But mostly I blame it on the kids.)

Here again Philip Pullman says it so well: "In a book for children you can't put the plot on hold while you cut artistic capers for the amusement of your sophisticated readers, because, thank God, your readers are not sophisticated. They've got more important things in mind than your dazzling skill with wordplay. They want to know what happens next."

This was my major concern in Wendelin Van Draanen's first novel, *How I Survived Being a Girl*. I remember reading the book as an unsolicited submission and falling in love with the main character's voice. The daring exploits of Carolyn and her brothers as they spied on the neighbors and dug up someone's yard made me laugh out loud. I also remember grumbling quite a lot at the long and rambling sidetracks Carolyn went off on as she told her story. I found myself skimming and skipping ahead—*yeah, yeah, but what happens next?*

And so I wrote to Wendelin and said I liked her story but would she please cut it in half. If she was willing to try, then I'd read it again. I may have been nicer about it than that, a smidge more encouraging, but not much.

I stand by the advice. Cutting a story down to what's essential is as important in a novel as it is in a picture book. But I cringe now at how glibly I delivered my suggestion for such major surgery. How brutal I must have sounded. How easily she might have tossed my letter aside.

The story ends well. Wendelin did revise the book and it was the first novel I acquired on my own—a huge milestone for any young editor. Wendelin and I have now worked on thirty-four (and counting) books together. We are an awesome team. So when I think back on the terseness of my first letter to her, I feel the weight of all I would have missed out on had she responded differently.

I remind myself to be clear and kind and encouraging. Always.

For middle-grade novels I do consider the gatekeepers. I do think about what's appropriate for a young reader. Can we convey strong emotion without cursing? Usually. Do we need that graphic violence and gore? Usually not. I also think about the kind of world we're portraying. Do we need to pretend the world is sunshiny all the time? No. But do we need to depict it as unrelentingly bleak either? I don't think so.

This is not to say I think middle-grade books should shy away from tough subjects. On the contrary, I think a book can be the best place for a kid to first encounter some of the evils of the world. Better in the safe confines of a book than in real life. But I also think the author and editor have a responsibility to know when something might be shocking and to treat it with care.

Hope is essential.

Here again, I am guided by the wise editor Richard Jackson: "A [middle-grade] novel ends not with happily ever after, but with a new beginning, with the sense of a lot of life left to be lived."

For young adult novels, I let all those thoughts of gatekeepers go. What's appropriate is based solely on what feels right for the story. Teens can and often do read adult books. They watch the news. They survived junior high! They are well aware that the world is a flawed place. So why not give them stories about how characters respond to the worst that life throws at them? The censors disagree, of course, but they're fighting a losing battle. What could be more enticing to a teen than a book some adult thinks they shouldn't be allowed to read?

In the end, it turns out my advice for all children's authors is essentially the same: put a kid at the center of the action, look at the world through their eyes, and let the story flow.

. . . .

18 LIVES THAT MATTER

EDITING BIOGRAPHY, AUTOBIOGRAPHY, AND MEMOIR

· ·

WENDY WOLF

What could be simpler?

Writing a biography—the story of a life—means conforming to a pre-existing chronology, as life naturally lays down its own patterns and rhythms. An author just has to assemble the parts in the right order, make sure of his facts, and then get out of the way. If he is writing an autobiography—the story of his own life—he's won half the battle already (he knows how the story goes). The editor's job must be equivalently easy, pruning out a few errant details here and there, right?

In fact, after forty years of editing biography and autobiography—political, historical, academic, comic, literary, athletic, wistful memoir and hard-hitting investigative biography—I can assure you that nothing is more complicated than getting a life down on paper, making it real, and getting it right.

But regardless of whose life an author has chosen to document and which approach she has chosen to follow, I always begin with two simple, crucial questions: Why does it matter? And to whom? Without thinking through those questions, a writer is lost in the wilderness before she starts, so my counsel is to take some time and be honest. The answers will dictate everything from the author's vocabulary and voice, the sources she trusts, the notes she publishes, and the details she includes and leaves out, to the conclusions she draws and the editor she works with. And if she can't at least take a well-placed jab at the answers at the beginning, it will be impossible for any editor to help her find her way home from that wilderness.

Of course there's a third question: What's new here? Scholars in particular presume that's the *first* question, and certainly new sources or new interpretations are crucial to a biography, particularly in dealing with an already

WENDY WOLF is associate publisher at Viking, where she edits biography, history, science, politics, and other nonfiction. She was previously an editor at HarperCollins, and Pantheon Books before that. Her authors include Manning Marable, Nathaniel Philbrick, Nancy Isenberg, Steven Pinker, Jared Diamond, Blanche Wiesen Cook, Rebecca Eaton, Lynne Cheney, John Norris, Stacy Cordery, Allen Shawn, June Cross, Linda Greenwald, Jenifer Ringer, and Daniel James Brown.

well-scrutinized life. To me, though, novelty is a necessary but not *sufficient* premise.

As an editor at a major trade publishing house, I weigh projects with the same concerns as all my colleagues in other genres—who's going to care, or, to put it more bluntly, who's going to care enough to spend thirty (or fifty) dollars just because there's a previously undiscovered cache of letters, or an eyewitness produced after thirty years of silence? How much does this new information change what we know? Does this life have reverberations beyond its own confines? The answers to these questions help me determine whether this is a trade book, with the possibility of a broad readership beyond the university or the family (for memoir or family biography), or whether it's a valuable contribution in its field but probably for a limited set of readers.

Over and over, authors tell me that we *should* care about this person's contributions to neurobiology, or her experiences during the French Revolution, but frankly, few readers really do. With Wikipedia providing what most people want to know about most of the facts of most lives with enough accuracy to satisfy most casual inquiries, why bother?

Every time I see in a proposal the phrase "There's never been a biography of _____," I shudder. Usually there's a good reason why. The fact that there hasn't been a book on Y since 1954 may not be enough either, just on the face of it. And let's be honest, very few people who aren't professionally paid to do so are actually going to buy and read a book about an unknown horsemaster's daughter's life in fifteenth-century Morocco, even if there is a *really* good diary. Unless the author can bring her to life the way Laurel Ulrich did with an eighteenth-century midwife in *A Midwife's Tale.*

So yes, I do want to know what's new—but that's not enough. The books that I most love to publish offer new information and new interpretations but also, more urgently, something more than just documenting the life under scrutiny. I listen for passion in the writer's voice; I want to hear that the story of this life casts light on more than itself—if it reaches through history to explain something about *my* world to me, or is about a world that it's important, or entertaining, to know more about. To know why the author cares—and how he will make *me* care.

Remember, I'm a kind of gatekeeper, but only to one particular pasture. There are many others out there, and that's why an author must begin with his own passion and commitment; it's what will see him through. He may be writing for an audience of two—himself and his grandson—and there is no more legitimate motivation. Or because he simply loves researching and writing about the political lives in Ethelred the Unready's court. That's not a reason to stop. But it's a reason to gauge one's expectations.

The art of great biography is found as much in what the writer leaves out as in what she includes. There is nothing I dread more than reading (or worse, having to edit) what I call the "He went here, he went there" kind of life that simply records a litany of dates and events without interpretation or without emphasis. Not every day of my life is interesting, and neither was every day of FDR's, trust me. That litany, however, may be where one has to start. One of my great privileges was working with Manning Marable on his monumental biography *Malcolm X: A Life of Reinvention*. I came into the project after Manning had already devoted ten years to the documentation phase; when he decided it was time to get a publisher, he had written pages and pages, and he and a retinue of devoted students had assembled something known, in reverential terms, as "the Chronology"—a day-by-day, sometimes hour-by-hour, account of Malcolm's every known move, deed, appearance, conversation. It took up literally reams of yellow legal pads, scrawled in pencil and pen, taped together, stacked up, pinned across endless walls. On these pieces of paper, Manning was physically assembling a life.

But most nonfiction books generally begin with proposals, and this one was no different. Manning's was missing certain things we often expect now: ideas for marketing, or demonstration of media savvy, and if someone in 2001 had used the phrase "author platform," I would have expected plywood. But the proposal made clear, and my preliminary meeting in my office with Manning confirmed, that this was a once-in-a-lifetime chance to acquire the defining account of a towering figure of the twentieth century, and that there was no other writer who could bring together the background, the context, the insights—and the pigheadedness—it would take to write it. We signed a contract and expected to have a book to show the world in about four or five years, not an unusually long delivery date for such an ambitious project, with archives still to plunder and plot lines to wrangle into shape.

Of course, nothing works out quite as you plan—and over the next decade, we worked as a team to bring the book home. One of the first things we agreed on was that simply printing up Malcolm's life in real time was not the goal. We had to make what I would call the case for Malcolm as a uniquely American figure. We needed to understand the worlds through which Malcolm moved, the America that blacks lived in and the ones that whites lived in, in the forties, fifties, sixties. We needed to understand what Malcolm's options were so we could probe the choices he would make. We needed to get to know his family, his role models, his disciples, his enemies. We needed to know—and this was crucial given the looming shadow of his autobiography—when he was lying about himself, and why. What Manning knew from his years of immersion, and what he proved in his book, was that Malcolm was not just a foot soldier or a fire breather (though he was both at times), he was an agent of change. The record of the facts of Malcolm's life was necessary but not sufficient; the "why it matters" was delivered by Manning's explanation of what Malcolm changed and how he changed himself. A self-educated man with a thirsty brain and a huge heart, Malcolm embraced a faith and then had the courage to sever himself from its leader when its principles no longer made sense to him, pragmatically or spiritually. He began his political life counseling withdrawal from white society and at the end spent every day urging action and engagement. In the end, he proved to be a profoundly American figure in his utter belief that we could in fact remake our society.

The other great challenge, or opportunity, in a book like this, which occupies a pivotal era in history, is to re-create the context around the subject. Once again, how an author chooses to accomplish this will depend largely on what reader he's writing for. In the case of Malcolm X, we wanted to make sure that young readers and students in the twenty-first century really understood Malcolm's world, and we had to make choices about what we could assume or not. A typical younger white reader probably knows who Martin Luther King Jr. was but might not understand who Marcus Garvey was, or Frantz Fanon, or what the Los Angeles riots were, or why zoot suits were important. All this history fed into Malcolm's life, and would feed into the narrative of the book. In that way, my interests as someone who edits history as much as biography slide into each other.

Biography almost always means rebuilding an era, in both its light and dark sides, as with a biography of the great newspaper columnist Mary McGrory that I published in 2015. McGrory came of age in the early 1950s, when women in newspaper offices were expected to carry the coffee, not cover the president. I was surprised by how many of my younger colleagues found this eye opening. But I knew not to take for granted that the reader would know who Adlai Stevenson was. We had the blessing of a vivid writer to quote and hoped to demonstrate not just what a pathbreaker McGrory was for women but how she affected the way news was covered and commented on through her career, and how far we've fallen from so many of her high standards.

I often look at biographies also as a chance to teach—and not necessarily the expected inspirational lesson. With Malcolm X, I wanted to remind

....

people of the physical courage men and women in the civil rights movement displayed. It's always alarming to me how ephemeral the *experience* within history is, how the drama of a life is quickly reduced to dates and facts; the human anguish and other emotions are boiled out of it. A lot of my focus, and that of my associate editor, Kevin Doughten, who worked intensely on the manuscript with Manning and me for over a year, was to make sure that the human Malcolm could be seen behind the icon.

All of this leads, of course, to one of the thornier patches a biographer must cross: what do you know, what can you impute, what must you imagine? Here my rules are clear and immutable. The author's evidence is going to assemble into several distinct piles: the facts she can document, the assumptions she can rationally make or presume, the inferences she can create from context, and the vast tower of everything else, including unrecorded events, emotions, thoughts, motives—all crucial building blocks to a biography, but not all to be used with equal abandon. She is free to draw from all piles but must let the reader know why she knows or thinks what she claims. Sometimes this can be gracefully accomplished in the text itself ("no one knows what was said behind that door, but Napoleon emerged smiling from the room"; "her boots would have been gleaming in the light of the full moon that night"); in other cases a source can be cited in the back matter. We may quote a conversation where there's a reliable witness, but we ought to resist the urge to put words, and thoughts, in mouths where the record is silent.

Sources are the biographer's salvation, but they can be treacherous. In *Fallen Founder*, the biography of Aaron Burr I published in 2007, Nancy Isenberg faced the double hazard that a lot of Burr's personal papers were lost at sea and that the most voluminous documentation of his life was by his contemporary enemies. I likened it to the task of a biographer trying to write the life of Bill Clinton if the only record of his deeds were the *Congressional Record* from the time of his impeachment hearings.

Manning Marable's book in fact began with a question about a source— Malcolm's famous *Autobiography*, largely written by journalist Alex Haley, which Manning taught as a key text in a course on the history of African American political thought. But the more he examined it, and the more he tried to match it up to the facts and contours of what he was learning about Malcolm's life, the more questions he had about the integrity of that remarkable book as a reliable record of a life. Thus he had embarked on two decades of research, compelled by his fundamental belief that this life, this man, held the key to understanding some fundamental, if dark, truths about America.

This was a case where the primary memoir source had been relied upon for decades, but turned out not to be a good map for the real life. *The Autobiography of Malcolm X* remains one of the most extraordinary documents in American political literature, but now we can read it for what it reveals and disguises.

There is no magic rule for relying on memoirs or diaries any more than there is for any primary source, other than the author's own expertise and common sense—sometimes supplemented by the editor's. Given the controversies over the "artful" construction of memoir today, it is surprising to me how long it has taken so many biographers to question the veracity of their subject's own memoirs, when clung to as a source. I tell biographers, "Believe—but if you can, get a second source. If something smells like it's been cooked, it probably has been. You are the one who knows the material best, and yours is the opinion I'll rely on." The commotion these days over fictionalized memoirs reminds me of a blunt phrase my family applied to a clever uncle of mine: "He never let the truth stand in the way of a good story." I look for a biographer to parse fact from fiction and to signal when we're on dodgy territory or at the mercy of an unreliable witness.

The solution, of course, cannot be to litter a book with "might have" and "we could speculate." The author's research is the scaffolding, and the task in editing a well-researched, thoroughly documented life is to know what should remain in sight and what should get moved into the back or banished completely. That applies to both details and events, to the author's background research, and to her observations and conclusions. She should be confident in writing what she knows to be true, but be ready to explain to a skeptic (though not necessarily in the text itself) why she knows it. I encourage authors not to break the frame of their subject's time period, if possible—in other words, not to make direct reference to sources or to secondary accounts or modern books, if possible, in the text itself. She should present *her* narrative, *her* interpretation, and argue with her rivals in the back of the book.

The temptation for authors to load a book down with everything they know is huge. I urge them, Resist! Resist at all costs. There are long periods in any life which can be summed up as, essentially, "more of the same." The editor must stiffen the author's spine: more is not better, and showing off that you know what color dress the general's wife wore to the victory celebration is probably unnecessary. The vogue these days is certainly to go long, but I have to ask if we really needed—as we got in a recent writer's biography—752 pages recounting the life of a someone whose own work was always scrupulously spare and whose books rarely exceeded 300 pages. Scrutinize every detail, every anecdote, and ask, *Does this contribute to the interpretation of this life? Does it matter, really?*

Too many biographies in recent years have ballooned into bloated, soggy messes of undifferentiated facts stuffed into a narrative. I suspect it's the product of a number of factors—the depth of research that can be done from one's own desk, the ease of access to documentation and primary sources that the internet allows (if writers were transcribing all those quotes by hand instead of just cutting and pasting, there'd be a lot fewer of them), and even the quickness of typing on a computer and seeing a manuscript unfold only one screen at a time, instead of pounding away and watching it pile up page by page. Back in the typewriter age, physical labor kept books shorter.

I have over my desk a little typed quote given to me by one of my authors (I've never tracked its source, though he claimed it was Leslie Stephen): "Consider your reader's brevity of life." Over the years there have been any number of famous (and famously long) multivolume biographies, and almost all of them began as one-volume lives that billowed out of control. A biography should not become like Borges's map, the same size as the empire it depicted, and a biographer shouldn't let his subject's life take over his own.

My guiding principle for documentation inside the book is this: I want to know where the author got his stuff. In general, I don't actually care if he tags each quote with an archive box number; I'm content with a detailed essay on sourcing at the back that tells me that the letters of Andrew Jackson are in this library, that everything he tells us about how they built a redoubt in eighteenth-century Boston came from that book, that all those quotes about the Watergate hearings are from the author's interviews unless otherwise noted. Many authors now post their more detailed sources online, but as a reader, I'd still like the summary in the back of the book itself. More scholarly books demand, and many of my authors who are academics still prefer, the detailed quote-by-quote numbered endnotes. I weigh what kind of book it is, what we think the reader will most benefit from (a hundred extra pages of notes will drive up the book's cover price), and come to some mutual understanding.

In books that take on controversial subjects, and especially books about people who are still alive (and therefore can sue for libel), there is also the important distinction between what the author knows and what he can prove. If there are issues of libel or invasion of privacy—the great specters of publishing law (along with plagiarism)—my authors and I work closely with attorneys in our company whose expertise is navigating these gray zones. My experience has been that publishing lawyers are in the business not of forcing authors to say as little as possible but of allowing them to say as much as possible. I have actually heard an attorney say, when I explained that we simply could not get written permission for a quote from a particularly essential letter, "Let 'em sue." At the same time, no publishing firm or author should be cavalier about the accuracy or ethics of what they publish, and a good editor flags potential problems before legal counsel is required.

Not all biographies rescue lost or forgotten heroes, even when that was the original intent. Authors may have to make hard choices when they find out things that are unpleasant or unappetizing, or if they challenge the shining image of icons, or reveal unsavory facts about deeds or misdeeds. Maybe the biographer finds out her subject was a coward, or an addict, or a plagiarist. She must be prepared and be honest. If the problematic facts are material to the story, she has to be scrupulous. Maybe the families that gave access to their beloved ancestor's papers will be horrified to discover marital infidelity or substance abuse in the book. The biographer has to decide if it's crucial to her argument to include such facts or if it's just lurid detail. There are no hard-and-fast rules here other than the author's own moral compass and common sense. That said, it helps to have a clear arrangement for the use of any archive, public or private, before diving into it.

There will always be readers (and critics) who will howl if you tear down their long-held images. In the case of *Malcolm X*, what I call "the Malcolm Faithful" went nuts over a few lines about events in a difficult time in his younger days and about Marable's interpretation of Malcolm's political trajectory. I firmly believe we actually presented a Malcolm who was more heroic than the myth, because he was more human.

Also, I don't want to find out in the last stages of editing a manuscript that a widow has the right of review for her husband's biography or that an archive won't permit letters to be quoted in part, only as a whole. An author should be honest and take advice from his editor early on about legal guidelines and permissions and talk through any squirmy issues that arise in the process.

Because of the obvious risks, I've always been wary of publishing biographies of living subjects, especially ones in which the subject offers "cooperation." (Also, I like to know how the story ends . . .) Obviously, many editors are less cowardly. Sometimes it works out fine—the subject opens doors for the writer, participates in interviews, offers access to papers, has no right of review, and agrees to go on NPR with the author. Too many times, however, especially with a celebrity subject, you get miles down the road when suddenly a lawyer, manager, or publicist gets wind of what's going on and there's hell to pay. If a writer is basing his book on cooperation, it's critical he get the deal spelled out in writing up front or, at worst, fully disclose to his editor the project is a gamble.

Clearly the legal hazards of writing about the living are greater, and therefore one's sensitivities must be greater too—the dead can't sue for libel (though their families can for invasion of privacy, and copyright to unpublished documents survives their writer's death). Again, forewarned about the law is forearmed; it's a tricky area, and no one wants ugly surprises.

So what about memoir, a noble genre which has lately come under such fire? There the issue of what is truth can be murkier. Memory can be highly unreliable. The more scrupulous memoirists actually fact-check themselves, consulting other sources to make sure their memories are accurate (and sometimes finding useful details to supplement their recollections).

Beside the matter of factual accuracy, there is the matter of emotional honesty. What sets some memoirs apart is that the author turns a really unsparing gaze on him- or herself, connecting with readers by exposing feelings we might all have shared even if they are ugly or shameful. I've sometimes found even very thoughtful and articulate writers resist this, or don't push themselves to dig beneath their own surface that way. Again, not every memoir has to be a searing self-exposé, but many writers need to be pushed to take their introspection beyond the level where they're first inclined to settle.

And there are inevitably conflicting memories, as I find every time I try to reconstruct some simple event from my own family history. Each memoirist has choices about what to believe and what to present, and must set her own tone and her own rules. I ask only that she be honest with the reader about the choices she has made.

Also in memoir, the author may well be close to squeamish about exposing or offending *other* people and may elide events or pull punches because "old so-and-so is still alive." That problem exists in biography too but is obviously more acute when the writer is also at the center of the story.

In my mind, though, in the end, it's pretty simple. The author knows what's a fact and what's made up, or improved, or embroidered; she knows when characters are real and when they've morphed into something more convenient. She knows when things happened and in what order. If she wants to rearrange the facts to get to the "truth," okay. But she has to tell her reader that's what she's doing. If this is how she remembers it and we know others disagree, fine. She can say so up front, in an author's note. I'm uncompromising on this subject. If she's not comfortable with that, if she think it's too restraining to her art, fine. She can write a novel.

Any author–editor relationship is based on trust. I trust that an author is representing the facts, knows what he's talking about, and has done his job. He is the author, his name is on the book, and it's his expertise that I've relied on, his knowledge of the subject, his honesty in approach, his doggedness in the endeavor. For his part, the author trusts me to read, counsel, advise, offer a smart opinion, help sort out the important from the detritus, highlight the foreground and push the rest into the background. He may have come to know his subject too well, and I'm here to bring him back into the real world.

A close colleague and accomplished editor, Tom Engelhardt, was once asked in an interview, "Publishing is a business, but editing is a profession, one might also say an art. What does an editor do?" He answered, "All fine writers lay down a path for you, the editor. All you have to do is find it in the verbal undergrowth, set foot upon it, and then it's all remarkably simple. You're doing your best to slip inside another mind and help unknot the words and thoughts that stood between a writer and the book he or she imagined."

The task of the biographer is related. A life unfolds before her, but she has to find the most graceful footing through it. She has a responsibility to the life she is observing, to present it accurately but appropriately, but she has an obligation to the reader as well. There is a broad spectrum from satisfying to inclusive to comprehensive to exhaustive to exhausting. Wherever the author chooses to land, and for whatever audience she's writing, the most important thing is that she knows why that life mattered. The task of the editor is to make sure her readers know that, too.

19 OF MONOGRAPHS AND MAGNUM OPUSES

EDITING WORKS OF SCHOLARSHIP

. . . .

SUSAN FERBER

First, do no harm.

While it may seem strange to apply a well-known motto of medicine to the realm of publishing, it seems to me the first and foremost responsibility of an editor is to not inflict damage while improving the health of a body of scholarly writing. The scholarly book editor is akin to a medical subspecialist: she focuses on acquiring titles within a discipline that is a niche within the larger scholarly community—not simply fiction or nonfiction but typically an area of scholarship mastered by a relatively small portion of the global population. Authors she meets are therefore highly trained professionals who have spent decades in preparation for a given book, often delving so deeply into their particular subjects that they have become less and less able to speak to others about it. The editor thus must think about how to best present this material to a broader yet still primarily academic audience and to respect the specialized nature of advanced scholarship. Overly simplifying, or "dumbing down," the author's text may ultimately result in alienating its core audience without realistically replacing it with a wider one. And so not harming that piece of work, esoteric as it may be, must be the first goal.

Very few people enter the world of publishing with the goal of working on scholarly books. The job perks of academic editors do not include swanky book parties filled with well-known writers whose work appears in mainstream literary magazines. The books they edit are not the ones found in airport bookstores or on best-seller lists. The lists they manage can be quite

SUSAN FERBER is executive editor for American and world history at Oxford University Press USA. Her list includes academic and trade titles, by both junior and senior scholars, on topics ranging from ancient history to contemporary history. Books she has edited have won numerous history awards, including the Pulitzer Prize and Bancroft Prize, and five have become national bestsellers. She also teaches at the Columbia Publishing Course and speaks to audiences regularly about academic book publishing. She has written for a variety of publications, including *The Chronicle of Higher Education, Passport,* and *Perspectives on History.*

large—several dozen to a hundred a year, perhaps. Relatively few editors are primarily educated in the disciplines in which they publish—there are simply not enough literature lists for every English major in scholarly publishing. More common is for a scholarly acquisitions editor to learn to acquire in a discipline, with its own jargon, its own trending issues, and its own celebrity authors who are known only in these niche communities; there is often minimal crossover to scholars in other fields, let alone readers outside of the academy.

So why do scholarly editors do what they do? At least for me, the chief satisfaction comes in the editing process itself. I believe that each project adds unique knowledge to the world, and intellectually engaging with that work is what helps me to translate an author's scholarly contribution to a wider audience, consisting of at least his peer group. Most authors tend not to think about their manuscripts first and foremost as stylish, engaging, accessible pieces of prose. Helping them to step back from their research, to prevent scholarly detail and the findings of other academics from overwhelming their voice, and to produce a work of a reasonable length for the intended audience occupies my evenings and weekends. The ability to diagnose what a manuscript needs comes with experience, but each project has its own unique challenges, and it is impossible to apply a one-size-fits-all approach.

For many academic editors, manuscript development is a secondary, or even unwritten, part of the job description. We are typically assessed on quantitative goals, such as signings and sales; "quality" is a difficult output to measure. Critical acclaim or book prizes may serve as a proxy metric, and most of us believe a well-crafted book will outsell a mediocre one. But how much better can a book be made by editing, and what percentage increase in sales will result? These effects are unquantifiable. And in each discipline, even for different types of books, the answers may significantly differ. If a book on, say, criminology has a lyrical voice, will that alter its eventual sales or reception? Some topics simply do not have a large audience. There is more opportunity for American history titles to find a crossover audience than, for example, those on literary theory or linguistics or biochemistry. The broader public buys more books on Lincoln and Kennedy than on molecules or modalities. And frankly there is not time in a scholarly editor's schedule, given the sizes of lists and all the other tasks involved in publishing, to engage in detailed developmental work for every book equally, or even all books on her list. So the editor must decide what kind of editorial intervention is necessary—or possible—within the constraints of her own list and workflow. Giving broad-based advice to authors about introductions may be all that is

. . . .

feasible; in some cases, author and editor may be mainly relying on the feed-back from the peer readers' reports or advice from a series editor.

It helps to parse types of scholarly works in terms of what kind of edit-ing might be most beneficial for them. There are traditional monographs, by which I mean very narrow, highly detailed, and thoroughly researched stud-ies intended only for a specialist audience. The aforementioned "crossover" books are not necessarily any less thoroughly researched, but their topics are part of a more public conversation outside of academe, be that in the profes-sional world, a niche audience (such as yogis or birders or Civil War buffs), or a general-interest audience, perhaps because of current events (such as al Qaeda after 9/11, Ukraine after the Orange Revolution, or Gulf Coast flooding after Hurricane Katrina). A book may also be classified as crossover because of the author's platform, particularly if she is a known figure in the media or has written other works that have given her name recognition beyond a discrete scholarly circle. As these books seek to reach a wider and less expert audience, they may repay (and demand) a greater investment of editorial time to make them accessible to those readers.

Assessing the role of a given book in an author's career also helps deter-mine the type of editing that is appropriate for the text. If the author has, by choice or by circumstance, decided to leave academe or is not aiming for tenure-track employment, then he may be open to editorial suggestions that a tenure-track assistant professor in a conservative, heavyweight research university may not be. This can manifest itself in numerous ways, starting with the title. One author insisted to me that a book with a "How" or "Why" phrase in its subtitle would never be acceptable to colleagues in his elite de-partment, while others have felt that titles suggested by the publisher might sell the book but raise the eyebrows of academic readers for being too broad and overhyping the contents.

First-time authors with a strong dissertation in hand who are staying on an academic path may wisely deem their key audience to be peers in their specialist field, the very individuals who will likely be asked to write letters about their corpus of work for their tenure files. They may be thinking primar-ily about establishing their scholarly credentials in the eyes of their depart-ment. Their books may have a core audience of scores or a couple of hundred readers, in which case an editor might be less likely to invest the publisher's resources or her own finite hours in significant editing of their manuscripts.

At the opposite end of the spectrum, I have worked with authors who think of themselves as writers first. They care most about the narrative quality of their work and only secondarily about engaging explicitly with the scholarly literature. Often it is tenure that gives such authors more freedom to speak expansively and permits them to pursue a desire to reach a wider audience. So an accurate sense of where a project fits into an author's career arc, how the manuscript fits into an author's self-identity as a writer, and what her goals are for the work is critical before I engage with the text. This is not to say that any work can be turned into one for a larger audience; there are topics that are necessarily far more limited in reach, no matter how accessible the writing is. Nonetheless, that a book is scholarly is no reason for it to be badly written, unreadable, or beyond improvement.

At a bare minimum, most scholarly manuscripts I encounter benefit tremendously from a fairly substantial revision of their introduction. It is in these opening pages that the author is most obviously working out how to position the project amidst the mountains of surrounding literature, often coming to the point of the book toward the end rather than beginning with a statement of its argument. My recommendation is most often to simply excise the existing introduction and begin writing from scratch. The quotes and citations can be added in, but writing free form, rather than getting distracted by tracked changes and the ways that the project has long been framed, can liberate an author to express compellingly what the work is meant to do and what its contribution is.

Like Goldilocks, writers need to find the introduction voice and length that feel just right. Many introductions present perfunctory information and demonstrate all too clearly that an author has hurriedly written up something to put at the beginning of a manuscript after devoting virtually all his energy to the rest of the chapters. Other introductions—and not only by first-time authors—are extremely long and wind tediously through the dreaded "literature review" before finally discussing the contribution of the present work (often in the form of an equally excessive road map to the contents of each chapter). In these and other cases, authors can often forget that readers need to be captivated and guided into a subject that they, unlike the authors, have not spent years working on. The best way to start may be a case history of a key figure in the work, or a telling anecdote, or an ethnographic description, or a big question that the author has set out to answer.

Rather than generalize about the other parts of scholarly manuscripts that most frequently need editorial attention—such as transitions, the webbing between chapters, and overlong notes—I will illustrate the diagnostic challenges and treatments of a few types of projects using examples from my own discipline, history. Once a book has been published with extensive revisions, there is no way to quantify how it would have performed if left largely un-edited. But I have selected these projects to discuss because on publication they achieved recognition for the quality of their writing.

Microhistory is a particular genre whose popularity has ebbed and flowed, but that has attracted many a scholar who has discovered a story in an ar-chive while working on a broad study and found that following an individual or small subject has been more fascinating. Oftentimes microhistories can revolve around a compelling event, such as a courtroom trial, an urban crisis, or another revealing episode, and their organization can appear to flow nat-urally from the research. I have edited several such works: they are tremen-dous reconstructions of *what* happened, and figuring out where the stories begin and end is one of the key challenges the authors faced. So too is piecing together the lives of the people who intersected in these events, which is es-pecially difficult if they never became household names and appear in the historical record only fleetingly.

While the scholarly excavation involved in the research for such books is no less deep and intense than for many a monograph, these works may have a more limited time frame and scope. Editorial intervention can be valuable in helping the author figure out where the chapter breaks should fall, whose perspective(s) should come to the fore in different parts of the story, and how to connect the narrative with larger interpretive questions. What larger un-derstandings of the period and the field these microhistories can speak to is central to what audiences the book can reach.

A story that is intriguing to the author, even one in which she has invested years of wide-ranging research, does not in itself make the book worthwhile, readable, or, frankly, necessary. When scholars undertake these works, the results may be quite different from what happens when writers or journal-ists with a nose for a good story dive into them. Nonscholarly writers often spend a good deal of time thinking about plot, pacing, setting, character de-scription, and other elements of narrative for which a scholar may have less-developed writing muscles. Academic historians, if they wish to be praised for their scholarly contributions, must convey longer-term meanings and larger relevance for their narratives, while highlighting what makes their in-terpretation orginal. But this imperative can be in tension with the effort to attract nonspecialist readers or students.

There's a second type of book I'll simply dub the magnum opus, the work whose scope and ambition make it a capstone to a scholarly career. The mag-num opus is a species familiar to editors in every discipline, and it comes with its own challenges. First, there is the issue of length. When an author who has signed a contract on proposal delivers years—or decades—later a manuscript four to five times the contracted length, it usually signals that my job as an editor is going to be of a different order. Not only is the actual editing work much more time consuming, but so too is convincing publishing colleagues that the sales and market expectations and publishing plans for the book deserve to change. It becomes even more incumbent on editor and author to ensure that the depth and scope of the study live up to the promise of the work and that there is no unnecessary fat in the manuscript.

Frequently in these long-gestating tomes, the introduction sets out an ambitious argument but the chapters themselves have become overgrown with examples and the chronological or thematic scope of the work overall has expanded well beyond what was initially planned. The narrative threads may be strong at the granular level but not connected to the interpretive argument driving the overall work. Finding narrative momentum both within and between individual chapters and adding signposts through the work are essential to making the "big book" work. Editing this type of manuscript cannot involve a slash-and-burn approach but requires very close line-to-line microsurgery. Recognizing that each archival detail has been hard won means making careful choices about which are most colorful, which best support the author's point, and which are not essential, no matter how intriguing.

One of my authors referred to this editing as putting his manuscript on a Jenny Craig diet. It is often much easier for an editor to see that a manuscript needs this reduction in order to become a stronger, healthier version of itself than for the author who has invested so many years of work and writing in it. The magnum opus often requires a particularly challenging editorial letter: praising the author's mastery of the topic and respecting the enormous amount of work that the research and writing have entailed, while at the same time insisting on surgical intervention before a work can be published.

It is somewhat unpredictable how long a work the market can bear. A definitive work is often by necessity long—but how long is too long for its intended readership? Given that manuscript length directly correlates to production and manufacturing costs, does cutting by 20 percent suffice to attain a feasible length, or is more pruning needed? Will the core audience of scholars feel that some of the muscle of the project has been damaged by this editing? The answer, again, must be determined case by case, factoring in the publisher's best guess as to the size of the market, the editor's stamina, and the author's willingness to "kill her darlings." The latter is unpredictable, because for each author this is her lifetime of work. She may argue that her eminent colleagues say that the book cannot be cut. Or that it can be published in two volumes. Or that some other editor knows better.

The editing process can take months or sometimes longer, depending on the degree of revision and the author's workload of teaching and other responsibilities. It may also be prolonged by peer review, which is discussed elsewhere in this collection, though procedures for this vary so widely from one press or even one project to another that it's hard to generalize. Some projects are reviewed as early drafts or even proposals, and the feedback may help guide the editing; in other presses or other situations (perhaps when the original manuscript has been heavily revised), peer review may occur after editing.

Once the one-on-one work of manuscript revision is complete, the collaborative process between author and editor shifts to focus on other elements of the book and expands to include others in-house as the manuscript enters the publishing pipeline. It may, for example, entail walking an author through how to acquire art or prepare tables and graphs that the production department can work with, an area that may not be his forte. Scholarly publishers do not have staffs to prepare and handle these details for authors, nor are they (generally) able to pay permission costs. Scholarly book budgets are close to the bone and cannot cover what may be routine expenses for a college textbook publisher, such as specialized cartography or outside developmental editing.

Working with the author and with marketing to plan for publication also begins long before the book goes to production—in fact, at the moment of acquisition. Indeed, the author's input and active involvement are essential to tapping into the networks of specialists she is a part of. Thinking about general audiences and mainstream review publications is of much less use than identifying how to reach niche audiences. Indeed, it is perhaps a golden age for promoting books to niche academic audiences, given the print publications, blogs, specialized societies, Twitter feeds, social media outlets, and other networks that exist to bring together far-flung individuals with esoteric interests.

Unless this groundwork is laid, the moment of publication can often seem like a letdown for a scholarly author who has often spent many years of a career preparing to write this work. It can take a few years for a print review to appear in the flagship academic journal in the field; it may be fiscally impossible for the publisher to advertise as widely as an author would like—say, via a solo ad in the *New York Review of Books*. The sales numbers may take considerable time to build, given the buying patterns of libraries and wholesalers, let alone individual buyers. These are not books bought in large quantity on spec by bookstores—but neither do they have the subsequent mass returns that commercial titles often suffer. They are also not books that are only "for the moment." Often the product of many years of research, they can have a long tail, finding interested readers years after initial publication.

How scholarly manuscripts are selected and become finished books is a process one of my authors has compared to the mysteries of the Ouija board. In my experience, it is not hidden spirits guiding the hand of the editor but a number of specialists all coming together—the author as scholarly expert, the editor, other academics as peer reviewers, and numerous publishing professionals with different areas of expertise—to make accessible and lasting, in print and in pixels, a body of specialized knowledge that others can in turn build on to create new scholarship. But between the initial selection of a work for the list and the book's debut in the world, the editor's diagnosis and treatment of the text's weaknesses represent a quiet, even intimate way in which she helps create a fitter and more enduring version of the book.

20 RELIABLE SOURCES

REFERENCE EDITING AND PUBLISHING

ANNE SAVARESE

In the early decades of the twenty-first century the notion of editing or even using reference books might sound quaint, if not anachronistic. Do people still need those things anymore? Doesn't everyone just look everything up online?

Reference is an elastic term in publishing. In its most generic sense it refers to books and digital products (databases, apps, e-books), often multi-authored, that have a practical purpose—dictionaries, encyclopedias, companions, atlases, guidebooks, and other sources in which you can look up useful information. Students might consult a reference work as a first stop in a research project; instructors or scholars might consult one to learn about a subject outside their specialty or for a quick refresher on a topic they are teaching. Broadly defined, reference includes books like the one you're reading now.

Reference publishing started moving into digital formats in the 1990s, much earlier than most other publishing categories, and with good reason. Reference works are particularly well suited to digital platforms. The information they provide is what people in the field call "granular": part of a well-designed whole but organized in stand-alone units, such as encyclopedia entries or dictionary definitions. *Content* is a word that reference publishers use more frequently than *book*, because the product is not format specific. Content is the material, the information, the knowledge that readers want. The editor's job is to make sure that content—whether in print or digital form—is as authoritative and useful as possible.

In digital form, reference works can be updated and expanded quickly

ANNE SAVARESE is executive editor for literary studies at Princeton University Press, where for ten years she acquired and developed reference books, among them a winner of the Dartmouth Medal, *The Princeton Dictionary of Buddhism* by Donald Lopez and Robert Buswell, and seven *Choice* Outstanding Academic Titles, including *The Princeton Encyclopedia of Poetry and Poetics*, fourth edition, edited by Roland Greene and Stephen Cushman, and *The Princeton Encyclopedia of Islamic Political Thought*, edited by Gerhard Bowering. Previously she was a reference editor at Oxford University Press and Facts On File, and a trade editor at St. Martin's Press.

compared to the time it takes to produce a printed book, though significant revisions and additions generally need to go through an editorial process similar to that of existing content. A collection of reference works can be cross-indexed, allowing users to search across sources. The content is not static: it can develop over time, as with such crowd-sourced projects as Wikipedia or such scholarly works as the *Stanford Encyclopedia of Philosophy*. The digital format allows for greater flexibility in length and number of illustrations, and can include links to primary sources, video clips, and related material. Electronic resources also don't take up shelf space as multivolume print encyclopedias do, and they allow remote access: the user does not have to be in the library to use them. Some well-known reference works that began as books now have print and digital versions, such as *The Chicago Manual of Style*; some have become primarily digital resources, such as the *Oxford Classical Dictionary*. But while digital publishing has many advantages, cost is not necessarily one of them, particularly when the original creation of a digital version is accounted for. Most publishers do need to charge subscription or other fees for such works to recoup the costs of developing and maintaining them.

In bookstores, the trade reference category doesn't exist in the way it did twenty years ago: the reference section of stores and online vendors usually includes an assortment of language dictionaries, study guides for standardized tests, quotation books, and collections of unusual words or fun facts.

That said, a variety of print reference is still out there and still can sell successfully, but not in the general, catch-all "reference" section. A historical atlas, for example, will be shelved with other books on history. *The Princeton Companion to Mathematics* is shelved with other books on math.

Something similar has happened to print reference in libraries. Many public and academic libraries have reduced or phased out their print reference collections. It's not that the material is no longer necessary but instead that the same book, or an updated version, is available as part of the library's digital collection, so the reference room or section of the library has become less central.

Search engines and online databases have greatly reduced the demand for books that simply collect basic facts. To attract an audience, contemporary reference works must provide much more: context, analysis, bibliographies, or collections of data otherwise not easy to find with a few clicks.

As a result, the number of publishers that produce traditional reference works has declined, particularly among trade presses: these days, reference is the domain of commercial academic or reference publishers and university presses. But even if relatively few people in contemporary publishing will be full-time reference editors, a larger number will have an opportunity to develop reference content. University press editors, for example, might commission the occasional reference work to complement a list of monographs, textbooks, and general-interest works. Knowing some basic details about the editing of reference works can save a good deal of time and effort—and can make the work as useful as possible for its intended audience.

ACQUISITION

Most reference works originate with the publisher: the acquiring editor researches and develops the idea, then commissions authors or volume editors, usually scholars, to carry it out. Occasionally an author or institution develops a reference proposal and submits it to publishers, but this is more common for practical, how-to reference books than for large-scale projects.

The acquiring, or commissioning, editor must consider how the work would serve readers and how it would complement the publisher's list as a whole. Is there a need for a new reference work on this subject? What would make it distinctive? Is the subject sufficiently broad? Is it widely taught at the university or secondary level? What is the potential size of the audience that is likely to find the work indispensable? If it is a one-volume print reference book, will it appeal to scholars or students, or both, as well as to libraries and other institutions? Will it take a comprehensive or selective approach? Does the content lend itself to more than one use, in spinoff volumes, databases, or apps? Even single-volume reference works can generate spinoffs: for example, Harvard University Press published *Religions of the Ancient World: A Guide* in 2004 and later collected some of the major entries from that volume into a paperback, *Ancient Religions*, suitable for course use.

Reference editors should be aware of competing reference works from other publishers, as well as what kind of work makes sense for a press of their size. Because most reference works take significant time and resources to develop, a new reference project should be unique and authoritative—essentially, a must-have for some clearly defined group of readers.

As part of their research, reference editors often consult with scholars or librarians to try out ideas or solicit reactions to proposals. Some reference publishers have permanent advisory boards of librarians; others assemble a group of advisers to consult on a specific project. It's customary to pay these advisers an honorarium in return for their comments.

Before approaching potential volume editors, it's wise to sketch out a preliminary budget and try to anticipate the questions from potential editors and contributors. The clearer you can be about the intended length, format, timeline, price, and sales potential, the easier it will be for editors and contributors to understand their roles in the project.

Reference budgets typically include an advance for the volume editor; fees for the associate or section editors and advisers; fees, free books, or both for the contributors, and the cost of professional proofreading and indexing, as well as funds to acquire or redraw illustrations or maps. Sometimes major reference works, such as those with a heavy or complex illustration program or a multimedia digital component, require subventions to cover the costs. In some cases volume editors are able to secure funding through their institutions; in others, the publisher applies for a grant.

CHOOSING THE TEAM

Major reference works are complex to plan and develop. A typical encyclopedia might have an editor in chief and several associate or section editors; contributors, who can number in the dozens or the hundreds; a corresponding number of articles, ranging from a few hundred to ten thousand words each, depending on the project; and often a group of advisers as well.

No matter how strong the subject of a reference work, the right author or editor is one of the keys to its success. The ideal editor, or editorial team, should have outstanding credentials and contacts in the field, as well as the interest and vision to lead a project that will take considerable time and energy to complete. You'll know when you've found the right people if they understand the idea right away and offer thoughts that refine the idea and make it stronger.

If the appropriate volume editor for your project is a university professor, look for someone with tenure and sufficient seniority. Midcareer and senior scholars will have broad knowledge of the field and a network of colleagues and former students they can call on to contribute. Their personal relationships as well as their professional standing will encourage others to contribute to the volume. The volume editor should want to take an active role in planning the project; this will result in a much stronger project than you would get under someone who plans to serve only as a figurehead, no matter how well known.

Most scholars who agree to edit a reference work have never done so before, and some might be wary about the amount of work involved. It's important for you, as the acquiring editor, to explain the steps, as well as the support—administrative as well as editorial—that the publisher intends to provide. Discuss the division of labor and who will be responsible for what,

....

from making the initial contact with prospective contributors to reviewing the proofs.

Few people agree to edit a major reference work for the money, which usually is modest and paid out over time: the motivation is more likely the opportunity to create a valuable resource for students and colleagues or to make a mark on the field. If the volume editors are confident that their publisher shares their vision and will offer guidance and support at each stage, they are more likely to sign on and to persuade others to contribute to the project.

Reference contracts for multiauthor reference works developed and commissioned by the publisher usually are works for hire: the publisher owns the copyright. Each contribution is part of a collective work, and this arrangement allows the publisher the ability to license, revise, and repurpose the material over the life of the work, which could be decades long. Reference contracts for volume editors also typically include a list of the editors' specific responsibilities and contain delivery and payout stages in order to keep the project on schedule.

DEVELOPMENT

Once a reference project is under contract, you'll need to work with the volume editor to develop a table of contents or list of entries (sometimes called a headword list). If the project will involve an editorial team and many contributors, schedule a planning meeting with the editors, including advisers if you have them, to plan the scope of the project, flesh out the scope of the planned entries, suggest contributors for those entries, and iron out how the process of assigning articles, setting deadlines, sending reminders, and so on will work. Gathering everyone in the same room for a day or two allows the editors to get to know one another and generate ideas. By the end of the planning meeting, everyone should have a strong sense of personal investment in the project and a commitment to the collective mission.

Before you start to invite contributors, it's helpful to develop contributor guidelines that include a description of the project, the planned contents, style and format points, submission instructions, schedule, and sample entries or articles. Post the guidelines on a web page and give contributors access. The more detailed the guidelines, the easier the editorial process will be: even if contributors don't follow the instructions, the guidelines will make the copyeditor's and proofreader's job easier.

Once the articles have started to come in and the volume editors have approved the content, developmental editing can make the difference between a coherent, consistent reference work and a hodgepodge of articles written for seemingly different audiences. This level of editing is not always something that you, as an acquiring editor, will have time to do yourself. Whether you will delegate to a development editor or packager, work with a hands-on team of volume editors, or manage the process yourself, a strong editorial eye on the entire project is crucial.

Even if you will not be the one to edit the majority of the entries, spend some time editing the sample entries, along with the contributor guidelines, and request sample editing from the development editor or packager so that you and the volume editors can review it carefully. Accessibility and clarity are essential. Unless you're preparing a highly specialized, technical reference work for professionals, a reference work for adults should speak to the "educated nonspecialist"—generally, upper-level undergraduates and beyond. Some entries might be more technical than others, but the writing level should remain consistent, even for the entries on more sophisticated concepts. Put yourself in the user's shoes and query anything you don't understand. The preface or introduction should articulate clearly the scope of the book, how it is organized, and how the editors expect readers to use it. Consider that reviewers will read this, even if many readers skip it, and make sure the work delivers what it promises.

Make sure you have a clear plan for the day-to-day management of the project as well. Reference works require heavy correspondence, the preparation and trafficking of contracts and articles, careful recordkeeping (with the help of a shared spreadsheet or database, depending on the complexity of the project), and attention to the schedule and budget. As the acquiring editor you know the project best and have the greatest stake in it. Contributors tend to be overcommitted, and a reference article can fall to the bottom of their to-do list, especially if the deadline is a few months off. Make sure they receive regular reminders that request a response, so that if a contributor goes quiet you can investigate further. Allow plenty time for revision and for chasing or reassigning articles that run late.

PRODUCTION

Reference works often are large, and it's rare that the entire manuscript comes in at the same time: articles usually are assigned and delivered over a span of several months. Invariably some contributors deliver late, and some articles will need substantial revision; still others have to be reassigned. It is not unusual to begin the production process before the entire manuscript is in final form, so that you have batches of articles in progress at different stages: in

....

draft form, in copyediting, and with the compositor. A digital project might edit and post articles in batches as they arrive or on a designated schedule.

Reference manuscripts are more time consuming to produce than conventional books not only because they tend to be longer but also because they've been written by a team of contributors. Expect to get involved in resolving questions related to style and content. The copyeditor, for example, might find inconsistencies both small (disagreement over the precise date of an event or the translation of a foreign term) and large (apparent contradictions in facts or analysis from entry to entry).

PUBLICATION

Reference books attract little traditional review coverage beyond trade publications such as *Choice* and *Library Journal*, and it can take several months for those reviews to appear. But if the project is unique, or unusual enough, it might encourage reviews or features in print media and notice on social media as well. The intriguing title and subject of the 2014 book *Dictionary of Untranslatables*, for example, helped attract publicity that ranged from a one-sentence review on a humor page in the *New York Times Magazine* to a substantive discussion in a *New Yorker* article on the challenges of translation. The fourth edition of *The Princeton Encyclopedia of Poetry and Poetics* (2012), a significant revision of a well-known resource by a new editorial team, inspired a "virtual roundtable" in which several poets responded creatively to individual entries for the online review *Public Books*.

You can help your colleagues in marketing, sales, and publicity by distilling your long immersion in the project into bullet points that will help them spread the word with enthusiasm. In addition to preparing a detailed table of contents, a list of contributors and their affiliations, and some sample material to use in promotion, think about the questions they are likely to have.

Who is the audience for the book? Reference books often serve a range of readers, but you should be able to identify who they are and why this book is for them.

What's in it? How is it organized? List the reference features, including the number of articles and contributors and any other elements, such as bibliographies, appendices, an index (or more than one), topical list of entries, and other features that demonstrate the project's ease of use.

Who is the author? If it's a collectively written project, will the volume editor or members of the editorial team help promote the book by participating, for example, in panel discussions or interviews?

What's the story behind the book? What makes it unique—is it, for example, an atlas of the ancient world more than ten years in the making; a dictionary of concepts essential to a particular discipline; the first guide to an emerging area of study; the most comprehensive or authoritative encyclopedia on the topic?

You might be asked to create sample material for a promotional website or to provide material—sample entries, interesting facts, etc.—suitable for social media. Encourage the volume editors and contributors to post about the work on their own social media accounts.

WHY REFERENCE?

Reference publishing continues to change, but certain characteristics of the category remain. Reference content synthesizes current knowledge about a subject. It provides a gateway to further research. It can help frame or define a broad subject, academic field, or emerging area of interest, and it can make scholarship or archival material accessible to a broad audience of students, scholars, and researchers.

Despite a common image of reference works as dry, dull, or antiquated, well-executed reference works are none of these things. The really good ones serve readers for years, even decades; the best are indispensable. And the best of the best are those that readers actually enjoy: they're rewarding to browse. They make us feel smart. They contain plenty of well-organized information and analysis. They are balanced, covering topics in proportion to their importance; they tell us why the selected topics are important.

In return for the challenges that come with editing reference—among them the constant demands of managing each project and the long-term investment in building it, piece by piece, until it is greater than the sum of its parts—the reward is in the finished product. An enduring resource filled with reliable, well-written material, professionally organized and edited, serves readers in ways that endless search-engine results never will. In an ever-rising sea of information, reference editors offer readers a lifeline.

21 THE PINK SHOULD BE A SURPRISE
CREATING ILLUSTRATED BOOKS

. . . .

DEB AARONSON

Before I begin, you should know that I did not sign and return my contract for this essay in a timely fashion. I also missed the deadline for submitting the essay itself by well over a month. Illustrated books have their own special problems and rewards, but managing authors is a challenge you'll have no matter what kind of books you work on. Getting a contract signed, and a deadline met, by your author is often no small feat.

There are other ways in which the publishing process is similar across all categories of books. This is an idea-driven industry, and a book always begins with an idea—whether it's your own or one pitched to you by an author or agent. Then there's the process of convincing your colleagues it's a good one, followed by the task of making an offer and negotiating a contract for the book.

The tenor of the contract negotiation is often a strong indicator of how the project will unfold. If the negotiations are relatively easy (they are hardly ever *truly* easy), if you and the author can articulate and hear each other's concerns and come up with practical compromises to manage your different needs, then the process of making the book itself will likely be a gratifying one. If you struggle with these things, if the author has difficulty putting minor points in perspective or trusting that you will stand by your word even though you can't insert that promise into the contract, then chances are that dynamic will continue through the creative process. When you believe in an author's work, you likely want to be a part of that person's creative development over time and even after the book is finished, and you hope the inverse is true as well. In the ideal scenario, the trust that is built on the foundation of one book will result in collaborations to follow.

The beauty of making books is that the final result almost never hints at the wear and tear it took to get there. The pleasure of seeing the final

DEB AARONSON is vice president, group publisher at Phaidon. She is responsible for Phaidon's art, photography, fashion, general interest, and children's publishing programs, as well as overseeing the design department. She came to Phaidon from Abrams, where she served as publisher for the adult trade group.

result—seeing your idea transformed into a physical, tangible object—can't be underestimated and is, especially in this digital age, universal. No matter how long I've worked in publishing, no matter how many books I've worked on, that feeling, thankfully, is a dependable reward.

While those dynamics are common across most categories of book publishing, there are plenty of ways in which creating illustrated books is strikingly different. When I was an editorial assistant in 2000, few houses published illustrated books apart from those who published them exclusively. Aside from cookbooks and children's books, most trade houses invested limited resources in these kinds of projects and the staff to make them. The lack of interest in illustrated books from the big trade houses suggested that the commercial possibilities of these titles were limited. Only a select number of houses, a few of them university presses, focused on acquiring them, and fewer interested parties often meant smaller advances. As a result, there was little incentive for literary agents to represent illustrated projects and the authors who wrote them.

Editors had to be both creative and savvy, not just in developing ideas for books but in imagining how these ideas would take shape as objects and making decisions about how they'd look and feel. How big should the trim size be? How many pages is ideal? Should it be hardcover or paperback? Should it be slipcased? And how does all of this relate to the book's potential audience, where they shop, and how much they are willing to spend?

Illustrated books are not defined by their subject matter but rather by the capacity of that subject matter to be expressed visually. That means that any idea that can be, literally, pictured is on the table for potential publication, and not just ideas related to traditional illustrated book subjects, such as art, photography, design, and architecture. I've published books about the history of punk music, the American Civil War, and a woman who dressed up her pet parakeets in tiny little outfits and photographed them against elaborately staged representations of historical events and domestic scenes. This is a good problem to have: the pool from which book ideas can be drawn is unlimited, but it is also mildly overwhelming.

Like many industries, publishing is built on relationships. Ideas and projects grow out of forging new and nurturing long-standing connections with people and organizations—museums, foundations, galleries, archives, and agents. Ideas for books have also come to me from (in no particular order) roaming the internet, reading magazines and newspapers, drinking whiskey, watching television, traveling, visiting galleries, listening to NPR, hanging

. . . .

out with friends, brainstorming with colleagues, and a hundred other places. Believe me, most of them weren't good, and only a very small percentage of them became actual books.

The first project I acquired was as an editorial assistant at Harry N. Abrams, my first job in illustrated book publishing. I wanted to publish a monograph with Gregory Crewdson, a contemporary artist whose work I admired and who had been featured in the *New York Times Magazine*. His inclusion in the influential general-interest magazine suggested his appeal went beyond the narrow margins of the art world and that a book by him might appeal to a wider audience. He was teaching at Yale at the time, so I reached out to him by email. To my surprise, he responded positively, and after a lunch, a meeting with his gallery, a few coffees, and a bit of negotiating, we agreed we'd publish a book together.

Although it didn't seem so at the time, the acquisition was pretty straightforward. Of course it's easy to be nostalgic about the simplicity of the past in the face of the challenges of the present. As the culture at large has moved toward the highly visual, more publishing houses, including the big trade houses, have increased their investment in illustrated book publishing, focusing on traditional categories as well as subjects such as popular culture, style, interior design, and humor. But the direct and overhead costs of producing such books can be high, increasing the risks involved.

Meanwhile, the flourishing of the digital marketplace, which coincided with and accelerated the consolidation of chain bookstores while threatening the existence of independent ones, has also led to the rise of specialty retail outlets, shops that display and sell books as part of the growing "lifestyle" industry. In an age of e-books, physical books, especially expensive ones, not only *can* but also *need to* justify their existence. Illustrated books don't carry the same appeal as text-heavy books in e-book format, though occasionally publishers will produce them as enhanced e-books or apps. More generally, this has led to an increasing focus on the object-ness of books and created a renaissance in design and production in this segment of the industry.

These circumstances have also resulted in a sharp increase in the number of illustrated projects pitched by agents, as well as other potential partners, including leaders of not-for-profit and commercial organizations, who see illustrated books as not only a way to bring in revenue but also a way to expand their presence in the global marketplace. This has, inevitably, resulted in a more crowded field in which projects are now frequently subject to stiff competition, preemptive offers, and bidding wars, and to a more congested marketplace where everyone needs to work harder to distinguish any given book from all the others out there. Without tie-ins to big shows at museums and similar outlets, such books do not necessarily attract attention in traditional review media.

What this also means is that more and more nonprofessional authors are creating books and being represented by agents. Such authors have always been a staple of illustrated book publishing, adding a dimension to the editor's role unlike that in much of fiction and narrative nonfiction publishing. Although every editor has at one time or another probably rolled up her sleeves and rewritten a manuscript from beginning to end, this happens with greater frequency in visual book publishing. Often a frustrating experience, it requires skill, patience, and sometimes forbearance on the part of the editor.

Collaborating with authors who are not writers and who are also working full-time jobs—their book by necessity a side project in addition to their regular workload—is typical in illustrated book publishing. Such authors (among them artists, designers, photographers, and curators) may not be used to or proficient at expressing themselves in writing. Part of the editor's responsibility is acting as a translator—helping authors express ideas in a language that's not necessarily their primary one. Often their native language is a visual one, with its own vocabulary and grammar. And an important part of the editor's job is to create a lingua franca that serves as a bridge between the visual world of the author and the audience of readers.

Early on at Abrams I assisted our editor in chief on an exhibition catalogue of the work of a revered photographer that we copublished with a distinguished museum. The curator who organized the exhibition contributed an essay to the catalogue and submitted her first draft. Although the curator was a scholar—exceptionally talented, smart, influential—writing apparently did not come easily to her, nor was it her first priority. Her primary job was to focus on the exhibition, to get it done on time while keeping the photographer happy (no easy feat). Our EIC spent days rewriting her essay, refining the larger argument while laboring over individual sentences. He sent the extensively marked-up version to her for review and she came back to him with one comment, remarking on a phrase, like many others, that he had struggled to rework: "Dear Eric, I truly dislike this sentence. Please try again, only simpler."

Every book needs to tell a compelling story, which requires a narrative arc that takes the reader from the beginning to the end providing context, pacing, and meaning. Creating this arc for visual books is accomplished by selecting the images and organizing and sequencing them in such a way that the reader is led through the pages of a book with grace, style, and momentum.

. . . .

The written content of the project, whether in the form of an introductory essay, running text, or captions, is folded into the existing storyline, adding a dimension to the book that can't be achieved by the visuals alone. Of course there are books in which the text drives the narrative, and images are added to enhance the meaning and understanding of the text, but much of the time it is the opposite.

Building this arc involves the author, editor, and a third person, the designer of the book. The importance of the role of the designer in illustrated book publishing cannot be overstated. His goal is to create the container in which the content of the book is held and to ensure that this container provides an appropriate and dynamic counterpoint to the visuals, bearing in mind the aesthetics of the material and the author's subjective preferences. The visual concept that he creates for the book includes, but is by no means limited to, typographic choices (what font or fonts will be used), image treatment (cropped, full bleed, or neither), page layout (single or multiple images per page, where the text sits relative to the images, placement of folios and headers or footers), sequencing of images to form the narrative, and the jacket, cover, or packaging design (what is the best way to visually articulate and sell what's inside the book). A designer's aesthetic intelligence and engagement with the content inform the balance and interplay of these elements and profoundly impact the way the book will be seen and received. Alongside the editor and designer is the production manager, whose responsibility it is to transform these ideas into a physical object. These professionals' ability not only to execute this shared vision but also to provide creative input, guidance, and solutions to manufacturing challenges is crucial to the outcome.

Todd Selby is a photographer with whom I've worked on a number of books. We've established a collaborative process in which the various elements of the book—images, text, design—are developed simultaneously. It is, in a sense, a moving puzzle. Todd is known for photographing creative people in creative spaces, and every one of his books is broken into chapters, each featuring a single subject. Every chapter requires a self-contained narrative (who is this person, what is his space like, what is her day/job/life like), which includes photographs, typeset text, handwritten captions, and illustrations. Todd makes a first go at the image edit, and the designer places the photographs in the layout, anticipating and leaving space where illustrations and captions might fit. Todd and I then review each page, suggest changes to the sequence, point out images that should be added, deleted, or swapped for new ones, and pass those comments to the designer, who then executes the next pass, making additional adjustments and suggestions. This process is repeated until we're all satisfied with the result; sometimes it happens quickly, other times there's a lot of back and forth. It's only when the edit is finalized that the text and captions can be written, the illustrations drawn, and the layout completed.

In each of the books I've mentioned, there was an outside author involved whose responsibility it was to provide a basic editorial framework and visual material. That isn't always the case in illustrated book publishing.

Recently at Phaidon my editorial colleagues and I developed an ambitious book, *Body of Art*, whose premise is to explore the ways the human body has served as subject, inspiration, and medium for artists around the globe over tens of thousands of years. We not only conceived the editorial premise of the book but also undertook the job of developing the content, selecting the images, and writing or closely directing all of the text—no small thing as the book included over 450 images and 100,000 words.

The images were gathered from different and sometimes little-known sources—tracked down, cleared for use in the book, and quality-checked to ensure they were submitted in a format that could be reproduced in print. Each part of that process has its own challenges. Sometimes you find an image that you want to reproduce but you can't figure out who it belongs to, how to secure the rights to reproduce it, or how to access a print-quality version. Sometimes you know who it belongs to but they simply won't give you permission for reasons that seem, at least to you, random, opaque, and frustrating. Other times rights holders are happy to grant you permission if you pay them, say, $10,000, which may be more than your entire picture budget. In the worst cases, sometimes you are under the belief that you have permission to use a photograph only to find out later that you sort of didn't, after all. Unfortunately, rights problems—or other issues even harder to anticipate—often come to light only after the book has been printed. In one memorable example, a person who provided personal items as props for an artist's work was horrified to find out that, in one image, the label on a bottle of pills detailing her prescription for an antipsychotic medication was fully legible to the reader. Most of the time, though, all goes smoothly: the rights holders are happy to have their images included in a book and are available and willing to negotiate their use.

The publisher's obligation to a rights holder doesn't always end with the grant of permission. As recently as a decade ago, images were provided as prints or transparencies, the goal being that the reproduction in the book mirrored the hard copy in hand. Sometimes the prints were faded or the color in the transparencies had shifted, making accurate reproduction a challenge. With the transformation of visual material from the physical to the digital, reproducing images is easier in some cases (digital files can be worked on and refined to meet an author's exact taste and specifications) and more difficult in others, as the expectations of how these files will translate into published form is often unrealistic given the limitations of the printing process.

I'll never forget standing in a color correcting room with the director of my production department reviewing the fifth round of color proofs with a well-known painter. (It's not unusual to go through two or even three rounds of proofs until you get the color right, but five is pretty extraordinary.) He pointed to the proof of one of his paintings, a portrait of a woman, specifically at a spot next to her nose and asked, "Do you see that pink right there? That pink should be a surprise." What wasn't a surprise was that his book never made it to press: after almost a year of trying, we weren't able to satisfy the artist's expectations and had no choice but to cancel the book.

Other production issues can arise, sometimes related to how complicated the book is and sometimes not. I've seen signatures sewn in upside down, ribbon bookmarks cut too short to extend beyond the bottom of the book, and laser-cut slipcases riddled with hanging chads. Although these problems will mystify and sometimes haunt you, most of the time they get sorted out early and pale in comparison to the triumphs of an exquisitely produced book that thrills on sight.

So now we're back at a moment that all editors experience—when the creative process is complete and the book emerges from the publisher's warehouse into the world. But because the illustrated book is an object with a presence, it situates itself differently in the world from a novel or memoir. These books are often large, expensive, ambitiously designed and produced, and left out or stacked on tables in the home or in shops. They are not built to be hidden. Readers seem to form a different relationship with illustrated books, picking them up at will, with less pressure because they can drop into them for a minute or an hour or three. These books activate our minds, our eyes, our sense of touch, and, hopefully, our sense of pleasure in the variety of wonders the world has to offer. No small thing for an idea that came to you over a cup of coffee.

PART FIVE

Pursuing a Publishing Career

. . . .

VARIETIES OF EDITORIAL EXPERIENCE

22 WIDENING THE GATES

WHY PUBLISHING NEEDS DIVERSITY

. . . .

CHRIS JACKSON

I'm often asked to speak about a thing that doesn't actually exist: diversity in publishing.[1] Ironically, I don't think this is because people get any pleasure from hearing me talk about this thing that doesn't exist, any more than they get pleasure from hearing strangers tediously relay the details of their dreams. And yet we keep talking about this abstraction, this thing that doesn't exist, as if it could be conjured through the power of lectures and panel discussions. The word itself has suffered from its failure to describe a reality. *Diversity* has become an empty, ugly, punishing sound, like a wave of coughs or the revving of a stalled engine. It's in the category of thing that people generally agree with in principle, although they're not exactly sure why they're nodding their heads, and are confused about how to actually achieve—or perhaps not confused at all but worried that it will cost more than they're willing to bear, which for many people might be any cost at all. But I think there are ways to anchor the question of diversity in publishing in reality—and ways to achieve it that will only grow the work we do to greater abundance, with no meaningful loss.

My own story of getting into publishing, a story about my own luck and the generosity of others, is illustrative in some ways. My first attempt at a real job in publishing was when I was called in for an interview at a strange small (now defunct) publisher called Paragon House. I had just graduated from high school when I came in for that interview and hadn't yet enrolled in college. While still in high school I interned at a small book-packaging company, and the summer after I graduated, I freelanced for other small, weird publishers of the kind that used to dot New York City. It was a strange job choice for an eighteen-year-old, but I'd loved books and libraries and bookstores all my life. I had been raised in the projects, raised in an apocalyptic religion,

CHRIS JACKSON is vice president, publisher, and editor in chief of the One World imprint at Penguin Random House. Previously he was executive editor at Spiegel & Grau. He has worked with authors including Ta-Nehisi Coates, Wes Moore, Trevor Noah, Matt Taibbi, Bryan Stevenson, Jill Leovy, Victor LaValle, and Jay Z.

1. This essay originated as a talk given to the Association of American University Presses at its annual meeting in June 2016 and has been expanded and adapted for this collection.

primarily by my mother and a host of old ladies who still talked with south-ern accents and retraced the Great Migration every summer. Books had been my salvation on project playgrounds and in the backseat of our beat-up car driving back to North Carolina and back—first fantasy epics, then the hodge-podge of popular fiction my mother brought home from the library, then Kurt Vonnegut, which led to Joseph Heller and Herman Hesse and Celine, and then, awakened by hip-hop, I took a turn into the black arts movement, to Baraka and Sanchez and Nikki Giovanni, and then back to Ellison and Wright and Baldwin, and then forward again to Lorde and Reed and Bambara and Morrison.

There was little popular publishing for black readers, at least from main-stream publishers; what there was was done by small houses like Holloway House, who published thrillingly well-crafted pulp like *Pimp* by Iceberg Slim and the works of Donald Goines, which I found on the book tables of 125th Street in Harlem, where I lived. Up the street from those tables was Libera-tion Books, where I found works by Afrocentric scholars like Molefi Asante and John Henrik Clark. New York's tonier independent bookstores back then used to look on black boys with the same suspicion, contempt, and fear as the rest of the city in that era of the Central Park Five and Bernie Goetz. I would mostly go to Barnes & Noble—there was only one in Manhattan back then, on Eighteenth Street and Fifth Avenue—a store large enough that no one really took mind of my presence. You could go to a Barnes & Noble and go to the black books section and see nothing but great literature. I'd just go through the books in that section one by one. All winners. These weren't writ-ers who were necessarily taught in my classes in school, but their work awak-ened me and transported me and reframed my own vision. I would dive into the worlds the books created and then look up from every page and notice that my own world was changing, too.

But I wasn't ready to go to college—my father died when I was four, and my mother was very sick in my last year of high school and died that summer. The religion I was raised in forbade college—a prohibition which was an al-most unnecessary additional impediment to most of the kids who were in it, or at least the ones I knew, who were already stuck in low-income housing and failing schools and living at the peak of the most murderous period in the city's recent history. Still, I needed a job. I thought about driving a bread truck, like one of my close friends, or learning how to repair air conditioners. I tried to get a job as a security guard or loading freight or answering phones for the Better Business Bureau. I could not get any of these jobs.

But I did get that job at Paragon House. My high school internship led to

. . . .

summer work, and that led to an interview with the editor in chief at Paragon House. He came right out of central casting, or out of my own imagination of what an editor in chief might look like —I remember him, an impishly mischievous white man, jaded and ruefully grinning (or grimacing) all the time. Bald and round and always in rolled-up sleeves; in my memory he's chomping on a cigar, but that seems unlikely. He told me in the interview that the company was owned by Korean businessmen. He laughed about the creative ways he was burning through the "Korean investors'" money, publishing the idiosyncratic books he loved in beautiful, award-winning, expensively designed packages. He hired whomever he wanted (as long as they wanted to work at Paragon House, which narrowed the field), and knew he could get away with it all as long as the company also published a series of esoteric conference proceedings the Korean investors insisted on.

I was eighteen. It sounded like fun, although I found his glee at sticking it to his investors peculiar and maybe a little racist—this was 1990, a time when fear of rising Asian power was at one of its periodic peaks. I sat in his office for hours. We talked about the books we were reading. He pulled some books about publishing off his shelves and gave them to me—Scott Berg's biography of Maxwell Perkins among them. I found the whole scene intoxicating— the buzzing office, the book talk, the idea that I was following in the footsteps of Maxwell Perkins, whoever he was, and that I was looking, finally, at literature's workshop up close and possibly taking a place in it.

The editor in chief asked me to immediately do some part-time work on a probationary basis, filling in for an assistant editor who'd gone off on a some long, exotic-seeming journey. I walked out of the interview into a cubicle, and the first task I was given was to type a rejection letter, the first, maybe, of millions. A busy-looking editor came over and quickly dictated the letter to me while I scrambled to write it all down on a pad. Then I pulled my chair up to the typewriter, eager to prove myself, and realized that I had no idea how to type a letter. I'd never typed a letter in my life. Where on the page do you start? I decided to start at the upper left-hand corner of the page, tight against the edge of the paper. I didn't really understand margins, so the whole letter sat up at the top left corner of the page. I typed the letter quickly—I was at least a fast typist—and handed it over to the editor, who, I remember, was smoking a cigarette in her office at the time. She looked at the letter—in my memory it was stained with the sweat of my anxiety—and shook her head. "You have no idea how to do this, do you?" she asked.

And then she told me how to do it. And then they hired me.

Now the job, it turned out, was a little crazy. The Korean investors turned out to be Sun Myung Moon's Unification Church. The back-office staff was made up entirely of church members, many of whom were married to each other. But the editorial staff was made up of secular, frankly godless, publishing romantics. A French editor who handled our translation projects took me out once a week for a lunch of mimosas and a little book club—she wanted me to read all of Faulkner with her. A freelance lawyer with whom I worked to create a contract boilerplate—well, I typed it—taught me all about publishing contracts and law. Two exotically beautiful assistant editors—one a salty, militantly bohemian English man who'd just graduated from the University of Pennsylvania with a degree in advanced mathematics, the other a young black woman with dreads who'd just finished at the New School—did their best to corrupt me after hours and with more reading assignments: Anaïs Nin, Rimbaud; Didion, Hunter Thompson; Luc Sante, Barthes, Ngugi wa Thiong'o, Amos Tutuola. I worked there for less than two years, mostly part time, and eventually enrolled at Columbia, but I never looked back; I worked in and around books and publishing more or less from that point forward.

So what does this say about the way publishing can diversify? Well, a few things. First: I was not, to put it lightly, qualified for the job in a technical sense. I was a recent high school graduate. I'd never worked in an office before. I didn't have a résumé and didn't even know how to type a letter. I'd read deeply in certain areas but in the style of an autodidact, not a scholar. But I was passionate about the work. I was willing to learn. And I became an asset to that strange company, instead of a likely terrible security guard.

Publishing, it turns out, is a job you can learn while doing, if people are willing to help a little. I was lucky to find my way into a publishing house that was not constrained by corporate hiring practices, so they could take a risk on someone like me. Those of us in publishing are here—at least this is what I believe, in my heart of hearts—because we love literature and ideas and we want to share those ideas. There is a kind of generosity at the heart of publishing: in fact, that generosity is the engine of the business—our work is premised on our irrepressible impulse to share ideas and art, to tell stories. And this impulse—the sharing of knowledge, the sharing of art—is what allowed me to get a foothold in the business itself. The people I worked with didn't expect me to arrive fully formed, and they loved the opportunity my massive ignorance presented: they could teach me even as I was assisting them. It gave them a chance to articulate and rethink and even question how they worked, what they thought they knew—and whether Faulkner was actually any good or not. It was an exchange that strengthened all of us.

. . . .

Today, too often I see the opposite in book publishing. It is, despite its periodic challenges, a competitive business to get into, and editorial assistant openings usually generate a pile of great résumés and recommendations from colleagues. But I try to think about my job as not just hiring the person whose credentials add to my own status; or even, necessarily, hiring someone who is ready to do the job on day one. The job is fairly uncomplicated at the technical level—what's important is that you be able to read and write exceptionally well and that you think and care deeply about art and ideas and stories, traits that people with multiple degrees might never cultivate, but that an eighteen-year-old for whom books and stories and ideas are a salvation might. It takes five minutes to learn how to format a letter; it takes a week to learn most of the internal systems of a company. Every new hire is a chance for me to learn something new in teaching them—to question something I thought I knew, to have my ideas challenged, to have my status quo in some way shifted. And in publishing, those opportunities are far more valuable than a premastery of technical knowledge that can be easily learned on the job. And yet a lack of credentials, connections, and certain forms of experience can sometimes bar people *at the entry level.* They never even get in the door.

I've taught at the City College Publishing Institute—and I also work sometimes at the Columbia Publishing Course—and can see firsthand how brilliant students at CCNY are sometimes handicapped by a lack of social capital and certain forms of easily acquired technical knowledge, by a lack of confidence, and by not even knowing what's expected of them, whereas the kids who come through the far more expensive Columbia program are more polished and likely to be hired, but no smarter or more likely to contribute in substantive ways to the mission of a publishing house. Educational institutions should do more to prepare those students from less wealthy backgrounds—and publishers can contribute to helping schools that serve working-class and poor and African American and immigrant students—but on our side, the hiring side, we should think about what the true qualifications for these jobs are, what can be taught and what can't. We're all strapped for time and resources, but there's no better way to sustain the status quo than to refuse to take chances, even chances that might put us as some risk.

What's the payoff of having a more diverse workforce? Well, there's obviously the moral case to be made—and that's a case that I think applies to any industry. But in book publishing, I think we have a special obligation, given our central role in shaping the culture. I hope a couple of stories will show how I've come to this idea.

One of the authors I've worked with is Eddie Huang. Eddie is Taiwanese American and a cultural sponge. He's a brilliant polymath, and as a writer he's trying to build a fresh idiom out of the languages that mix and merge in his own consciousness. The language is sometimes obscure, sometimes vulgar—it takes from Mandarin and hip-hop and feminist theory and a million other idioms. But it's also often beautiful, and using this new language he is able to say new things about the world.

I published his first book, *Fresh off the Boat,* at the house where I worked before my current one. Some readers loved the book—it was a bestseller—but some people found the language jarring. One of my bosses at that publishing company actually asked me to go back into the now-published, bestselling book and edit out the more obscure references and the passages she found vulgar. It was pretty astonishing. I refused, of course, because I felt like what Eddie was up to was something that I kind of *wanted* her to find vulgar and maybe even obscure. Because for a certain audience, reading Eddie's work was the moment when they finally felt their own language reflected in a book.

One night recently Eddie and I had a public conversation about his second book, *Double Cup Love.* The event was in a packed room full of black readers, and Asian American readers, and white readers, and Native American readers, who all responded with passion and gratitude to the same language that this colleague of mine had found so vulgar that she thought some of it should be excised from Eddie's work. For this second book Eddie appeared on NPR and *The Daily Show* and hip-hop radio stations and on the front page of the arts section of the *New York Times.* The world was catching up to what he's doing—and even as he evolved, at no point did he feel like he had to compromise his voice to achieve this effect, which was part of what I thought of as my role: to protect him from the pressure to conform to the gaze of the dominant culture. I knew from my own life experience as an outsider what can be lost when we aren't allowed to speak our own languages—the ways meaning and nuance are diminished, the way some stories go untold altogether, or are told wrong.

In 2015 Marlon James wrote about how writers, sometimes without realizing it, pander to the person they imagine to be the gatekeeper and how we are all poorer for it. Marlon, who won the Booker Prize that year, has since told me that there were books he wanted to write but never did because he knew they'd be written in vain, because that imagined gatekeeper would reject them. And based on my experience, he may have been wise not to try. When we expand the range of the industry's gatekeepers, we expand the range of our storytelling, which expands our ability to see each other, to talk and listen

. . . .

to each other, and to understand each other. It allows more people to see themselves represented in literature; and it allows the rest of us to listen in, to understand our neighbors and fellow citizens, their lives and concerns, their grievances and their beauty, their stories and ideas, their language. The empathic bridges this creates between us is one of the essential functions of literature in a democracy. But it can only happen if we widen the gates of literature and diversify the gatekeepers.

Another quick story about the value of diversity: In 2015 I published a book called *Between the World and Me* by Ta-Nehisi Coates. I had met Ta-Nehisi a dozen or so years earlier—we were set up on a lunch date by his agent, the remarkable Gloria Loomis, because she felt like we should get to know each other. We were both youngish black men, from somewhat similar backgrounds and with some of the same tastes and interests, so she thought we should meet. We met by his office at the *Village Voice* and talked for hours about a book idea he had about his own father, a Black Panther and a radical publisher and an aggressive proponent of free love. We eventually shaped that idea into his first memoir, *The Beautiful Struggle*, which I bought for a few thousand dollars—I was, it happens, the only person who even wanted to bid on the book. I thought Ta-Nehisi was a brilliant writer and a fascinating thinker, if not particularly well credentialed at that point in his life. But he was a writer. What he didn't know about writing a memoir—which was a lot—he would learn or, better yet, ignore. By the time he started working on *The Beautiful Struggle*, Ta-Nehisi had quit the *Village Voice* and lost a pretty terrible job at *Time* magazine. He was blogging to an audience of dozens. But I felt like the story he was telling—of growing up in a radical household in the drug and murder-scarred 1980s in a Baltimore not so dissimilar from the Harlem of my own childhood—was a vital and largely untold one. So together we took a chance.

That book has now sold over a hundred thousand copies, but when it was first published, it didn't do much business. But Ta-Nehisi and I had developed a creative connection and spent some years concocting another book idea, one about the Civil War based on his immersion in history and scholarship of that era. By this point Ta-Nehisi had been brought onto the staff of the *Atlantic*. While we contemplated that Civil War book, Ta-Nehisi wrote one blockbuster magazine piece after another, culminating in his award-winning "The Case for Reparations." As the drumbeat of murders of young black folks—starting with Trayvon Martin and then on to too many men, women, and children to name—got louder and louder in recent years, Ta-Nehisi and

I talked about attempting a book that would address the crisis and the anguish we were feeling about it. At Ta-Nehisi's recommendation, we decided to reread, together, Baldwin's *The Fire Next Time*. When he finished his reading, Ta-Nehisi called me and asked: Why don't people write books like this anymore? And I said, You should try. So he did.

We went through several drafts and many more arguments—Ta-Nehisi and I always argue, but, I like to think, we argue like brothers, people who fundamentally believe in each other's integrity and our sense of common cause. And, of course, he wins most of the arguments because it's his book—and I'm usually, eventually, grudgingly, grateful to take the loss. Eventually the book—*Between the World and Me*—came out and became a sensation: selling over a million copies, winning a National Book Award, and in some ways changing the conversation about racist violence in this country.

Would that book have been the same without a black editor working on it? I'm not sure. I really don't know and wouldn't want to speculate, but what I do know is that the relationship I developed with Ta-Nehisi was rooted in his trust that I was not trying to soften his message or channel him into a position of pandering. He knew that I understood in an intimate way the human consequences of white supremacy. It allowed for a deep collaboration and, I think, a special book.

At the time of writing this piece, I'm preparing to relaunch an old imprint at Random House called One World. Rather than just cranking up the engine on a typical publishing imprint, my dream is to treat it in a prefigurative way—to create, in a small corner of the Random House building, the model for what I think all of publishing should look like, what the world in some sense should look like. It will be an attempt to bring some meaning back to that shell "diversity," to actually put the concept into action, to give it blood and life. That will inform the way we hire, the way we acquire, edit, and publish books, and the ways we cultivate audiences. This will require some work and time, but what it won't require is a diminution in the quality, or even commercial prospects, of the imprint. It will only make it stronger. I believe in book publishing, in its capacity to help us all retrace our paths back into history, to see the present in all its complexity, and to imagine different futures. To do that we have to build a publishing industry—at all levels of publishing—that honors the potential, the complexity, and the fullness of the world itself.

23 THE APPRENTICE

ON BEING AN EDITORIAL ASSISTANT

· ·

KATIE HENDERSON ADAMS

In an era with few true apprenticeships left, publishing still has something approaching that old tradition: the job of editorial assistant. The assistant—shepherding manuscripts through every step of publication, reading alongside his boss, managing communication between all of the house's departments, and building professional relationships out of house—is an editor in training as well as an invaluable contributor to the process. The assistant handles plenty of tedious tasks—photocopying, form-filling, mailings, and the like—and the details of the job vary from one publisher or industry sector to the next, but the work is never just secretarial. Many if not most editors keep their own calendars and answer their own phones, while some assistants will find themselves reading submissions virtually from day one. When the relationship is working best, the editorial assistant will have instant recall for deadlines and due dates, nuanced understanding of each author's specific needs and styles, and an ever-growing awareness of both the house's list and the business in general.

Plucked from a heap of newly minted BAs, editorial assistants are frequently English majors with aspirations to write. Many realize quickly that publishing is not for them, and more than a few end up on the well-trodden path to law school. Others discover that sifting through the contents of another writer's brain is excruciating when one's own writing beckons. Those that come in citing their favorite books as *Cranford* or *Malone Dies* find early on that an undergraduate knowledge of Western literature, though useful, is woefully inadequate for understanding the contemporary publishing marketplace. Clever new hires immediately begin trolling new release tables, scanning best-seller lists, and following industry websites and newsletters for a crash course in what makes authors and books successful.

As the job title implies, the editorial assistant's primary role is to support one or more editors. As an editor builds her career, the volume of

KATIE HENDERSON ADAMS is an editor of literary fiction and nonfiction at Liveright, a division of W. W. Norton. She lives in Manhattan with her husband and two young sons. Twitter: @KatieANYC.

work that only she can do—especially evaluating submissions and editing manuscripts—increases until it reaches a critical mass, so delegation becomes essential. Though a good editor must be involved in all aspects of book making, must have an eye for design, a brain for publicity and marketing, and an ear for good copy to help describe the book, a busy one will find that the tasks offering the most significant value to the company must be prioritized. It's in these situations that a good editorial assistant becomes a precious asset. Authors and agents know that when they need a quick, reliable answer they can call or email the EA and get it with a smile, and when coworkers need an update on an author's copyedited manuscript or the most recent version of a jacket, they can skip the editor altogether and go right to the all-knowing assistant.

At almost every step of the process, the editorial assistant has the opportunity to both execute a task and learn something valuable about a future career as an editor. For example, when the first copies of a finished book arrive from the printer, I will often ask my assistant to overnight one to the author immediately, with a personal note of congratulations from me. The author will eventually receive a contracted quantity of copies from the warehouse, but this first book fresh off the presses is something special. The publishing business is a fickle one with relatively little in the way of guaranteed rewards; the editor should help the author celebrate every victory, however small. The finished cover, the first galley, the first good prepublication review, and certainly the arrival of finished books—each happy moment should be feted. To an assistant, mailing this book might seem a menial task, but for one interested in learning about the business and sharing the joy of the job, it's a lesson in taking good care of our authors and making sure they know that their book is as special to us as it is to them. Publishing their work is a sacred trust, and it's important to be worthy of it.

These low-level tasks can also be the building blocks of long-term relationships within the business. Sometimes that box of author's copies (or a finalized contract, a new version of the book jacket, etc.) can take a while to arrive, so it's not uncommon that an agent's assistant will check in with the editorial assistant for a status update. The best-case scenario would be that these two communicate with friendly authority, handling the small issue with minimal input from either boss. In this way crucial connections are formed. Many a high-powered editor and super-agent who seem to publish dozens of books together started their relationship in the trenches as assistants. An editorial assistant of course should be as helpful and professional with agents as possible, but those agent's assistants can be industry peers for decades to come.

. . . .

Though acquisitions are primarily the responsibility of the editor, in some houses the editorial assistant will begin reading submissions for her boss almost immediately. Due to the volume of submissions most editors receive, they need their editorial assistants to be an extra set of eyes to either read submissions first—flagging those that are worth extra attention and drafting rejections for those that aren't—or evaluate promising projects alongside their boss. The discussions that follow—about strengths and weaknesses of a project, the author's expertise, the book's marketability, etc.—are a way for the editorial assistant to absorb the taste of her boss as well as a range of insights into what makes a successful book. The volume of reading can be overwhelming, but it's also—for most of us—the reason we got into this business in the first place. The editorial assistant who doesn't enjoy reading submissions is probably not long for the publishing world.

No part of the job is more important, or unrelenting, than manuscript tracking: moving the author's work into and through the production process. Usually the editor is the one who knows when production can expect the manuscript in the first place, when it will go into copyediting and begin its transformation from Word file to physical book. But after that, it's the editorial assistant's job to keep track of this winding, often halting, journey. When the copyedited manuscript goes to the author, when it comes back, when first pass is ready, when it's due back from the author—these deadlines are all essential to keeping the schedule moving, and at any given moment there are several books in the pipeline at different stages of completion. Procedures vary, and in some houses the managing editor's staff will handle back-and-forth with the author through production. But the EA will still need to keep on top of progress and field queries from other departments or the author. It's a challenge in both organization and communication.

Publishers' production departments are for the most part incredibly flexible, and though they try very hard to keep editors and authors from wandering off schedule, when that occasionally does happen, Production can be counted on to shift and maneuver to minimize the damage. Their superhuman skill set stops short, however, of mind reading. If the editor wants to read through the ending of the copyedited manuscript again before passing it along to the author, or if the author needs an extra week reviewing first pass because she just had a baby—this can be accommodated only if everyone knows about it. The editorial assistant's alerting colleagues to each exception and request ahead of time, instead of waiting for someone to notice the manuscript is late and begin chasing it down, not only prevents myriad delays and missteps but also keeps the editor in good standing with her coworkers.

Each editor has a reputation in-house, good or bad, for timeliness, professional courtesy, realism, honesty, and communication. No editor—or editorial assistant—can prevent unexpected changes to a manuscript's schedule. But when the editorial assistant initiates the conversation, checking in or passing along an update, everyone involved in the process is assured that someone's in control and that Editorial understands the concerns of other departments. It's an absolutely crucial element to ensuring that everyone involved feels like a valued, respected member of the team. Not only does this elevate the finished product, but it banks goodwill for those inevitable occasions when editors find themselves delayed and asking someone else to pick up the slack. (When an excellent editorial assistant leaves a job, one of the greatest compliments he can receive is to see sheer despondency in the production department; a great EA will keep the trains running so well the managing editorial staff won't believe it can happen without him.)

Manuscript tracking is laborious, but the most tedious work an EA will face is undoubtedly the dreaded permissions log. Publishers take seriously the responsibility of securing permission to use excerpts and images from their original copyright holders, and every song lyric, quotation, and photograph must be evaluated for fair use. It's a lot of painstaking work. Contractually, determining whether something requires permission, requesting it appropriately, receiving it, paying for it, and documenting it in an organized way are all responsibilities of the author. In reality, many authors don't turn to this until they've finished the involved and taxing process of revising their manuscript with their editor. They're often exhausted and hoping their delivery and acceptance payment is close at hand, so it can be delicate to introduce a new project of this magnitude. Often it's the EA's job to break the news, relay the requirements, and sometimes even step in to help with some of the legwork. I've known EAs to work for months with authors on tracking down errant heirs and combing multilingual archives for permission to use a vital piece of text. It's exhausting work with little reward, but every editor who's worked her way through the ranks has been there too.

The job itself will teach the editorial assistant a great deal, but extra interest, enthusiasm, and curiosity are rewarded with extra knowledge. When I'm working on our title information sheets (TIs, called tipsheets or sellsheets in some houses), on which we list not only a description of the book but key selling points and relevant comparative titles, I will often give a list of similar recent books to my editorial assistant so that he can look up the sales figures on those titles. If they're strong, I'll ask that they be added to the TI. I'm always pleased when the editorial assistant takes that opportunity to

....

ask me why I've chosen those titles. Perhaps it will be obvious—the comp titles are recent entries in the same category, such as Civil War histories or popular biographies of women scientists—but sometimes it's more subtle. If I'm working on a novel about a family of women in Jamaica, I may look for a range of comp titles, some of which have a similar setting (books by Marlon James or Tiphanie Yanique, perhaps) while others have similar emotional content (those by Vaddey Ratner or Alice Hoffman). I'm happy to explain my thinking, and as the process continues and we seek endorsements from other writers, get the sales team's reaction to the manuscript, and see reviewers compare the book to others like it, a richer understanding emerges about the interconnected web of writers and readers within which we're working.

This ever-growing knowledge of both how to position a book and the network of similar books into which it's being published comes in especially handy when writing the many rounds of copy each book requires. Often editorial assistants are responsible for at least early drafts of TI copy, catalog copy, and finally jacket copy. Each description of the book may require something slightly different, as each has a different audience in mind (sales representatives, critics and booksellers, and consumers, respectively). Finding the most effective way to describe a book, using evocative prose that doesn't distract from the writer's work, and developing a style that the editor appreciates all take time, but once conquered this can be one of the most impactful contributions to a book's publication. Go into a bookstore and watch readers browse the shelves, poring over the cover blurbs as they decide which books to buy, placing many back on the shelf; it's a bracing reminder of just how important it is to master writing good copy.

Even more useful, if less common, is when an editor can mentor an EA in the editing process itself. When I was an assistant, I was fortunate enough to have a boss who was willing to let me learn how to edit using one of his authors' manuscripts. He chose a veteran author who needed little in the way of tinkering, and he assigned me a chapter to edit, then edited both the chapter itself and my comments before passing them along to the author. The author got his notes, and I learned a lot about how to help a writer reframe an argument and how to gently correct a mistake (preserving the author's morale is as important as fine-tuning the words on the page). This kind of careful mentoring is time consuming, and as the demands of the business get even more arduous, that time can be difficult to find. But this is how the editorial craft is learned, honed, and passed on. An EA who shows a burgeoning passion for the work will tend to benefit from such opportunities.

As the assistant gains experience and the relationship with her editor evolves, it can become increasingly beneficial to each party. An EA will start to suggest strong comps and insightful blurbers. She may be able to build buzz about certain titles among publishing's youngest generation or advocate for a galley mailing to the Young to Publishing Group. She should look to turn her youth into an advantage, and in this era, that includes as much awareness and understanding of the internet and social media as is humanly possible. As others discuss in this book, the editor's role is evolving to include further publicity, marketing, and general publishing responsibilities, and an EA who can offer digital savvy is invaluable and will soon be imperative. Many publishing relationships are now being built online, and when I'm hiring an assistant, looking at a stack of résumés from smart readers with relevant internships and strong educational backgrounds, those who also demonstrate an understanding of how to use the web as a pivotal tool rise quickly to the top.

No matter how dedicated or fastidious they are, assistants make mistakes. Tasks slip through the cracks, deadlines are missed, messages are forgotten. Even the most eager assistant can make a big mother of a mistake, one that can have serious consequences. When I was an assistant I once emailed a deal memo—a sheet confirming all the relevant points of a negotiated deal including total advance and royalty rates—to the UK publisher from whom my boss had acquired US rights to the book. Or had I? Actually, I'd accidentally sent it to a literary agent who had the same first name—one of the toughest, most successful agents in the business. Not only did I embarrass myself in front of a powerful agent, but I also revealed to her that the author in question didn't have an agent and was working directly with publishers. In the coming months she snapped him up and undoubtedly made my boss's life much more difficult in subsequent negotiations. I felt sick when I discovered this mistake and immediately apologized and took full responsibility. My boss saw that nothing he could say could make me feel any worse than I already felt, so he generously forgave me. Lesson painfully learned. The wise assistant will own up to mistakes before they become crises, and the humane boss will recall that he has a blunder or two on his own record.

Of course, not all bosses are humane. The quality of life for an editorial assistant is defined in large part by the quality of his boss. The publishing world is full of generous, attentive editors who willingly share their time and insight. But as in any other business, there are also some temperamental, demanding bosses who can make the editorial assistant's life hell. I've seen assistants insulted for their education, taste, intelligence, beliefs, and even physical appearance. I've heard tales of editorial duties pushed aside in favor

....

of filling out a boss's child's preschool applications or returning a boss's designer dress with no receipt. The more mercurial the editor, the harder it can be for the editorial assistant to evaluate the appeal of the job itself, so the question whether to stick it out and climb the ranks or flee for greener pastures can be especially difficult. Those who stay, though, can be sure they've found their passion.

A time will come when the assistant has absorbed these hard-won lessons, the rhythm of the publishing schedule has become second nature, and the assistant moves from rookie status to trusted veteran. She gets promoted to assistant editor, then perhaps associate editor, and by this point may have had the opportunity to make a few independent acquisitions. Given the ratio of work to employees in today's publishing industry, even the "associate" is probably still assisting a senior colleague. Almost every assistant I've ever spoken to on this subject has hoped that several years of devoted service will result eventually in a promotion to editor and an end to assistant work. For a lucky few, this works out. If the assistant is able to acquire enough books that she makes a strong case for her fiscal contribution to the company, perhaps she'll get her own list. Sometimes serendipitous timing will see one editor exit just when a younger colleague is ready for promotion, and a transition is possible.

Most of the time, however, you have to move out to move up. No matter how conscientious or supportive your boss, no one is going to manage your career for you. Especially if you're great at your job, no one is going to help you leave. But they'll understand if you do. There are advantages to starting as a newly minted editor in a new professional environment. All of your relationships in-house will be defined by your current position, not the one you held for years before. It's an opportunity to tell agents a new story about yourself: this is my new gig and my new address, and this is the kind of book I want to acquire and publish. And if you've done it right, you've left behind nothing but strong, deep relationships with your colleagues and friends at the publisher where you cut your teeth.

24 THIS PENCIL FOR HIRE

MAKING A CAREER AS A FREELANCE EDITOR

. . . .

KATHARINE O'MOORE-KLOPF

Rarely do editors start their careers by deciding to be self-employed, but many do end up freelancing. Their role in book publishing often goes unnoticed by authors and by people outside publishing because there is no centralized source to count them or document what they do. Freelance editors may also do different types of editing, as discussed throughout this collection, and may have a variety of clients including book publishers, authors, and other organizations or types of publishers.

WHY FREELANCE?

Because of the major changes to traditional publishing since about 2007—including the advent of electronic publishing and the associated opportunity for editors to work remotely—many more editors freelance now than ever before. But there is no "one true path" to becoming a freelance editor, though it might have once seemed that way. My own route to freelancing might be broadly similar to that of many in my generation: Fresh out of university with a bachelor's degree in journalism at the beginning of the 1980s, I intended to be an investigative journalist like Bob Woodward and Carl Bernstein. I spent two years as a reporter in Texas and thoroughly enjoyed it. When I became a parent, however, I realized that working the night shift wasn't going to allow me to care for a baby, be a good reporter, *and* get any sleep. After a move to Colorado, I left journalism to take a job in the public relations department of a hospital.

But public relations and I weren't a comfortable match, so I moved on to working for a tiny, family-run publishing house, editing manuscripts and

KATHARINE O'MOORE-KLOPF is a self-employed medical editor specializing in editing journal manuscripts written by nonnative speakers of English. Her editing has helped researchers in more than twenty nations get published in more than fifty different medical journals. She owns KOK Edit, at www.kokedit.com. She is the owner of the email discussion list Copyediting-L, at www.copyediting-l.info. She blogs at *EditorMom*, at http://editor-mom.blogspot.com. On Twitter, she is @KOKEdit. You can find her on LinkedIn at www.linkedin.com/in/KOKEdit, and on Facebook at www .facebook.com/K.OMooreKlopf.

then typesetting them. Two years later, I ended up in New York as a production editor for a major trade publishing house. By that point, working with books and journals had become my true love. I later became a production editor for a medical publisher in New York City. After four years there, I had another child and decided to try freelancing full time. That was a good decision: shortly afterward that publisher was bought by a larger one, and later in turn by a yet larger one, and many staff members were laid off. I started freelancing in 1995, beginning with projects from my former employers, and as of this writing I'm still doing it. I'm pretty sure that means I've succeeded.

But why do others go freelance? There are several common reasons.

The majority of editors who become freelancers do so because they have been laid off from publishing jobs. This continues not just with traditional book publishers but also with digital media. For example, in 2016 Yahoo, IBT Media, and Mashable laid off large numbers of employees. It's a good bet that a number of their former editors are now self-employed.

Not all freelance editors are former employees of publishers, however. Some may be seeking a career change from a profession that is no longer as satisfying as it once seemed or that no longer has as many staff jobs as it once did. Often they come from professions at least somewhat related to editing: teacher, librarian, writer, journalist, translator. It is possible to become a freelance editor without a publishing background, but it requires additional training and hard work to convince potential clients that the new editor can edit. Taking courses through professional associations, training organizations, and universities and attending the annual meetings of associations are excellent ways to learn about the business of editing and about editing itself. Some of the entities offering in-person and online training or annual meetings in the United States are listed in the Further Resources list at the end of this volume.

Rather than freelance because they've been laid off or want to change careers, some editors choose self-employment for personal reasons. Some may want to more closely integrate work and the rest of their life. Commuting to and from a job can be exhausting, put stress on family relationships, and decrease time available for other life interests. Also, employers don't always offer enough sick days or other time off for editors with chronic health issues, but self-employed editors can adjust their work schedules to make up time lost to illness and visits to health-care providers. Some editors may have to provide care for children or other family members. (As a freelancer, I have at times edited while breastfeeding an infant who was sleeping in a baby sling across my chest, and later edited while bouncing a grandchild on my knee.)

These editors go freelance so that they can be at home when their children are not in school, be at home with a high-needs child, or be available to help provide care for aging parents. Having the ability to rearrange work hours can make caretaking easier.

THE BUSINESS OF FREELANCING

To succeed as a freelancer, editors must learn how to run their own business. They must determine what business structure should they use—sole proprietorship, limited liability company, or some type of corporation. They have to decide who their clients will be—publishers, individual authors, editorial services (also called packagers), or a mix of these. They have to know when to pay estimated taxes to the federal government and, in many cases, to their state government. The questions continue: How do they create a business budget? What office equipment, tangible supplies, and intangible (e.g., digital) resources will they need? What about work flow? Do they work on one project at a time, or can they arrange their schedule to juggle projects that are each in a different stage (e.g., editing, author review of editing, cleanup after author review)? Helpful sources of information about these topics include professional associations through face-to-face meetings, online courses and webinars, and subscription-only email discussion groups; books written for the self-employed; the US Small Business Administration; online editorial communities within Facebook and LinkedIn; mentors found through serendipity or through professional associations; materials and tools accessed through links in the Copyeditors' Knowledge Base; and university courses and degree programs.[1]

GENERALIST OR SPECIALIST?

Whether a self-employed editor should be a generalist or a specialist has long been hotly debated in the community of freelancers. Generalists can take on any subject matter they like. But specialists can often command higher fees because of their expertise. If editors are easily bored by working with one subject all the time, they'll fare better, interest-wise, as generalists. But if they have a passion for a subject such as politics, education, medicine and health

1. For more specific guidance on many of the topics covered in this essay, see the relevant postings in the Copyeditors' Knowledge Base, http://www.kokedit.com/ckb .php; on my blog, http://editor-mom.blogspot.com; and in the *Copyediting* newsletter and its blog, http://www.copyediting.com.

....

care, chemistry, or biography, they will likely gravitate to clients who can offer them projects in that subject.

Sometimes freelancers don't consciously choose a specialty; they fall into it. Most often they develop specialties because clients note that they are talented at editing in certain subject matters, the way actors become typecast because of specific roles they handle brilliantly. But sometimes they want to develop a specialty because it sounds interesting or because they know it will allow them to bring in higher fees. To break into a new niche, freelancers may have to take courses, possibly earn certificates or obtain certification, read books on their desired field, and then convince some current clients to let them try their hand at editing manuscripts in that field. Publishers will often give such opportunities to freelancers whose work they have come to trust. And freelancers should not be afraid to *ask* for opportunities rather than wait for them to fall from the sky.

Other types of specialization involve the kinds of editorial tasks freelancers handle and the broad areas they focus on. There are freelancers who do developmental editing, line editing, production editing, or copyediting. Few do all of those tasks, because each task requires a different mindset and focus. Some freelancers choose to focus on manuscripts for university presses, textbooks, or fiction.

Sometimes editors will go freelance and already have specialized knowledge and experience. This can help them target clients who will offer manuscripts in their specialty. As an employee, I started out as a generalist. I became a medical editor because a lifelong interest in medical topics led me to take a job as a production editor for a medical publisher. I learned on the job because my university degree is in journalism rather than in any of the sciences. After a few early years as a generalist freelancer, I decided to capitalize on that medical editing experience. I continued educating myself about the field, and I sought and achieved board certification as an editor in the life sciences. Though there is no certification available in the United States for other editing specialties, some professional organizations in other nations offer general editing certification exams.[2] After obtaining certification, I began marketing my services as a medical editor. I get the manuscripts and clients

2. The certification offered by the Board of Editors in the Life Sciences helps authors and publishers find practitioners with the needed expertise. Meanwhile, Editors Canada / Réviseurs Canada offers five professional credentials for editors who can pass its exams: in proofreading, copyediting, stylistic editing, structural editing, and one that encompasses the other four areas.

that I want, can turn away those that don't seem a good fit, and can charge much higher fees than I could as a generalist.

OTHER BUSINESS ISSUES FOR FREELANCERS

As is the case for editors who are employees, work life for freelance editors is affected by such factors as the state of the national economy, changes in the publishing industry, the need for continuing professional development, and the necessity of learning to use new work tools.

Finances

The US and world economies affect how well freelance editors do financially. For example, the financial crisis that began in the United States in 2007 caused a global recession. Because of it, some publishers reduced the number of new book titles produced each year. There were also huge layoffs in the industry in 2009, creating a large new pool of potential freelancers to compete for fewer assignments. In addition, some publishers even took editing work back in-house as a cost-cutting measure. Early in the following decade, however, the general sense in the freelancer community was that business was picking up again.

In the short term, freelance editors can experience business cash-flow issues in these instances: clients don't pay their invoices within an agreed-on time span; clients push back project schedules, leaving a gap in freelancers' work flow; freelancers are not vigilant about maintaining a consistent level of marketing of their services to clients; and freelancers have unexpected illnesses or disruptive life events, such as a death in their family. To mitigate problems such as these, freelancers must set aside funds for lower-income times, plan ahead, stay in constant communication with clients, and have a backup network of colleagues they can refer their clients to if necessary. They also need to spend some time each workday on marketing activities, to keep projects coming in.

What are those marketing activities? Freelancers should network, keeping in touch with former employers who may need their services, making new connections with potential clients, and consulting with and helping colleagues, often through social media, professional associations, and professional email discussion lists. They also need to market their services by (1) acting like the business owners that they are and (2) building a robust online presence within social media platforms (most often Facebook, LinkedIn, and Twitter) and having a business website that they update often to draw visitors.

....

Freelance editors are generally not required to carry professional liability insurance, which is also called errors and omissions insurance, because they are not responsible for the final content of publications; authors and publishers are. However, freelance writers, as content creators, are sometimes required to have this kind of insurance.

A Global Work Pool and Outsourcing

Thanks to electronic technology, US publishers can now lower their production costs by seeking out editors from other countries with costs of living lower than those in the United States. Such editors will generally accept lower fees than US freelancers will.

Another way that publishers cut costs is to outsource projects to editing and production services, often called packagers. For each project they take on from publishers, these services line up freelance editors, proofreaders, indexers, book designers, and other self-employed editorial professionals. In return for handling these administrative tasks, packagers take a cut from the fees that they pay freelancers.

In the self-publishing arena (sometimes called indie publishing), authors may use bidding services, such as Upwork and Reedsy, to find the editorial professionals they need. The authors, who are the clients in this setting, post project descriptions online with the bidding services and then review all bids from freelancers. Within the community of freelance editors, these services have poor reputations because the bidding process and authors' expectations often mean that the freelancers chosen will be paid extremely low fees. Also tarnishing these services is that they often do not allow direct contact between freelancers and authors, which takes away the collaboration that can make the author–editor relationship most beneficial for manuscripts.

Continuing Professional Development and Work Tools

Like all professionals, freelance editors must engage in continuing professional development and keep up with new technologies if they want to continue garnering projects. Freelancers can sharpen their skills and learn new ones by attending editorial associations' annual conferences and taking short courses. For example, at the 2015 annual meeting of the Council of Science Editors, whose members include both in-house and freelance science editors, there were sessions about topics such as preparing manuscripts written by nonnative English speakers, disclosure of conflicts of interest by authors and editors, and plagiarism. Similarly, in spring 2016, online courses and webinars offered by the Editorial Freelancers Association were on topics such as developmental editing in fiction, basic copyediting skills, numeracy skills for editors, and basic business skills for freelancers. Past courses by the organization have taught the use of such tools as the Evernote application for managing a freelance business, Word macros for automating routine editing tasks, WordPress for building a freelancer's business website, and social media platforms for marketing an editing business.

PUBLISHERS VERSUS AUTHORS AS CLIENTS

For freelancers, editing for publishers can feel both very similar to and very different from working directly with authors. With both types of clients, it's necessary to build good working relationships based on clear and appropriate communication, tact, and mutual respect. And with both types, freelancers must ask for the types of projects they want to work on and for the fees they want to be paid, instead of hoping that clients will read their minds. But there are many more differences than similarities.

Publishers

Publishers generally have settled on their own definitions for various levels of editing, and they instruct freelancers on what level is necessary for each project. Along with good two-way communication between publisher and freelancer, these definitions increase the chances that freelancers will do the work that the publishers have in mind rather than the level that the freelancer thinks is necessary, which might blow the project's budget and annoy both the publisher and the author.

Publishers are more likely than individual authors to insist on specific fees rather than being open to freelancers' desire to negotiate them. In addition, publishers often are unwilling to issue payment on invoices until at least thirty days after invoice date, and when the US economy (or their business) isn't doing well, they sometimes change that period to forty-five, sixty, or even ninety days. Some publishers require freelance editors to sign a formulaic contract for each project, but others use the instructions in their cover memos and emails as contracts.

Publishers also act as a buffer between authors and freelancers, since they usually tell their freelancers not to communicate directly with authors. This arrangement offers freelancers the chance to focus just on editing rather than on soothing the souls of authors with poor interpersonal skills who take out their frustration about the publishing process on their editors. Freelance editors expect that publishers will stand up to such authors on their behalf. However, the involvement of publisher staff members as go-betweens means

....

that it may take much longer for freelancers to get answers to their questions than when working directly with authors.

Authors

In an increasing number of situations, authors may need to hire freelance editors directly:

- when they are self-publishing and do not have access to a publisher's editorial staff to polish their writing
- when their manuscript needs developmental help
- when they are subject-matter experts but good writing is not one of their strengths
- when they are nonnative English speakers who have been asked to contribute chapters to a book and their manuscript requires language polishing
- when they are unsure of their skill in putting together a book proposal for submission to a publisher
- when they have a book contract with a publisher but their manuscript needs more attention than the publisher's acquisition editor can provide
- when their agent has said that their manuscript needs an editor's touch

Unlike publishers, authors may not be aware that there is more than one kind of editing that freelancers can do (developmental or substantive editing; technical editing; light, medium, and heavy copyediting), so freelancers may have to spend some time educating them in order to get appropriate fees. In addition, freelancers will have to spend a good deal of time clarifying with authors what outcomes the authors want from editing. It's best for both freelancer and author that the results of such discussion be described explicitly in a project-parameter document that both parties sign. If there are disagreements later when the editor is deep into editing, that document will help settle issues. If necessary, it can always be revised to reflect the evolution of the work required, and then both parties should sign it again. Having project parameters set out also prevents project scope creep, a situation that means freelancers do more work than planned and earn less money than expected.

Individual authors are more likely than publishers are to want written contracts. If authors don't ask for contracts, freelancers should provide them, for their own protection and for the protection of their authors. Also, authors are generally quicker to pay than publishers are. After all, it can take longer to push an invoice through a publisher's accounting department than it does for an individual author to write a check or send an electronic payment. Although in general publishers have larger budgets than authors do for contracting with freelancers, this is changing because of the popularity of crowdfunding publishing tasks, including editing, through personal online fundraising pages. Authors who have already been published are sometimes willing to pay higher editing fees than publishers are, because they've learned through experience that a well-edited book or article pulls in more readers than a sloppily written one does. Authors are thus more heavily invested in good editing, whereas publishers generally want to keep editorial fees in a narrow range, regardless of the depth of editing needed.

A freelancer working directly with an author with objectionable personality traits can decide to "fire" that author, whereas a freelancer working with a publisher can't. That autonomy can be satisfying and can cut down on freelancers' expenditures on medications for heartburn and depression (figuratively and literally). But far more fulfilling is the joy of working closely with an author to make the manuscript the best that it can be. Such a relationship spurs personal and professional growth for both parties.

CONCLUSION: THE PROS AND CONS OF FREELANCING

Freelancing has changed so much over time that it has become a viable career for many editors instead of something that only a few choose. Some editors may be forced by layoffs to become freelancers, but many more editors now choose self-employment deliberately. In fact, because of budget cuts necessitating staff reductions, it is the wide availability of freelance editors that permits publishers to still offer editing to their authors. Unlike staff members, freelancers are paid only for each project they do; publishers do not have to maintain employee-style benefits year-round for freelancers.

It is not necessarily automatic anymore for all editors to spend time working in-house for publishers before becoming freelancers. Professional associations for a wide variety of editorial niches offer networking, training, and listings of project opportunities. There are online communities that allow freelancers to learn from one another and market their services without traveling to client meetings. Technological advances have eliminated the need for working face to face in shared offices, allowed for freelancers to afford their own work equipment, and sped up publishing processes.

Editors who are considering going freelance must be honest about their desires and their abilities. If they freelance, they will have two jobs rather than one: they must edit, and they must run a business. If they wait to be handed projects the way employees are, they will go broke quickly. Are they self-starters, or do they need externally provided structure? If they aren't good at setting schedules for themselves, they should remain employees. Do they chafe under an office chain of command and so need more autonomy? If they do, they will want the freelancer's ability to turn down projects and authors or clients. Do they need frequent face-to-face contact with colleagues, or are they comfortable with a lot of alone time? Yes, the internet makes video visits and quick written discussions possible, so that makes freelancing less lonely than it used to be, but those who crave in-person contact should remain employees. Do they want an employer to provide opportunities for continuing education, or are they willing to seek and pay for it themselves? Education that freelancers pay for can be tax deductible in the United States. Do they want an employer to provide job equipment and keep their computer running well, or are they okay with serving as their own information-technology expert or purchasing such expertise? Freelancers have to find ways to deal with the feast-or-famine cycles of self-employment: Can they put savings aside, and can they market themselves consistently to decrease gaps between projects? And finally, do they want an employer to provide health-care insurance for them, or are they willing and able to take on that tax-deductible expense themselves?

I've been self-employed for more than two decades, and I wouldn't give it up for an in-house job unless financial survival for my family depended on it. I love getting up in the morning and setting my own schedule; not having to attend nonproductive in-house meetings called by an employer; being exempt from someone else's dress code; and taking breaks in my schedule without anyone's permission when I am ill, have errands or personal appointments, must provide care for a family member, or just need a mental-health day. I enjoy running a successful business of my own and being known in the publishing industry by name as an expert instead of being an anonymous employee. Most of all, I take satisfaction in building and maintaining excellent relationships with my corporate clients and my authors.

. . . .

ARIELLE ECKSTUT AND DAVID HENRY STERRY

If you are surprised, confused, or insulted by the idea of a chapter on self-publishing in a book that is devoted to the craft of editing, we implore you to read at least the two following paragraphs before you skip ahead. Yes, most of the other essays in this book focus on how editors in publishing houses do their jobs. But in today's rapidly changing and ever more democratic book marketplace, it's increasingly likely that your publishing house may have a staff of one: you! You and you alone may decide to become an author by publishing your own work. Or you may decide to set up shop as an editor who helps those who self-publish, after a career in traditional publishing or otherwise.

Self-publishing and editing have always had a rocky relationship. Or sadly, often no relationship at all. Too many writers self-publish books with mis-spelled dedications, sentences that should be arrested by the grammar police, narrative arcs that feel more like straight lines. Above any other failing—bad covers, bright white paper, terrible titles—the lack of editing has consistently distinguished most self-published books from traditionally published ones. Or rather, *un*distinguished them.

We are publishing professionals who strongly believe in self-publishing and want self-published authors to succeed, and very little makes us as sad as a self-published book in need of a stiff edit. The inverse is true as well. Very little has brought us as much relief and excitement as a well-edited self-published book. It sings PROFESSIONAL. It gives us hope that this is an author who wants to and can succeed.

When you self-publish, of course, the editing responsibility falls to you, the self in self-publishing. But what exactly does it mean to edit a self-published book? Is it up to the author to edit his or her own work? Should she depend

ARIELLE ECKSTUT and **DAVID HENRY STERRY** are cofounders of the Book Doctors, a company that has helped hundreds of authors get their books published. They are also coauthors of *The Essential Guide to Getting Your Book Published*. Arielle has been a literary agent for over twenty years at the Levine Greenberg Rostan Literary Agency. She is also the author of nine books and the cofounder of the iconic brand LittleMissMatched. David is the best-selling author of sixteen books. His first book was translated into ten languages and optioned by HBO, and his latest book was featured on the cover of the Sunday *New York Times Book Review*.

on beta readers or writers' groups? Should he hire outside help? The answer to all these questions is *yes*.

SELF-EDITING

Whether you're self-publishing or not, self-editing is necessary unless you happen to be one of those rare geniuses who is able to spit out a perfect first draft. We've yet to meet someone who fits this bill. The editing process for self-publishers is different from that with agents or editors in that you don't get professional feedback on your draft unless you seek it out yourself. Editorial feedback helps you know if you've successfully completed the self-edit stage, whether you have more self-editing to do, or whether you've lost all perspective and need to hire someone. It's impossible for you to see your book objectively. It simply can't be done. So once you've absorbed all the wisdom in this book and edited your manuscript until you just can't look at it one more second, it's time to get some outside help. Just one question before you do: have you read your book out loud yet?

Reading your *entire* book out loud is a crucial step in the editing process that most people simply don't take. You won't believe what you hear that you weren't able to see when you finished your "final" edit. We're not just talking about fiction here. We're big believers that nonfiction should be every bit as interesting and entertaining as a novel. That's why we read our five-hundred-page reference book *The Essential Guide to Getting Your Book Published* out loud three times before we handed it in to our editor. And every time we do an updated edition, we read the whole thing again from cover to cover, out loud.

It takes us about three full days to do so. It could be considered an excellent form of torture down in literary hell, but there's a very good reason for the slog. It never ceases to amaze us how the awkwardness of a sentence may conceal itself completely until it has to pass between your lips. Most of the time when we stumble on a sentence, it's because the sentence isn't as good as it could be. It doesn't roll off the tongue. Repetition becomes obvious—on both the micro level (for example, we found we were using the word *altogether* altogether too often) and the macro level (the book lagged and sagged in the middle). Opportunities for jokes, interesting wordplay, more abundant storytelling present themselves. Which is all to say, reading your book out loud will make your book better. Period.

WRITERS' GROUPS AND BETA READERS

Before you spend a dime on hiring editorial assistance, it's best to have the help of a writer's group or beta readers. Let us break these out for you.

Writers' groups. We can't tell you how many people we've seen get successfully published (self or traditionally) with the help of a writers' group. It's especially helpful if you're in a group with people writing in a similar bookstore category. The feedback, the forced deadlines, the networking all feed a writer's career. On the editing front, group members can give you crucial information about what's working and what's not. Sure, there will be big mouths who harp on the ridiculous, and other members whose taste you don't share. But if everyone says your ending stinks, well, your ending stinks.

Beta readers. The *beta* in "beta readers" comes from the software world and refers to the phase when a product is complete but still has errors that may or may not be known to the developers but that need to be fixed before it can go to market. Beta readers can be your saving grace—or your yes-men who do nothing to help you. It all depends on how you use them.

Most people, when asked to read your book, will tell you, "It was great!" This kind of feedback will get you nowhere. That's why it's helpful to develop a sheet of questions to hand out before or after your betas complete their reads. Some people like to hand out questions beforehand so that their readers can think about the issues you've brought up while they read. Other people don't like to put ideas into their readers' heads and want them to have an unbiased experience during the reading process. But either way, you want to give your readers some prompts. The questions should range from the very general to the very specific. If you're writing fiction or narrative nonfiction you could ask everything from *Were there points in the book where you felt bored and wanted to skip ahead?* to *Did you find it unrealistic when Aunt Tallulah revealed she spent her youth as a spy for the CIA?* With practical nonfiction you could ask everything from *Were there points in the book where you didn't understand what I was explaining?* to *Was it going too far to ask my readers to videotape themselves sitting silently in front of a mirror for ninety minutes?* The point here is to get a range of responses that will serve in subsequent edits. It's also helpful to get multiple answers to the same questions. If a majority of readers found the same section dull or felt uncomfortable with the ninety-minute videotaping, chances are that other readers will feel the same. If you get very diverse answers to the same question, then you might want to stick with what you've got or take what speaks to you from the various answers. Often someone else's criticism will initiate a creative spark that might lead you down an entirely new path. But it might be a breakthrough path that you never could've gotten to without the feedback that sparked your new idea.

....

Who makes for ideal beta readers? Probably not your grandma and your best friend—*unless* they happen to be avid readers of your genre. You can't give your romance novel to your little brother who only reads books about poker. You want to find readers who live and breathe your particular kind of book. If you don't know any of these people, let us introduce you to a cool new invention called the World Wide Web. When in doubt, always go see your librarian or local independent bookseller, which gets us to the next category: People you can pay to read your book.

PROFESSIONAL READERS

Between us, we are the authors of twenty-five books. We almost always pay an editor before we even turn our books in to our agents or publishers. And we *always* pay an editor when we self-publish. We are going to get into how to find and hire an editor, but first we want to delve into a gray area of editorial help, *professional readers*. The people we typically pay as professional readers are librarians and booksellers—and not just any librarians and booksellers. As with beta readers, you want to find those who specialize in your category of writing. Find the bookseller who buys your category for her store. Find the librarian who is known for his love and deep knowledge of your subject. If you're writing a children's book, for example, you will be hard-pressed to find anyone more literate in nearly any section of the children's shelf than a children's or school librarian.

But a professional reader shouldn't be limited to these two distinguished groups. If you're writing a business book, you might look to colleagues in your field. If you're writing about a local issue, then a local reporter might be the perfect match. University professors, high school teachers, food critics (if you're writing a cookbook!) are all great potential professional readers.

OUTSIDE EDITORS

If you have the budget, an outside professional editor can be your most important investment in your book. If you don't have the budget, then you should consider waiting to self-publish until you do. Thankfully, we live in a world where Kickstarter campaigns can fund a penniless entrepreneur very quickly, if you have a persuasive enough pitch. That's what all self-publishers are, after all. When you take on the role of publisher, you are creating a startup where you're wearing all the hats of a publisher's staff—editor, publicist, marketer, salesperson, and more. The problem is, most self-publishers do not have any training in these areas, and that's why it's essential to have the money to hire outside help. Editor is number one on the list.

How do you find a great editor? A person doesn't have to pass any kind of test or get a license to call herself an editor. All she has to do is say she is one. But don't be fooled by a shiny, sparkly website or slick, enticing come-ons—especially if the business or person promises publication. In the world of self-publishing, there are, unfortunately, many shysters who are just waiting to rip you off. They whisper sweet nothings in your ear and then deliver exactly that: nothing. And they're not actually sweet.

So before you hire anyone, you must do your research. Are there any complaints about the person/business online? Are there positive reviews? Who exactly is going to edit your book? What is that person's background? Was she an editor at Random House for twenty-five years or a copywriter for a gaming company during college? If she *was* an editor at Random House for twenty-five years, did she edit your category of book?

Ideally, you're looking for an editor with deep experience in your particular category. The editor doesn't have to have been at a big-name house. There are numerous amazing independent publishers out there, but no matter where an editor has worked, he needs—let us say this again—experience editing books like yours. Other important questions for potential editors are these: (1) Can you talk to their clients? Best to first check out their client list and ask to speak with people whose books look similar to yours. (2) Will they edit a small sample of your work before you hand over your check? (3) Will they put fees, deliverables, and deadlines in writing? The reason for this last question is that there are a number of different kinds of edits, with different deliverables associated with them, and you want to know exactly what you're getting, for how much, and when it will land in your inbox. These different edits break down as follows (for more detail on each kind, see other chapters in this book).

Developmental Edit

A developmental edit usually occurs fairly early in the process; the vast majority of writers need this for their manuscripts before even contemplating a line edit. It is also significantly cheaper than a line edit, because it's less time consuming.

The purpose of a developmental edit is to evaluate the big picture of your book. For fiction, that's everything from pacing to character arc to plot to voice and more, and for nonfiction, everything from voice to clarity to structure to marketability and more. A developmental editor typically delivers an editorial letter, and he may annotate individual pages too. Then you should have the chance to have a conversation with your editor to go over any questions you may have. This is one of the most fruitful parts of the process. Some of our best ideas come from questioning feedback from an editor. Often when we say "Yes, but this is what we meant!" it's a signal that what we intended is not clear in the document.

If you start with a line edit, much of it may become moot after the development work, which may well call for major changes throughout your manuscript. Better to pay less money to learn about the big issues and seek out a line edit only *after* any problems with structure, character, and voice have been discovered and addressed.

Line Edit and Copyedit

A line edit dials down to the paragraph/sentence/word level. As we said, it's usually a much more expensive job than a developmental edit. A line editor will go through the pages of your book with a fine-toothed comb, looking for dialogue that feels awkward, sentences that don't quite work, repetition, and more. Obviously this happens when the bulk of the work in terms of plot, character, beginnings, middles, and ends is done. It's not that a line edit can't address the bigger picture. But in most publishing houses an editor simply won't do a line edit until the bigger issues are addressed, so as not to have to do the same work twice. It's smart to stick with that order in self-publishing too.

Line edits may or may not come with an editorial letter. But be sure that the fee includes time for you to meet in person or talk on the phone once you've had a chance to digest the edits.

Often the same person could do both a developmental edit and line edit, if that's what you decide to pay for, but you will also need a copyeditor. Copyeditors are the grammarians, the fact-checkers, the formatting gurus, the identifiers of repetitive words and phrases. They are the ones who make a book as smooth as a fresh jar of Skippy. The one instance where you might not need a separate copyeditor is if you hire someone to do a line edit who does a copyedit simultaneously. Some people have both skills and can pull this off, though it's rare.

Proofreading

Last but not least, there's the proofreader. Though not technically an editor, the proofreader is the eagle-eyed person who makes sure that any silly typos along the way get fixed, that a weird line break gets unbroken, that a chunk of text that got inadvertently removed gets put back. It may sound like overkill, but please listen: the last thing you want is to open your precious book that you've spent thousands of hours on, and possibly thousands of dollars, only to find out that you dedicated it to your beloved moth instead of your beloved mother.

Taking Criticism

The self-published author is in a unique position when it comes to taking criticism. When you have an agent or editor, you're often forced to take criticism whether you want it or not. When you self-publish, it's easy to ignore criticism because you can. Here's our advice: don't. The ability to take criticism is the mark of the professional writer as opposed to the amateur. This isn't to say that you have to make every little change that is suggested. That would be silly. Take the time you need to let the feedback sink in and to get past your natural defensive reaction. Imagine you had a traditional publisher and the information was coming from your editor there, or your agent. How would you respond if this was the case?

For those of you who are not inclined to look outside yourself for editing, we beg you to seek the help you need and open yourself up to outside critiques. The point of writing a book is to have readers. The sooner you bring readers on board, the sooner you get a feel for what resonates and what does not. Yes, it can be deeply uncomfortable, infuriating, humbling. But if you want people you don't know to actually read your book, criticism is necessary. It will make you a better writer and your book a better book.

ALL THOSE OTHER HATS

As you've read throughout this book, editors do much more than just "editing." In a publishing house the editor is also responsible for acquisition decisions and for supplying a lot of marketing intelligence—positioning the title in the marketplace, writing tipsheets and copy, coming up with publicity hooks, etc. The self-publisher is also, of course, responsible for all of that. And just as a lot of self-publishers don't edit themselves as well as they should, many of them aren't very adept at the design, publicity, marketing and sales sides of the job either.

Just as we've suggested getting help with the editorial side of the self-publishing process, we can't leave you without saying the same about these other jobs. If you happen to be a graphic designer, then you're golden when it comes to the cover and the interior layout. But if you're not a professional publicist as well, then you probably don't know how to effectively reach out to the media (which, by the way, is even harder when you self-publish).

When you decide to self-publish, you are making the choice to become an entrepreneur. And the more you understand about the business of publishing, the more success you will find. But first you need a great book. And that's why self-publishing begins with self-editing.

26 A NEW AGE OF DISCOVERY

THE EDITOR'S ROLE IN A CHANGING
PUBLISHING INDUSTRY

· ·

JANE FRIEDMAN

In 2013 Bowker, the bibliographic information service, released an eye-opening infographic on retail book sales in the United States. It showed that—regardless of print or digital format—between 2010 and 2012, book sales shifted dramatically to online retail, away from physical retail. In 2010, chain bookstores accounted for 31.5 percent of all book sales; by 2012 that figure had dropped to 18.7 percent, partly due to the bankruptcy of Borders.[1]

While the growth—or stagnation—of e-book sales is a topic often highlighted in publishing trend headlines and tends to prompt the loudest debate, the bigger challenge for most publishers is not the shift to e-book format but the increasing importance of online sales and the ways books get discovered in a landscape dominated by digital media. For decades the bookstore has been the primary means of book discovery, but it's becoming less central to how books get marketed and sold. In 2007, Barnes & Noble retail sales peaked, and store count peaked in 2008. By 2016, Barnes & Noble sales had dropped by more than 22 percent and store locations by nearly 12 percent. And even those figures don't offer the full picture of how much bookstore sales have declined, given that Barnes & Noble's overall sales have been driven by growth of nonbook merchandise, such as educational toys and games.[2] Independent

JANE FRIEDMAN has twenty years of experience in the publishing industry, with expertise in digital media strategy for authors and publishers. In addition to being a columnist with *Publisher's Weekly* and a professor with the Great Courses, Jane maintains an award-winning blog on writing and publishing at JaneFriedman.com. She's spoken on the digital era of authorship at events such as BookExpo America, Frankfurt Book Fair, and Digital Book World, among many others.

1. "Online Retailers Gained, While Brick-and-Mortar Lost In Wake of Borders Exit," press release. Bowker, August 6, 2013. http://www.bowker.com/news/2013/Online -Retailers-Gained-While-Brick-and-Mortar-Lost-In-Wake-of-Borders-Exit.html.

2. Michael Cader, "Back to the Basics at Barnes: What's Been Lost in the eBook Era?," *Publishers Marketplace*, July 2, 2015. http://lunch.publishersmarketplace.com /2015/07/back-to-the-basics-at-barnes-whats-been-lost-in-the-ebook-era/.

bookstore growth has been much celebrated in the meantime, but its percentage of sales is minuscule in comparison to the growth of online retail—particularly Amazon.

In 2016, industry experts estimated that half of all books in the United States were sold through Amazon across all formats.[3] For e-book sales only, Amazon is believed to account for as much as 80 percent of all US book sales. Those figures have certainly only increased over time: in 2015, Amazon represented 51 percent of all growth in online retail and 24 percent of growth across *all* retail.[4] It's hard to overstate Amazon's effect on the book business at every level, including sales, marketing, and distribution, not to mention its role in shaping the e-book market. The launch of the Kindle in 2007 changed the face of book retailing forever, not only changing how books get sold and at what price but also opening up the field to self-published authors to get their work to market easily and profitably.

As book sales increasingly move online, different marketing dynamics take hold, such as search engine optimization (SEO), algorithm-driven recommendations, and social media conversations. The efficiency and accuracy of online search—and analyzing how to boost online word of mouth—becomes ever more critical as the number of books published each year continues to increase exponentially. For nearly their entire history, large publishers have focused their sales and marketing energies on servicing distributors, booksellers, and other businesses; now they're being compelled to develop the infrastructure and skills of direct-to-consumer companies and sell to readers directly.

While the number of published titles each year has been increasing steadily ever since the printing press came into existence—and especially during the emergence of desktop publishing in the 1980s—the title count skyrocketed after the e-book became a viable consumer format. From traditional publishers, the number of titles produced in 2001 was around 135,000. By 2013 that number was just over 300,000. Compare those numbers to what happened in the self-publishing market. Between 2006 and

3. Mike Shatzkin, "The Reality of Publishing Economics Has Changed for the Big Players," *The Shatzkin Files*, Idea Logical, September 19, 2016, http://www.idealog.com/blog/reality-publishing-economics-changed-big-players/.

4. Jason Del Rey, "Amazon's Complete Retail Domination in One Tiny Chart," *Re/Code*, December 23, 2015, http://recode.net/2015/12/23/amazons-complete-retail-domination-in-one-tiny-chart/.

2011, the number of titles tripled, with nearly a quarter million titles produced in 2011 alone.[5] By 2013 that number had risen to nearly half a million.
In September 2012, publishing consultant Thad McIllroy estimated that
more than fifty-six thousand e-books were released for the US Kindle in a
matter of thirty days.

So not only are traditional publishers competing with each other, but
they're also competing with the proliferation of self-publishing authors,
cottage-industry presses, and many forms of custom publishing output. It's
possible today for an author or a very small press to publish books that are
on an even footing with those of traditional houses because they have equal
access to distribution at Amazon, the number-one retailer of books. Any business or institution—such as a consulting firm, a school, or a church—can fea-
sibly start its own imprint, publish works that are in line with its mission and
values, and distribute or sell them to a target audience it likely knows better
than a traditional publisher does. This doesn't preclude the possibility and
likelihood of partnerships between traditional publishers and institutions (as
there are now), but certainly it's not a requirement for success to have such
a partnership, particularly if the content works best in a digital environment.
Industry consultant Mike Shatzkin has called the trend "atomization": "Publishing will become a function of many entities, not a capability reserved to a
few insiders who can call themselves an industry. . . . This is the atomization
of publishing, the dispersal of publishing decisions and the origination of
published material from far and wide. In a pretty short time, we will see an
industry with a completely different profile than it has had for the past couple
of hundred years."[6]

As author Clay Shirky has said, it is no great or important thing simply to
publish something in the digital era. You can publish at the click of a button.
The difficult work lies in getting attention in what he calls a world of "cognitive surplus"—the societal phenomenon where people now have free time
to pursue all sorts of creative and collaborative activities, including writing.
And they also have access to free tools to instantly distribute their work and

5. "Self-Publishing Sees Triple-Digit Growth in Just Five Years, Says Bowker,"
press release, Bowker, October 24, 2012, http://www.bowker.com/news/2012/Self
-Publishing-Sees-Triple-Digit-Growth-in-Just-Five-Years-Says-Bowker.html.

6. Mike Shatzkin, "Atomization: Publishing as a Function Rather than an Industry, *The Shatzkin Files*, Idea Logical, March 19, 2013, http://www.idealog.com/blog
/atomization-publishing-as-a-function-rather-than-an-industry.

make it public. Thus the avalanche of published materials we all now have to sift through.

Therefore the overwhelming problem for publishers, and ultimately for editors, is how to gain attention for their works in a world of dwindling bookstore retail space, and how to create sustained and meaningful word of mouth—all while keeping current with the technological advances and the shifting landscape of social media.

In a talk at 2013 BookExpo America, Phil Madans from Hachette said, "If you don't want your books to be found ever, use the *Fiction: General* category as your BISAC code."

If that comment had been made ten years earlier, no one would have much understood why they should care about BISAC codes—the book industry's standard set of subject categories—as long as a title had one and it was accurate. Since 2010, everyone cares. BISAC codes are just one of the many details in the larger landscape known as metadata—perhaps the biggest buzzword in publishing-insider circles since sales shifted to online retail. Metadata is all the information that describes a book and helps it come up in appropriate online searches; in some databases there may be more than one hundred fields for a publisher to use to define and describe each book, everything from its physical specifications to story themes and settings to author biographical information.

Metadata has different purposes depending on the context, but it's a hot-button concern because of its crucial role in helping readers discover books in the online shopping environment, where there is an unlimited selection of books but no personal guidance for the consumer. When readers run a search or browse titles, what they're shown is based on recommendation algorithms, and such algorithms are partly driven by the book's metadata.

In a talk at Frankfurt Book Fair's CONTEC 2013 conference, called "The Future of Metadata," German publishing expert Ronald Schild emphasized the need for semantic analysis, which relates to identifying the "core concept" of a book. Without semantic analysis, recommendations are less valuable; for example, your average reader is not searching for books by ISBNs or trim size but by themes, such as LGBT coming-of-age story, underground activity in communist Czechoslovakia, or other intellectual or emotional touchstones. But up until the growth of online retail, publishers had done very little thinking about this type of marketing.

One of the most fascinating aspects of the discussion is how much metadata can affect the sales of fiction. Conventional wisdom might lead one to believe it's most important for information-driven books, but a Nielsen study indicates just the opposite.[7] When publishers provide specific, detailed information about their novels instead of broad generic labels (which don't help readers), sales jump. For example, more readers are attracted to a title tagged with "historical suspense" "19th century" "London" "female protagonist" than to one simply labeled "mystery." The same discussions have also been happening in the self-publishing community, where authors have discovered that being meticulous with their categories, keywords, and summary descriptions have resulted in better visibility and thus better sales.

What do these trends mean for editors? To be the best possible advocates for their books, editors need to think about this larger picture throughout the book's development, starting in the acquisition stage. No one can count on quality bubbling to the top by itself—not that it ever did, but quality can't be discovered if the right readership is ignorant that it exists. Brian O'Leary, in his essay "Context, Not Container," makes a powerful argument that publishers can't focus on content or container (that is, the delivery format) alone; context is just as important. "Context" is the reason readers are looking for content (or a book) in the first place. Are they looking for a great beach read? Are they looking for recipes for entertaining over the holidays? Are they looking for personal essays about fathers by daughters? New startups in the publishing space often start with context first: solving a problem or satisfying a need that exists in the market. O'Leary writes:

> We treat readers as if their needs can be defined by containers. But in a digital world, search takes place before physical sampling, much more often than the reverse. Readers may at times look for a specific product, but more often they search for an answer, a solution, a spark that turns into an interest and perhaps a purchase. Publishers are in the business of linking content to markets, but we're hamstrung at search because we've made context the *last* thing we think about. When content scarcity was the norm, we could live with a minimum of context. In a limited market, our editors became skilled in making decisions about *what would be published.* Now, in an era of abundance, editors have inherited a new and fundamentally different role: figuring out how "what is published" will be *discovered.* To

7. Andre Brett and David Walter, "White Paper: The Link between Metadata and Sales," Nielsen, January 25, 2012, http://www.isbn.nielsenbook.co.uk/uploads/3971 _Nielsen_Metadata_white_paper_A4(3).pdf.

. . . .

serve that new role, we must reverse our publishing paradigm. We need to start with context and develop and maintain rich, linked, digital content.[8]

Figuring out context doesn't begin with metadata; it *ends* with metadata and filling out the fields appropriately when listing a book at wholesaler and distributor databases, a task often done collaboratively by editorial and marketing staff. Peter McCarthy, former vice president of marketing at Penguin, has argued that there are far more potential readers for each book than are ever reached, and that if publishers are to keep their value to authors, they need to be the best at connecting authors and titles to the most appropriate readers. When he develops a marketing campaign, he uses a range of data-driven tools to help him understand how "ordinary" readers (not publishing insiders) go about searching for things—and to make sure those people find the right book. For example, he might use a combination of reviews and conversations on Amazon, Goodreads, and LibraryThing to see how books get described or grouped together by readers. By doing some friendly "stalking" of reader conversations through social media and community sites, he might discover that people who love *The Bachelor* also love a very particular type of contemporary romance, which leads to ideas for how to better reach those readers and talk about a specific author or book.

One question that often bothers astute industry observers: do readers really have trouble finding books, or is discoverability a problem of the publisher? A reader's need for entertainment or information may be satisfied by many different books. The challenge for the publisher is to get the reader to buy *its particular* book: how to make one title stand out among many.

One strategy common in the self-publishing community is setting prices low (even at zero), which creates less purchase friction, attracts price-conscious buyers, and encourages a large number of readers to buy or download a title. However, this can be a double-edged sword, encouraging readers to load up with many more books than they could ever read, and reducing demand in the future. Still, traditional publishers are finding that a dependable way to increase the success of a new release is to offer another title, by the same author, at discount or for free in the immediate weeks leading up to publication, to create a rising curve of interest and attention. Discounting with a specific plan and strategy for marketing future work helps cut through the noise while retaining value.

8. Brian O'Leary, "Context, Not Container," in *Book: A Futurist's Manifesto* (Sebastopol, CA: O'Reilly Media, 2012).

In what are still, arguably, the early days of online retail and e-book marketing, self-publishing authors have been more nimble and experimental than traditional publishers in their efforts to reach readers through digital media. The most sophisticated and successful have even turned down lucrative publication deals offered by traditional houses. Editors must now bid for authors not just against their peers but against the greater profits and control that self-publishing offers. Best-selling author Sylvia Day, speaking at a 2013 industry conference, said she expects a comprehensive marketing plan that covers everything she's not doing herself. To pass muster with Day, a publisher's plan must hit a market she's not already reaching. "[Publishers] need to find me a new audience, to broaden my audience. As far as digital is concerned, [publishers] cannot compete with what I'm doing on my own. You have to knock my socks off with a brilliant marketing plan to be my publisher."

One of the unique effects of the digitization of the industry has been the call for traditional publishers to prove their value to authors. Anyone in publishing who doesn't see this as a growing problem might reflect on (1) the growing number of authors who are successful on their own, (2) the number of authors who have made exclusive deals with Amazon and therefore have deprioritized physical bookstore distribution, and (3) the growing footprint of Amazon's US publishing program. On this last point, while seen as a failure by some because it doesn't yet attract A-list authors, as of 2015, Amazon Publishing included fourteen imprints and more than twelve hundred titles; it had two thousand new titles planned for 2016. Its translation arm, AmazonCrossing, is now the number-one source of translations in the United States, and it has established foreign-language divisions as well.

In a development inconceivable even a few years ago, just about every head of every English-language publishing house now talks about the value it brings to authors and how it focuses on serving them. In 2015 at the BookExpo America industry trade show, Bloomsbury's Richard Charkin said, "The next few years will be about looking after our authors." But after an author gets his feet under him, gains credibility, and builds a direct relationship with his audience (a requirement for many authors to get published in the first place), of what use is the traditional publisher to an established author? It can't be *just* about publishing any longer. Anyone can publish, and publishing something doesn't guarantee attention like it once did.

Michael Bhaskar, in his book *The Content Machine*, argues that a publisher's value must come from its success at filtering and amplifying. Filtering, or *curation* to use another buzzword, means the careful selection of material that fits the mission or vision of the press and delivers value to its readers. Amplification is the ability to make that material visible and known to the target market. Prior to the internet, simply to print or to publish a book used to mean amplification. It was more difficult to publish something, and fewer things were published, so it was meaningful whenever someone invested in producing a book. That's no longer the case. So now a publisher has to find other ways of amplifying.

If a publisher is concerned about its potential to amplify a given title from the outset, then the acquisitions process should take this into account. Checking the sales of "comp titles" is the traditional way of assessing a project's potential, but now acquisitions research should also take the form of SEO and keyword analysis, so publishers can identify what people are searching for and quantify demand for a particular book concept or title. Online publications and magazines already use SEO and keyword analysis to determine what gets published, and such analytics have become extremely rich and detailed. Book editors and publishers will need to take advantage of these tools.

Acquisitions based on SEO and keyword metrics can sound deadening and offensive to anyone who works in publishing, especially those who believe that creative products are unique and aesthetic judgments trump number-crunching. But the two don't necessarily have to be in conflict, especially at publishers where the two key functions of filtering and amplification have a happy marriage. And when these two functions mesh, it increases value to the author as well as the publisher. So what does that look like?

Editors and publishers must push themselves to become leaders of the community of readers and writers who have matching interests. Publishers can add value and earn credibility within a community—through the act of publishing of course, but also through other forms of leadership and support that go beyond print publishing and extend into events, services, grants, fellowships, reading groups, and more.

For years, publishers have known that they need to build more relationships directly with readers, rather than relying on bookstores or e-tailers as intermediaries . The latter approach has led to an industry that has very limited ability to market direct to consumer, which is where a huge part of Amazon's power lies. In 2015 the chief digital officer of HarperCollins, Chantal Restivo-Alessi, told a group of industry colleagues, "Marketing has been the division most impacted by the need to change. There has been the change from analog to digital, but also the need to transform from trade marketing to relationship marketing"—that is, from marketing oriented toward industry partners to marketing aimed at earning the recognition and trust of individual consumers. The mission of community building is now getting under way in publishing circles: developing relationships with readers in a way that doesn't depend on large tech companies. But it requires intimate knowledge of and respect for communities of readers, combined with creativity and imagination in serving them. Publishers that survive, whether they focus on traditional print or on digital media, will need to become indispensable to the communities they serve.

While at one time a publisher might have become indispensable by delivering quality ideas and stories, a publisher who does that today—and nothing more—can be seen as merely adding to the burden all readers now face. There are too many wonderful things to read and too few signposts to what's worth our time. Thus the publisher needs to be a beacon, to offer a strong signal amidst all the noise and organize ideas, content, and stories within an identifiable and useful context.

Another term for this in a publishing context is *verticalization*. Rather than having a broad, generalist publishing plan across many imprints that don't have meaningful brands for readers, publishers should create imprints—or at least online communities—that have the potential to develop a loyal fan base around a single theme, idea, or genre. One of the oldest examples of this in traditional publishing is Harlequin, a name that equates to romance in the reading community. Other long-time examples include Rodale (healthy living), O'Reilly Media (technology), and Hay House (New Thought self-help). Some newer examples include Suvudu from Random House (science fiction and fantasy), Heroes & Heartbreakers from Macmillan (romance), and Cool Springs Press (home and gardening).

The marketing relationship with readers is just the start. A whole other level of engagement and interaction takes place when the community is involved in how and what is published—when fans may even serve as early readers *and* editors. Again, this is an area where self-published authors and the online publishing community has already been active and experimenting, ahead of traditional publishers, with collaborative models.

Some of the most provocative thinking in this area has come from Bob Stein at the Institute for the Future of the Book. His argument is that reading has always been a social activity and that our idea of literature as a solitary pursuit is fairly recent, something that arrived with widespread literacy. Now, as we move from the printed page to the screen—to networked environments—the social aspect of reading and writing returns to the foreground. Once this shift happens, we see something very interesting: the lines begin to blur between reader and writer. Stein suggests that authors will take on the added role of moderators and leaders of communities and as designers of complex worlds for readers to explore in fiction.

In the nonfiction arena, there are numerous examples of this social and collaborative aspect—the most iconic being *Wikipedia*, one of the grandest social writing and reading projects ever born. For some types of projects, crowdsourcing has become a replacement for development and content editing. Sourcebooks, a trade publisher, has experimented with this kind of authoring and editing process, which they call their "Agile Publishing Model." People in the technology world are already very familiar with this type of iterative framework, which makes content available faster, gets real-time feedback from the target audience, and shapes the final product through collaboration. CEO Dominique Raccah says, "The traditional publishing model—long schedules, creating in a vacuum, lack of involvement with the readers of the end product—drives some authors crazy. [The collaborative] model is a great fit for experts who are highly immersed in their field and where the field is evolving rapidly." Sourcebooks employed an agile model for *Evolution Shift* by David Houle. Other authors who have used unconventional means of writing their books (sometimes developing them publicly on blogs) include Chris Anderson and Dan Gillmor (*Mediactive*).

On the fiction or narrative side, the online community Wattpad and the burgeoning world of fan fiction represent potential models. Fan fiction is when readers take well-known characters and story worlds, such as Harry Potter or Star Wars, and create new stories for their own enjoyment and to share within the community. E. L. James's best-selling novel *50 Shades of Grey* began as a piece of fan fiction based on Stephenie Meyer's *Twilight* and was posted as a work in progress on a public fan fiction website. It gathered fans and feedback over time before being formally published.

Of course, one of the challenges of fan fiction is that to become a successful commercial project, it has to stand on its own as a new work and avoid claims of copyright infringement. Amazon recognized an opportunity in this challenge. In 2013 it launched Kindle Worlds to allow fan fiction writers to start publishing and earning money from their fan works through formalized licensing deals.

Thus far, however, activity on Kindle Worlds is fairly minimal when compared to a site like Wattpad, which has a user base of more than fifty million. While fan fiction is one of the most predominant areas of activity on the site, Wattpad is more broadly a community of people who love to read and write stories. Those stories are delivered primarily to mobile devices in serialized form—that is, in installments. If the fast growth of Wattpad and its youthful audience is any indicator, this type of interaction may shape the future of publishing.

One of the reasons Wattpad is attractive to emerging writers is that it offers a real chance to directly reach and grow a readership, even though it means giving away the writing for free. Wattpad can ping a devoted readership whenever a new story or installment gets posted. Unlike traditional publishing or even self-publishing through Amazon, where authors have limited insight into their readers and no means to have a conversation with them, Wattpad offers a platform for ongoing interaction. And Wattpad's larger vision is just that: to foster a stronger connection between the reader and writer.

There's another motivation for writers to use Wattpad. It can be very daunting to write a book, but it's not so hard to write a chapter. By building an audience and getting feedback right away (from ordinary folks—not editors), a writer may be encouraged to continue and build on his efforts rather than giving up when faced with a slump or self-doubt.

While serials and fan fiction are sometimes dismissed by industry insiders (and others) as low-quality work that won't affect how traditional publishing operates, these markets might be in a position to do exactly that. Wattpad delivers a social reading experience that some consider superior to that of the traditional e-book. Eric Hellman, an industry expert who specializes in economic models for e-books, wrote:

> It's worth paying close attention to the fan fiction sites. After all, 2012's biggest revenue engine for the book industry, *50 Shades*, was a repackaged fanfic. On an iPad with a decent internet connection, the fanfic sites work better than ePubs. . . . They deliver content in smaller, more addictive chunks, and they integrate popular culture MUCH more effectively than books do. . . . The authors are responsive and deeply connected to readers; they often ARE the readers! There's a fanfic site to appeal to every reader.[9]

While some career authors—who likely had to improve on their own and struggle for approval from the gatekeepers—may believe that emerging authors are publishing too early and too quickly without regard for quality, Wattpad offers a different model of how to develop as a writer. Authors benefit from getting those first manuscripts out in public and are willing to improve

9. Eric Hellman, "In 2013, eBook Sales Collapsed . . . in My Household," *Go to Hellman*, January 1, 2014, http://go-to-hellman.blogspot.com/2014/01/in-2013-ebook-sales-collapsed-in-my.html.

. . . .

as they go with the feedback of beta readers. As authors gain experience and titles under their belt, they may continue to use beta readers but also employ formal, paid editing teams.

Going yet a step further, it has even been suggested by Stein (and others) that the future of reading might look like gaming. One example is the Black Crown project, a work of interactive fiction produced by Random House UK. The story begins with a series of questions; then the reader is put into a number of predicaments, as in a Choose-Your-Own-Adventure novel. There is an author behind it, Rob Sherman, who said in an interview: "It's a scary thing because you need to relinquish control and allow for readers to have an experience different from the one you're expecting. . . . I think pretty much all authors have to accept now that readers are going to take things and manipulate them and make them their own. Whether you give them permission to or not. And they're going to share them with other people."[10]

If this all seems too far-fetched, consider how Amazon collects untold data through its Kindle reading platform, and already records exactly how people read a particular book: how fast, how slowly, and the exact paragraph where a reader abandons the story. E-book subscription service Scribd does the same; JellyBooks now specializes in collecting reading data for publishers to use in their marketing plans prior to book launch. Such flexibility recalls the long-expected, but never realized, dream of forking stories—books that have multiple endings, or alternative storylines. Previous attempts at this sort of "hyperliterature" have met with dismal failure because readers seemed uninterested in deciding the plot; they wanted the author to decide. But in recent years complex stories with alternative pathways have been wildly successful in video games, and some of the techniques pioneered in taming the complexity of user-driven stories in games could migrate to books. One publishing startup, Lithomobilus, is already exploring this possibility.

These developments don't mean the need for editors will diminish or that their gatekeeping role isn't needed. To emphasize again, publishers must filter and amplify—with intention and meaning for a specific group. Furthermore, with the rise of self-publishing, the demand for editors has only increased, with authors increasingly aware of the need for some level of assistance in rewriting and polishing their work. There are now two freelance marketplaces

10. Rob Sherman, in Rob Sherman and Dan Franklin, "Something Wicked This Way A) Comes B) Lurks," interview by Anthony John Agnello, Gameological Society, July 30, 2013, http://gameological.com/2013/07/interview-black-crown-project/.

focused on the publishing industry—Bibliocrunch and Reedsy—that help writers find qualified help, plus a range of boutique editorial-service companies that offer a package for every budget. Informal surveys always show that authors place top value on two people: their agent and their editor. Note that it's not necessarily the *publisher* that the writer is valuing, but the relationship with a specific person who is nurturing her craft and career.

Industry futurist Richard Nash wrote in his 2012 essay "The Business of Literature" that the editor is a source of great value in the economics of literature and will remain valued for two primary reasons. First, because the world still needs editors—people who filter and amplify. But second, because editors have relationship skills. Publishers of the future, regardless of what form books take or where they're sold, will always need to cultivate strong relationships with authors. Publishers can distinguish themselves with authors not necessarily by being the most technically advanced, or the most innovative in media creation and distribution, but by being trusted and respected partners. That partnership will start with the editor, as it has for generations.

CONCLUSION

....

AS TIME GOES BY:
THE PAST AND FUTURE OF EDITING

Anyone who has followed the book publishing business in the twenty-first century has heard, probably ad nauseam, that the industry is undergoing disruption—a voguish word for "big, scary change." The transformations in our time have been the more unsettling because in the past publishing changed so slowly. When I entered the industry in the 1980s, it wasn't all that different from what it had been since the 1950s. Change was happening, to be sure, but predictable and gradual change. Big publishing grew more corporate and consolidated; chains and big-box stores gained market share, and independent bookstores declined; scholarly publishers struggled with shrinking library budgets. Even the arrival of Amazon in the 1990s did not—at first—fundamentally change the landscape. But a revolution driven largely by technology soon followed—beginning with the massive growth of internet bookselling as more Americans moved online, and most obviously marked by the arrival of the Kindle in 2007, plus the explosion of self-publishing arising from the first two phenomena. The publishing marketplace, and the business of serving it, has changed more drastically in the past fifteen years than in the half-century before.

The era of rapid change seems likely to continue, for the forces stressing the industry as I write have not reached equilibrium. Independent bookstores, battle tested by combat with both chains and Amazon, have held their own, and many are flourishing, but brick-and-mortar retail in general is still losing ground to online sales. While Amazon and e-books have soaked up the attention of industry alarmists, another serious issue for publishers has drawn less notice than it deserves. For all their progress in online marketing and social media, publishers still rely heavily on traditional publicity channels like newspapers and radio. Those media are struggling badly, further challenging publishers' ability to make readers aware of new books.

Self-publishing continues to take market share from established houses, and while few best-selling authors have abandoned their publishers thus far, if blockbuster authors moved en masse in that direction it would truly change big publishing's business model. The essays in this book may suggest why such a move has not yet happened: the array of services, and of expertise, that editors and publishers provide is by no means easy for a single author to replicate. Even if the author has the funds to hire those services, finding and coordinating them all is a big job. Doing that job is another way that publishers provide value. But we might yet see consultancies bundling such services for authors on a larger scale. Meanwhile, even at the non-best-selling level, the sheer quantity of self-published books competing with those from traditional houses has eroded the latter's market share; we can't yet predict how far that erosion will go.

Indeed, the book itself may be an unstable category. We are already seeing the creation of electronic works that include sound, video, hyperlinks, and other interactive elements with booklike content; some of this is taking the form of smartphone or tablet apps. So far, these multimedia experiments have had modest impact: it seems that book readers prefer the immersive and imaginative experience where the author's words come to life in their own heads. But the ubiquity of other digital entertainment and communication, from Hollywood movies and music to group chat and Facebook live, available literally at consumers' fingertips, inevitably has reduced the hours available for reading, creating further headwinds for publishing. If future generations raised on screens come to prefer interactive books, editors may need to master an entirely new set of skills, just as they once mastered type-writing, word processing, or tweeting.

How, in this environment, can one foresee the future of book editing? It's hard at this moment to know whether the pace of change will slow down, as it has in the past, or just keep accelerating. And yet no matter how swiftly time goes by, on Publishers Row as in Casablanca, the fundamental things apply.

While working on this book, I happened to visit an exhibition in Venice celebrating the work of the city's revered printer, and one of the first great editors and publishers, Aldo Manuzio, or Aldus Manutius as he styled himself. He was a humanist—a scholar of the classics—who in 1494 started a business to publish the work of Latin and Greek authors. As an editor, Aldus took pains to produce the best texts possible. As a publisher, he innovated, creating the first italic type and pioneering the octavo volume—easy to hold in one hand—as a format for literature. Beautifully designed and far easier to read than most earlier books had been, Aldus's books helped establish reading as a leisure pastime, not just the province of scholars. They were also instrumental in the intellectual flowering of the Renaissance. Aldus's "brand" became such a powerful symbol of quality that even today some publishers copy his anchor-and-dolphin colophon—just glance inside a Doubleday book.

....

Publishing has seen a half-millennium of change since Aldus, but his labors consisted quite recognizably of the same three editorial functions we have explored throughout this book:

- *Acquisition.* Here Aldus distinguished himself first by curation, selecting ancient works he believed readers would value. Later he would publish groundbreaking original works such as the mythological romance *Hypnerotomachia Poliphilli.*
- *Text development.* Aldus's meticulous editing of classical works set his publications apart from others. He may have been the first to compare manuscript editions to establish the most accurate text. Though he was seldom working with new authors in real time, Aldus toiled to produce the best possible version of what each author created.
- *Publication.* Aldus showed genius in bringing his titles into the marketplace—creating new formats for books and realizing that elegant, readable design would expand the market of readers.

Looking at the paintings of Aldus's Venice by contemporaries like Bellini or Carpaccio (or trying to make sense of the phantasmagoric *Hypnerotomachia*), we can see Aldus inhabited a vastly different world from our own. Yet there he was, just like the editors and publishers of today, connecting writers and readers. And in doing so, he provided something of value to each, making a lasting contribution to culture.

So while it may be impossible to predict where the publishing industry is going or what shape it will take a generation from now, the essence of what editors do, and the need for it, will endure. To take just one of the major trends mentioned above, the continued expansion of self-publishing inevitably creates an ever greater need for curation—call it an equal and opposite reaction. For readers overwhelmed by thousands of books to choose among, trusted tastemakers who can identify and acquire work worth spending one's time on will surely be in demand. At the same time, the explosion of new titles means a growing need for editing in its most familiar sense—taking written content and making it better. Self-publishing authors who take their work seriously need such services, but so do the entity publishers, from institutions to church groups to restaurants, who want to produce quality publications. And authors of all kinds will still value professionals who can help connect them with their readers, identifying the likeliest audiences and using expertise to present their work in appealing ways. As we have seen, that too is the work of editors.

The career path for book editors in the future—perhaps for you who are reading this—may well be quite different from the one familiar to recent generations. Freelancing will be more common, and if large commercial publishers continue to consolidate, there will be fewer staff positions for editors in those houses. There is an equal and opposite reaction to this, too: the flowering of small independent publishers whose work is so well articulated in these pages by Erika Goldman and Jeff Shotts. Houses like Bellevue and Graywolf will attract authors by providing committed, attentive editing even if big corporations don't. Editing has never been the best choice for those who seek a highly lucrative job; that is unlikely to change, and, as elsewhere in the creative professions, steady employment may be harder to come by in the twenty-first-century economy.

But for those with a passion for books, editing offers rewards that are hard to improve on—including a community of like-minded colleagues. One effect of the mediocre entry-level pay in publishing is that those who enter the business, almost to a one, do it because they love to read. Though it may sound simplistic to say, I have found that a peer group self-selected in this way is an incredibly congenial one.

I have resisted, both in writing and in editing this volume, soaring rhetoric about the creative genius of editors, their selfless labors, or their mystical bond with authors. Those things are real, to be sure, but writing and editing are serious business, even when they are joyful, and I feel sentimentalizing the work impedes actually understanding it. Nonetheless, I do believe that editing is a noble calling. Authors do the hardest, loneliest work, the work of facing the blank page and drawing something out of themselves to fill it. But editors do something difficult and demanding too: putting their sensibilities in service to another person (and putting their own egos aside) to help that person realize a creative vision and share it with an audience.

The core—the heart and soul—of editing will always be the editor–author relationship. That relationship begins before, and extends beyond, the act of making editorial suggestions. It starts with the editor reading a manuscript and feeling the spark—that urge to share what he's just read with someone else. It continues with editor and author striving, sometimes happily and sometimes painfully, to turn that spark into a flame. And it reaches fruition when the flame becomes a fire, warming a widening circle of readers.

ACKNOWLEDGMENTS

. . . .

Editors are a busy lot. As these essays have probably made clear, to be a good editor usually means spending a long day at the office and then taking manuscripts home for nights and weekends; for freelancers, the workload is often similar except that home and office may be the same place. The writers of this volume wrested time out of their schedules, and probably away from friends and family, to set down their experiences and insights for the benefit of others. What they have done carries on publishing's honorable tradition of mentorship. As you may imagine, it was with some trepidation that I undertook to edit the work of some of the best editors in the business. But every one of them responded to suggestions conscientiously and graciously, which made *their* editor's job that much easier. So my first and most grateful acknowledgment is to my contributors. Thank you all.

In my own career, I have been fortunate to have several generous mentors. I owe to them much of what I have learned about editing and publishing, so I'd like to acknowledge them here: At Persea Books, Michael Braziller and Karen Braziller, who gave me my first job in the book business and from whom I learned firsthand how passion and commitment could drive an independent publishing house. At Crown Publishers, James O'Shea Wade, who, with Betty Prashker, gave me a chance as an acquiring editor, and who showed me the importance of maintaining both integrity and a sense of humor inside a conglomerate publishing house. At Oxford University Press, Laura Brown, a brilliant publisher whose vision enabled me to make the unlikely transition from a highly commercial house to a venerable scholarly one, and Ellen Chodosh, from whom I learned what humane and enlightened management is. Laura, Ellen, and some extraordinary colleagues at Oxford helped me discover how powerful genuine teamwork and esprit de corps can be in publishing. At Bloomsbury USA, Karen Rinaldi gave me the opportunity to launch an imprint, which was both an exhilarating challenge and a learning experience in even more ways than I anticipated.

I want to say a particular word of thanks to Thomas McCormack, who hired me as his assistant at St. Martin's Press. More than anyone else I know in the business, Tom took the job of nurturing young talent seriously and went out of his way to educate not just his own assistants but other young staff members in the ways of publishing. As a result, SMP served as a training ground for a remarkable number of leading figures in the industry. Tom taught me an enormous amount, not only by dispensing advice but, more importantly, by giving me enough responsibility that I could learn things for myself. That is the best kind of mentorship.

When I accepted my first job, I asked my new boss if there was anything I should do to prepare for my first day of work. He said, "Get a copy of *The Chicago Manual of Style* and start reading it"—still excellent advice for anyone who wants to learn how books are put together. In a sense, then, the University of Chicago Press began my education in publishing, and I'm honored to share a list with the *Chicago Manual* itself. I'm grateful to *my* editor at the Press, Mary Laur, and her editorial director Christie Henry, who invited me to put together this book and have supported it during a prolonged gestation period. Mary has been smart, patient, good-humored, sensible, and responsive—all I could have asked for in my first experience on this end of the process. More than once we got almost dizzy contemplating the complexities of my editing editors writing about editing, and her editing my edits of the editors . . . but I think it has turned out all right with her guidance. Ruth Goring has copyedited with a gentle touch and scrupulous care. Thanks too to contributor Cal Morgan, who also gave me invaluable comments on my own chapters.

This book is dedicated to my parents. When I was a boy, my father was a screenwriter and filmmaker, and my first insights into what made stories work came from talking about movies we watched together when I must have been in middle school. Later he became a book editor, and his palpable love of his work helped make it seem like a career worth pursuing. Now in his nineties and still reading and writing, he remains an inspiration to me. I owe just as much to my mother, herself a writer and editor and the most voracious reader I ever knew. And at the risk of cliché, I must close by thanking my wife, Susan Hewitt, and our children, Henry and Kate Ginna—who have endured many years of manuscripts encroaching on what should have been time spent with them. Christopher Hitchens once said that a friend of his "identified bliss with writing or reading very hard in the afternoon, knowing that someone really, *really* nice was coming to dinner." The only thing better is when the really nice people are in your house already.

account. An entity (bookstore, chain, wholesaler, or other business) that buys books in quantity from a publisher. In plural—"the accounts"—usually shorthand for a publisher's bookseller customers.

acquiring editor. An editor tasked with acquiring new books for publication. Sometimes called an *acquisitions editor, sponsoring editor,* or *commissioning editor.*

acquisition. The act of putting a work under contract for publication, or *acquiring* it. The work so contracted is also called an *acquisition. Acquisitions,* plural, refers to the overall, ongoing editor's task of acquiring new titles for the publisher.

advance, royalty. A sum of money paid by contractual agreement to the author in anticipation of **royalty** earnings. Royalty or **rights** income is credited against this advance and retained by the publisher until the advance is "earned out," after which it flows to the author. Sometimes called a *guarantee,* as the author keeps the advance money even if not earned out.

advance copies. Copies of a printed book sent out to the author, agent, media, or other industry contacts before its official on-sale date. *See also* **ARCs (advance reading copies)**.

agent, literary. A professional who represents an author's work to publishers and negotiates on his or her behalf.

agile publishing. A publishing model, emulating that of certain technology companies, in which some of the editorial process is iterative and crowdsourced; the publisher incorporates reader feedback on a book into new versions published more quickly than traditional updated editions.

analytics. The practice of studying patterns in business data.

ARCs (advance reading copies). Copies of a book printed and bound for prepublication distribution to reviewers, media, booksellers, and other opinion makers. They may be lavishly produced with the commercial book cover design or printed more simply. In the past these copies were printed from early **galley** proofs, and they are still often called *bound galleys.* Another older term for these is *BOMs,* because a key destination for bound proofs was the Book-of-the-Month Club's readers and judges.

art director. A person overseeing graphic and printing design in a publishing house, such as for book jackets and interior layouts. *See also* **creative director**.

art log. A record of a book's art program: a document listing each illustration to be included with a book's text, with information such as its size and placement. Supplied to the production editorial department as part of a manuscript's **transmittal**.

auction. A formal procedure, typically conducted by a literary agent, for selling a book to one of multiple competing publishing houses. Auctions may be "best bid" style, in which each house makes a single offer, or involve repeated rounds of bidding. Rules may vary widely from one auction to another.

author information sheet (AI sheet). *See* **title information sheet**.

back ad. The promotional copy on the back panel of a printed book cover or dust jacket.

back matter. Material included following the main text of a book, such as acknowledgments, endnotes, glossary, index, etc. Also called *end matter*.

backlist. A publisher's catalog of previously published titles. Generally refers to titles currently **in print**, excluding those in the **frontlist**.

beta reader. A reader recruited by an author to provide preliminary feedback and corrections on a work before it is exposed to the market.

bidding service. An online clearinghouse where freelance professionals such as editors or designers can offer their services to prospective clients.

Big Five. Industry shorthand for the five largest commercial publishing companies operating in the United States as of 2017: Penguin Random House, Hachette, HarperCollins, Macmillan, and Simon & Schuster.

binding. The covering holding the pages of a physical book together. *See also* **hardcover** and **paperback**.

BISAC codes. Standard subject descriptors agreed by the Book Industry Study Group, each one represented by an alphanumeric code—for example, LAN027000, Language Art & Disciplines/Publishing, the code for books like this one, or JUV059000, Juvenile Fiction/ Dystopian. *BISAC* stands for *Book Industry Standards and Communications*.

blurb. A favorable comment about a book supplied by a prominent author, celebrity, or expert. or a short excerpt from a book review. In older and especially British usage, may refer to any brief promotional copy, such as back ad or flap copy.

board book. A children's book printed with cardboard pages to withstand rough handling (or teething). Typically aimed at the youngest group of readers.

book doctor. A freelance book editor. *Doctoring* usually connotes extensive developmental and line editing, sometimes including rewriting, possibly shading toward **ghostwriting**.

BookExpo. The major annual convention of the US trade publishing industry, where publishers promote forthcoming titles and their authors to booksellers, media, and consumers.

Bookscan. A service of the marketing consultancy AC Nielsen that tracks current sales of books in the UnitedStates. Bookscan captures primarily sales at retail, so it does not include some library, bulk and **special sales**. Its figures are estimated to include roughly 75–85 percent of total sales for trade books

bound galleys. *See* **ARCs (advance reading copies)**.

break out. For a book, to sell above the expected level for its category or the author's previous **track record**. It may be said of a title that it "broke out" or of a house that it "broke [a certain title] out."

bricks-and-mortar stores. Retail stores in physical space, as opposed to **e-tailers**. These include independent booksellers and chains such as Barnes & Noble or Books-a-Million but also other stores that sell books, including Walmart and Costco.

buzz book. A book that attracts unusual prepublication attention. Certain titles are officially anointed as "Buzz Books" by being featured under that rubric at **BookExpo** or in industry publications such as *Publishers Lunch* and *Publishers Weekly*.

castoff. The projected length of a printed book based on the author's manuscript and a proposed type design. To make such a projection is to "cast off" the manuscript.

catalog copy. The description of a given title prepared for a publisher's catalog, typically also displayed on the publisher's website and in various other online venues such as e-tailer listings.

chapter book. A relatively short book with brief chapters, usually fiction, aimed at newly independent readers (seven to ten years old).

clothbound. *See* **hardcover**.

college publishing. Textbook publishing specifically aimed at the university-level market.

college traveler. *See* **sales rep**.

commercial fiction. Popular fiction (as opposed to **literary fiction**) thought to be more concerned with entertaining readers than with literary ambition. Which novels are "literary" and which are "commercial" is in the eye of the beholder. **Genre fiction** is a subset of commercial fiction.

commission. In the United States, for an editor to originate a book by finding an author for a topic or story the editor has conceived. In British usage, *commissioning editor* is another term for acquiring editor, but this does not necessarily require commissioning in the American sense.

comp. In art department jargon, short for "comprehensive layout": a designer's presentation of a proposed design for a book's interior layouts or cover.

comp titles. Books already published considered to be similar in audience to a given title under consideration. *Comp* is usually thought to be short for *comparable*, but may also mean *competitive*.

compositor. *See* **typesetter**.

con. Short for *convention*, a gathering of fans, as in Comic Con or Worldcon (World Science Fiction Convention); often important venues for genre fiction authors and editors.

copy. In publishing-specific usage, any text that is to be (or has been) set into type, including a book manuscript, back ad, or promotional description. Hence **copyediting**, **catalog copy**, cover copy, etc.

copyediting. Usually the final editorial stage of preparing a manuscript for publication—a meticulous read for technical errors, **style**, and internal consistency, along with marking or electronically coding the text to be ready for typesetting.

course adoption. The selection of a textbook (or other title) for use in school or university classes.

cover. In strict usage, the exterior of a printed book, as distinct from a **dust jacket**. But often used more loosely for the latter as well, as in speaking of a cover design, cover copy, or "**cover reveal**."

cover reveal. The promotion of a book by revealing its jacket or cover design before publication, often on a popular blog or magazine website.

creative director. The person in a publishing company responsible for visual design (including book covers and interiors as well as web pages, advertising, and company branding in general). A similar role to **art director**, though "creative director" connotes wider responsibilities, and in large organizations several art directors may report to a creative director.

crossover book. A work aimed initially at a scholarly or specialized readership that also appeals to a general audience. Some books are intentionally written as crossovers; others **break out** of their specialized category based on readers' responses.

delivery date. (1) The date agreed in a publishing contract by which the author must deliver a "complete and satisfactory" manuscript and any other items, such as images or permissions to reprint material, necessary for publication. (2) In some houses, the date on which finished books are scheduled to arrive in a publisher's warehouse, as opposed to the **publication date**, when the book is officially available for sale at retail establishments. Also called *bound book date, in-warehouse date,* or *in-stock date.*

developmental editing. Editorial intervention, usually at an early stage, to help the author with structure, substance, or other fundamental elements of a manuscript. Compare with **copyediting** and **line editing**.

developmental review. In textbook publishing, **peer review** of a manuscript or proposal aimed at enhancing its fitness for a target course market.

digital publishing. *See* **electronic publishing**.

distribution. The process of making books available to consumers and filling orders for them. In publishing, the word is most frequently applied to books moving through the physical **supply chain** but can also refer to electronic distribution of e-books.

dust jacket. The printed wrapper around most hardcover books and some paperbacks. Sometimes called simply a *jacket.*

earn out. *See* **advance, royalty**.

e-book. A book published in electronic form. Most e-books from established houses are published alongside printed editions, but many titles are released as "e-book originals" or "e-only" with no printed counterpart, especially in the self-publishing market.

edition. (1) A version of a book that has been created for the first time, as in "first edition," or one resulting from revisions to the previous version (updating of content, new forewords or afterwords, and the like), as in "second edition" or "revised edition." Sometimes a synonym for **printing** (or *impression*), as in "an edition of 1000 copies," but in contemporary book publishing, *edition* implies a version with significant changes to what existed before. *See also* **printing**. (2) One format out of several of the same text (e.g., "audio edition," "movie tie-in edition").

editor. A publishing professional whose responsibilities may include any or all of the following: book **acquisitions**; managing relationships with authors and **literary agents**; **manuscript** development and revision; **copyediting**; seeing works through the **production** process; involvement in their publicity and marketing, including writing **title information sheets** and promotional copy; and overall project management.

As a job title, "editor" varies with the specific responsibilities and the type of publishing house (as described throughout this volume), as well as the experience and managerial status of the individual editor. Above the level of **editorial assistant**, titles that reflect increasing seniority, responsibility (including **signing goals**), and autonomy generally include *assistant editor, associate editor, editor, senior editor*, and *executive editor*. At the top of the editorial hierarchy sits an *editorial director* or *editor in chief*. The latter is almost by definition a single person, but in some houses more than one editorial director may oversee individual **imprints** or specific **lists** (e.g., editorial director for fiction). Editors who are responsible for a manuscript from **transmittal** through prepublication stages to manufacturing commonly have the title *production editor, project editor*, or *manuscript editor*. They are usually members of a department separate from the one whose editors acquire and develop manuscripts, and the head of this department is commonly titled *managing editor*. *Copyeditors* have specialized expertise in **copyediting** and today are usually freelancers.

editorial assistant. A staff member, usually entry level, who works for one or more editors, performing clerical and editorial tasks (which may often be the same thing) in what often serves as an apprenticeship. *See also* **editor**.

editorial board (ed board). The group within a publishing house that approves proposed **acquisitions**, sometimes called a *publishing board* (*pub board*) or *acquisition board*; also, metonymically, a meeting of this group, as in "I'm bringing the proposal up at ed/pub board tomorrow." Some houses, especially smaller ones, may not have a formal board. University presses often have a board consisting of faculty members in addition to or instead of an internal one.

editorial director. *See* **editor**.

editorial letter. A document sent from editor to author with specific recommendations for revising the author's manuscript. It may accompany a detailed **line edit** of the manuscript or may stand by itself. Sometimes called an *editorial memo*.

editorial meeting. A meeting of a publishing house's editorial staff, sometimes joined by colleagues from marketing, sales, or other departments, to discuss proposed acquisitions, book ideas, and other business issues. Typically held weekly but may occur more often, or less. In some houses the editorial meeting and pub board meeting are the same thing; in others they are distinct.

editor in chief. *See* **editor**.

electronic publishing. Publishing works distributed in some electronic form, whether via an internet browser, e-book reader, or older technology such as CD or DVD. Publishers have long used electronic tools, from computer typesetting to optical scanning, to produce printed books, but *electronic publishing* implies the book itself is being delivered to readers by digital means. Used more or less interchangeably with *digital publishing*.

el–hi publishing. Textbook publishing specifically aimed at the elementary through high school, or "K–12," market.

end matter. *See* **back matter**.

enhanced e-book. An e-book that includes not just the text of a printed edition but additional features such as sound, video, or interactive elements.

entity publisher. An organization, such as a business or not-for-profit group, that publishes its own content (such as reports, guidebooks, cookbooks, or catalogs) for sale or gratis distribution.

ePub. A widely used format for electronic book files.

e-tailers. Online retailers. Amazon is the largest, but many other companies sell books online, including some that originated as **bricks-and-mortar stores**.

fact-checking. The practice of confirming the accuracy of factual statements in a work before publication. For a variety of reasons, unlike newspaper or magazine publishers, book publishers do not routinely check facts, though some individual titles may be fact-checked.

fair use. In copyright law, the doctrine that allows an author to quote or reproduce the work of another creator, in certain ways and for certain purposes, without compensating that creator.

fan fiction. Stories written by fans of an existing fictional work or series, using characters and settings from the model.

file cleanup. The process in which a copyeditor or production editor removes tracked changes, author or editor comments, and other extraneous material from a manuscript before sending it to typesetting.

first pass pages. The first set of typeset page proofs delivered by a compositor to the publisher, for proofreading and review by the author. Also known as *first pages* or *first pass proofs*. After house and author send any corrections to the compositor, the latter produces *second pass pages* or *revised pages* (and if necessary, further passes until all errors are corrected).

flap copy. The descriptive and promotional copy that appears on the flaps of a book's **dust jacket**. Also called *jacket copy*.

font. A set of type of a particular **typeface** and size. Widely used erroneously to refer simply to a typeface in any size.

Frankfurt Book Fair. The world's longest-established and largest annual gathering of publishers, booksellers, and others (dating back to the fifteenth century); the major international fair for book sales and **rights** deals.

freelancer. An individual hired on a contract basis to perform services for a company or an author. Freelance editors often specialize in one type of editing or one type of book and offer their services to multiple publishing houses.

front matter. The pages of a book before the beginning of the main text, including such items as title and copyright pages, contents page, and preface. Also called *preliminary matter* or *prelims*.

frontlist. A publisher's catalog of current titles, usually defined as those published within the past one or two years.

full bleed. Material printed across the entire surface of a book page or cover so that the design "bleeds" off the edge.

galleys. Historically, the first set of typeset proofs from a compositor, delivered on long single-column sheets. Until computerized typesetting arrived, type was not laid out in page format, with art or other design elements included, until after proofreading and correction. The term derives from the French *galée*, a long tray for holding type. Because galleys were for generations the first set of proofs received, the term *galleys* is still widely though inaccurately applied to any **first pass pages**.

genre fiction. Novels and short stories generally intended for a popular audience, plot driven, and fitting into a well-established category such as mystery, romance, science fiction, or fantasy. *See also* **commercial fiction**.

ghostwriting. Writing a book under the name of another person. Originally the term meant without credit (hence "ghost"), though today "ghostwriters" may be identified on a title page by "as told to" or "with."

guarantee. *See* **advance, royalty**.

handle, sales. A one- or two-line distillation of a book's key selling points. On **title information sheets**, frequently called a **keynote**.

hand-selling. The act of marketing a book to a customer with a personal sales pitch, as practiced most commonly in **independent (indie) bookstores**. *See also* **word of mouth**.

hardcover. A printed book with a hard exterior binding, usually of cardboard wrapped in another material. In the past the material was often fabric, so older publishing personnel still speak of "clothbound" books; today a sturdy paper is more common, but cloth is still in use.

house, publishing. Term often used interchangeably for *publishing company*, probably reflecting the traditionalism of an industry where many businesses began as dynastic family firms.

imprint. A publishing "brand" within a larger company identity, usually denoting a particular editorial vision or focus. Sometimes named for a presiding editor ("A Margaret K. McElderry Book") and nested under an existing house name; sometimes a market-oriented niche list (Harper Wave, Vintage Contemporaries).

in print. Currently listed as available for sale from a publisher. Before e-books, keeping a title "in print" meant a publisher had to maintain an inventory of physical books; when these sold out the publisher had to invest in reprinting or let the title go "out of print." Today publishers often deem titles to be in print even if they only exist in e-book or **print-on-demand** form, though agents and authors may disapprove of this.

in stock. Available for sale in physical, printed form from a publisher's or wholesaler's warehouse. Applies by definition only to conventionally printed books; e-books or **print-on-demand** books are effectively always "in stock."

independent (indie) bookstores. Bookstores not owned by large corporations. A relatively small sector of the overall book market, but one of outsize importance because of its diversity and the strong connection of local booksellers with their communities.

independent (indie) publishers. Publishers not owned by large corporations; some are constituted as nonprofit organizations. Some authors who **self-publish** consider themselves indie publishers, though this use of the term is considered inappropriate or confusing by others in the industry on the grounds that selecting authors is a key part of the publisher's role.

indexing. The process of creating an index, an alphabetically arranged list of people, places, and concepts discussed in a book. Indexes are generally prepared by authors or freelancers based on **first pass pages**.

inserts. Sections of a printed book where illustrations are grouped, bound between pages of the verbal text; typically printed on different stock for better reproduction. Also called a *gallery*.

ISBN (International Standard Book Number). A unique number assigned to each edition and format (though not each printing) of a published book, almost universally used by major publishers. (Amazon, however, uses only its own identifier system for many e-books.)

jacket. *See* **dust jacket**.

jacket copy. *See* **flap copy**.

jobbers. *See* **wholesalers**.

juvenile publishing. A somewhat old-fashioned term for children's book publishing, still used in some settings (for instance, in **BISAC codes** and some library listings).

keynote. The main selling point or sales **handle** for a book, typically identified by this term on a **title information sheet**.

keywords. *See* **metadata**.

launch meeting. A meeting in which editors present one or more upcoming titles to their colleagues to "launch" them toward publication. The timing of the meeting, and its focus and participants, may vary: in most trade houses, this is the first meeting at which editors present a future season's titles to colleagues in marketing and other departments, while in some houses it's focused more on the production editing and manufacturing process.

legal vetting. The reading of a manuscript by the publisher's counsel for the purpose of flagging potential problems such as libel, copyright infringement, or invasion of privacy. Also called a *legal read* or *legal review*.

license. To convey by contract the authority to publish or adapt the content of a book, as in "the publisher licensed the paperback rights." Also used as a noun, as in "the paperback license had a term of eight years."

line editing. Detailed editing of a manuscript—line by line, as the term suggests—but not necessarily correcting all fine points of grammar, punctuation, or **style**, which is the task of **copyediting**.

list. A publisher's complete catalog of titles, the output of the publishing house. Publishers also speak of seasonal lists ("the fall list"), or other specialized subsets of the overall list ("our cookbook list"), and an editor may speak of her acquisitions as her list. *See also* **backlist** and **frontlist**.

list price. The publisher's official price for a book before any discounts offered by retailers or wholesalers. Often used in calculating the author's **royalties**.

literary agent. *See* **agent, literary**.

literary fiction. Fiction considered to be more concerned with literary values than with entertainment. Compare to **commercial fiction**.

managing editor. *See* **editor**.

manuscript. As noted in the introduction, an anachronistic term still universal in American publishing for the document (physical or electronic) containing a book's text; the raw material that editors edit. *See also* **typescript**.

margin. Profit margin. As in other industries, *gross margin* refers to revenue after direct costs of goods sold—such as royalties, printing, and distribution—while *net margin* takes into account indirect costs such as overhead.

mass-market paperback. A paperback book, generally in **rack-size** format, designed to be widely sold in outlets such as supermarkets, drugstores, and newsstands.

metadata. Data about data—typically, information linked to a book's listing in the electronic database of a publisher, retailer, or other entity. A book's metadata include author, title, format, and price but also keywords related to its content to aid in online searching.

midlist book. A title whose sales expectations, or sales history, are below best-selling levels but high enough to be considered a viable publication. The "midlist" may be thought of as the middle of an imaginary bell curve of sales across a publisher's **list**.

monograph. A book-length academic work on a specialized subject.

option clause. A standard contract clause giving the publisher, within certain conditions, an option, or right of first refusal, on the next work written by the author.

out of print. *See* **in print**.

P&L. Short for "profit and loss." In editorial parlance, a worksheet showing the projected financial investment and return for a given title (or, retrospectively, its actual results). Publishing houses or their divisions also have P&L statements for their overall performance, but among editors "P&L" almost always refers to the former.

P.P.B. Paper, printing, and binding costs. "P.P.B." serves as shorthand for the bundled costs of producing copies of a printed book. Sometimes called *stock costs*. Compare to **plant costs**.

packager, book. A person or firm that originates books for publishers and that supplies, as well as the content, some of the work normally done within the publishing house, such as editing, design, or even printing—in effect outsourcing those tasks in advance. Titles involving complicated illustration and design or multiple authors are often packaged. Also called a *book producer*.

paperback. A book with a stiff paper or thin card cover, as opposed to a **hardcover**. Also called *softcover*. *See also* **mass-market paperback** and **trade paperback**.

paranormal romance. A popular genre combining elements of romance fiction with elements of horror, science fiction, or fantasy. *Twilight* was a **breakout** success in this genre.

peer review. The practice in academic publishing of obtaining assessments of a proposed acquisition from expert readers in the author's discipline (her peers). Often called simply *review*.

permission. Formal clearance from a rights holder, such as a publisher or a photographic archive, to reproduce copyrighted material.

plant costs. Costs incurred one time only in producing a book, such as a jacket designer's fee or typesetting costs, as opposed to manufacturing costs incurred each time a book is reprinted. Sometimes called *plate costs*. Compare to **P.P.B.**

platform. An author's capacity to command the attention of readers, based on her reputation, expertise, celebrity, social media following, etc.

preemptive offer (preempt). An editor's bid made to a literary agent before an **auction** for rights to a work, attempting to "take it off the table"—acquire the book before formal bidding starts.

prelims. *See* **front matter**.

press. In publishing usage, either (1) a publishing organization (as in **university press**) or (2) a printing press used to produce books, as in "press date," the date at which a book is due to be printed.

printing. A quantity of books printed by a publisher at one time, as in "a first printing of 25,000 copies." Also called an *impression*. Publishers may make changes to a text between one printing and another (such as correcting errors), but if it is changed significantly the revised text is called a new **edition**.

print-on-demand (POD). The practice, enabled by digital technology, by which book copies are not printed until a publisher or retailer receives orders for them—typically one copy, or a small quantity, at a time.

producer, book. *See* **packager, book**.

production. Broadly, the part of the publishing process involved in making the edited **manuscript** into a printed or digital book. Encompasses both *production editorial* (**copyediting**, design, typesetting, and **proofreading**) and *manufacturing* (the printing and binding of physical copies).

production editor. *See* **editor**.

professional publishing. The sector of publishing aimed at readers who seek information for their professional specialties, such as legal publishing or **STM publishing**. Often includes journals, newsletters, and databases as well as books.

proofreading. Checking typeset or printed material against the author's manuscript for errors. Compare to **slugging**.

proofs. Printed copies made from typeset electronic files, plates, negatives, or positives used to examine and correct a work's text or visual elements before final printing. *See also* **first pass pages**.

proposal. A summary and prospectus, sometimes with sample text, of an unwritten or uncompleted book offered by an author to a publisher for a contract.

publication date (pub date). The date when a book is officially available for sale at retail establishments, usually several weeks after the bound books are delivered to the publisher's warehouse, allowing time for copies to be distributed in the marketplace.

publisher. As a job title, the head of a publishing house or imprint, the person ultimately responsible for both editorial and business decisions.

publishing board (pub board). *See* **editorial board (ed board)**.

query. A message from an author or agent to an editor describing, and inviting the latter's interest in, a book project. If such interest is expressed, the author/agent will submit a proposal or manuscript.

rack size. The standard format for mass-market paperbacks, designed to fit in the wire racks common in newsstands, supermarkets, and other such locations.

reader's report. A written assessment of the strengths and weaknesses—normally from both editorial and commercial perspectives—of a possible acquisition. May be prepared by editorial staff members (commonly assistants), but in special cases (e.g., translations) and in scholarly **peer review** may come from outside readers.

reference publishing. A category of publishing focused on books and, increasingly, digital products, often multiauthored, that have a practical purpose—dictionaries, encyclopedias, atlases, guidebooks, and the like, including works like this one. Most trade and scholarly publishers have some reference works on their lists; a few publish such titles exclusively.

retailers. Businesses that sell books directly to consumers, whether online, by mail, or in physical stores (as opposed to **wholesalers**, another kind of **account**). In addition to traditional booksellers, merchants such as Walmart and Target and many specialty accounts—gourmet shops, craft stores, etc.—hold a significant share of the retail book market.

returns. Unsold copies of a books returned by accounts to the publisher. Most returns from retailers or wholesalers receive full credit from the publisher.

rights. The contractual authorization to publish, adapt, or distribute a work in a certain format, language, or territory (as in "movie rights," "German rights," or "Canadian rights"). *See also* **subsidiary rights** and **volume rights**.

royalty. A contractually agreed sum paid to an author for each copy of a work sold, or as a percentage of income from other **rights** sold. *List royalties* are computed on the **list price** of a book, in which case they do not vary with the publisher's discount to customers; *net royalties* are a percentage of the amount received by the publisher for each sale, called *net receipts*. See also **advance, royalty**.

royalty statement. A publisher's accounting, delivered to an author at contractually agreed intervals, of book sales and **rights** income.

running heads. Copy set at the top of printed pages, usually containing information such as the author's name or the book or chapter title; when set at the bottom of pages, called *running feet*.

sales meeting. Generally, a meeting at which editors present forthcoming titles to **sales reps** and marketing staffs. A *sales conference* is a large formal meeting at which an entire season's list and marketing plan is presented.

sales rep. A sales representative, generally one who calls on booksellers or other **accounts**. A sales rep who visits higher-education faculty members to sell books for courses is a *college traveler*.

scholarly publishing. The sector of book publishing dedicated primarily to publishing works by scholars for other scholars and their students (and the libraries that serve them). Also called *academic publishing*. Includes both **university presses** and some commercial firms that publish for this market.

season. A specified period of time during which a publisher releases a batch of new titles. Traditionally book publishers divided a year into two seasons, fall and spring, though book seasons begin before and end after their meteorological counterparts; large houses may have three four-month seasons in a year.

self-publishing. Distributing and marketing a book one has written at one's own expense, rather than through an existing publishing house. In the past, authors sometimes paid **vanity presses** to release their work, but many services now exist allowing authors to control the process themselves. Compare to **independent (indie) publishing**.

setting copy. The unique copy, paper or electronic, of a manuscript, prepared by the copyeditor and designer for typesetting, with all edits and design specifications indicated.

signature. A segment of a printed book formed from one printed sheet of paper folded into multiple pages. Commonly thirty-two pages, but may be fewer.

signing. Synonym for **acquisition**. To "sign" a book is to acquire it, though editors also speak of "signing" an author, meaning to acquire his work.

signing goals. Specific numerical targets, usually measured by projected sales in dollars, for an editor's annual level of acquisitions.

slugging. Checking a stage of typeset **proofs** against an earlier stage, such as second against **first pass pages**—as distinct from proofreading, when proof is checked against **manuscript**.

slush pile. The supply of **unsolicited submissions** directed to a publishing house but no specific editor—originally a physical "pile," now including both paper and emailed material.

small press. A small publishing house; the term usually connotes one with a literary bent. (What is small, like what is literary, is open to discussion.) Small presses are **independent (indie) publishers** by definition, but not all independent publishers are small.

special sales. Sales outside of regular book-retailing channels, such as through specialty stores, mail order, corporate accounts, or charitable organizations. Special sales have different sales terms, and royalty rates, from regular sales.

specs. Shorthand for specifications for typesetting, design, or printing—determinants of the physical or visual presentation of a title.

sponsoring editor. See **acquiring editor**.

STM publishing. Abbreviation for scientific, technical, and medical publishing; a large and profitable market sector aimed at specialists in those fields. STM publishing includes books but is dominated by journals and online products.

style. In publishing-specific usage (as distinct, say, from "literary style"), an agreed, consistent standard for usage, punctuation, spelling, references, and other elements of the content presented in a book. Part of **copyediting** is ensuring that a work consistently follows the same style throughout. Publishers typically use a given style guide, such as *The Chicago Manual of Style*, as a reference point.

style sheet. A document made up by a copyeditor recording the **style** adopted for a given book—later used by typesetter and proofreader as a reference.

subheadings (subheads). Titles for sections within a book chapter, set off typographically from body copy. Some chapters have subsections within sections, creating a hierarchy of subheads: *A heads*, *B heads*, etc.

submit. To present a book, in proposal or manuscript form, to an editor for possible publication. The material presented is a *submission*. *See also* **unsolicited submission**.

subsidiary rights (sub rights). Rights licensed by the publisher and author to a third party to adapt or publish other versions of a book. These may include paperback or audio rights, dramatic rights, book club, translation rights, or even video game rights. Revenue from the sales of such rights is split between publisher and author at contractually agreed percentages (*sub rights splits*).

supply chain. The system of people, companies, and processes involved in creating a book and delivering it, in print or digitally, to a consumer—that is, a reader.

In book publishing, "supply chain" refers principally to the production and distribution process—printing, warehousing, sales, shipping, and retailing—though technically it includes writing, editing, and design as well.

territory. A defined geographical area within which contracted publishing **rights** apply, such as "North American rights" or "UK and Commonwealth rights."

textbook publishing. The sector of book publishing devoted to producing works specifically for use in courses. Generally divided into **el–hi publishing**, for elementary through high school students, and **college publishing**.

tipsheet. *See* **title information sheet (TI sheet)**.

title. In publishing-specific usage, a book considered as a work for publication, in any or all of its varied formats. As in "we published large-print and audio editions of that title as well as hardcover and paperback."

title information sheet (TI sheet). A document containing a description, specs, sales keynote and other selling points, and author information for a given title. A key tool in sales, marketing, and publicity. Also called *author information sheet (AI sheet), tipsheet,* or *sellsheet.*

TOC. Abbreviation for table of contents.

track record. An author's title-by-title sales history; an important factor in assessing the sales prospects for a new title by that author.

trade paperback. A paperback book, generally in a format similar to a hardcover edition except for the binding, intended to be sold in bookstores and other book retail, as opposed to mass-market, channels. Sometimes called a *quality paperback.*

trade publishing. The sector of book publishing devoted to general consumer titles—books of the kind sold in regular bookstores, or what was historically called "the book trade." Though such books are now sold in many nonbookstore outlets and online, the term *trade* endures to distinguish this market sector from textbook and other kinds of publishing.

transmittal. The formal handoff of an edited manuscript, agreed by author and editor to be ready for publication, to **production**. The *transmittal manuscript* is the unique printout or electronic file that must pass through the production editorial process, with annotations from the copyeditor and book designer.

transom, over the. A phrase indicating an **unsolicited submission.** It dates from the days when offices had transom windows above their doors, and desperate authors were imagined throwing their manuscripts through them: one way of getting past the gatekeeper. If not sent to an individual editor, an over-the-transom submission lands in the **slush pile**.

trim size. The outer dimensions of a printed and bound book page. Given in inches in the United States, millimeters almost everywhere else. Standard hardcover and paperback formats in the United States are commonly referred to by trim size, e.g., "6×9."

typeface. A set of text characters that share a consistent and distinctive design. A typeface may include roman, italic, boldface, condensed, and other **fonts**.

Typefaces are designated by name, such as Baskerville, Times Roman, or Helvetica.

typescript. The term commonly (and inaccurately, for the most part) used in British publishing for what American publishers call (equally inaccurately) a **manuscript**.

typesetter. A person or company that prepares books for printing or digital publication from an author's manuscript. Almost all typesetters now use computers, but originally pieces of wooden or metal type were set or "composed" by hand to create pages; hence the synonym for this term: *compositor*.

unit cost. The cost of creating a single printed or digital copy of a book. An estimated unit cost is an important component of a book's preacquisition **P&L**. Unit cost is also an important factor in considering how many copies of a book to print or reprint.

university press. A publishing house connected to, and usually sponsored by, a college or university. Typically university presses specialize in academic **monographs**, but they may also publish textbooks, trade books, and reference books.

unsolicited submission. A work submitted to an editor for publication directly by an author, unrequested by the editor, and without benefit of an agent.

urban fantasy. A subgenre of fantasy books in which speculative elements are combined with recognizable real-world settings.

vanity press. A house that charges fees to authors, rather than paying them, to publish their books. Publishing through a vanity press is effectively a form of **self-publishing**; before the advent of e-books and print on demand, it was one of the few methods available to authors who had not found a traditional publisher or preferred not to try.

verticalization. The practice of focusing a publisher's list or an imprint around a certain community of readers, genre, or subject (such as romance fiction or sustainable living), called a *vertical*.

vetting. *See* **legal vetting**.

viral marketing. Publicizing a book by means of social media. It may mean spreading **word-of-mouth** book recommendations or, less directly, creating internet-friendly content related to the book that will be widely shared, raising awareness of the title.

volume rights. A common term loosely denoting the main publication rights to a title, usually the right to publish in hardcover, paperback, and e-book form, as distinct from **subsidiary rights**.

wholesalers. Businesses that serve as intermediaries between publishers and retailers by buying large volumes of books at a high discount and supplying them to booksellers at a lower one. Wholesalers serve the market by providing convenience, speed, and customer service in fulfilling demand, versus ordering directly from publishers. Some wholesalers also serve libraries or other specialty customers. Also called *jobbers*.

word of mouth. Personal recommendation of a book by one reader to another by oral or written means. Long considered the best, as well as most cost effective, method of generating sales and consequently the Holy Grail of publishers' marketing efforts. Word of mouth practiced by retail booksellers is, perhaps confusingly, **hand-selling**; *see also* **viral marketing**.

young adult (YA) book. A title intended for older children and adolescents, usually defined as ages twelve to eighteen. As with all children's literature, there are fluid and sometimes contested boundaries between age categories. Many titles published as YA have have been popular with adults, such as the Harry Potter and Hunger Games series.

FURTHER RESOURCES

· ·

What follows is not an exhaustive list but a selection of books, other publications, and online resources that may be useful to a reader who wants to learn more about subjects discussed in this book. I have included my own comments about some items that I think are particularly valuable or noteworthy. Some of the online resources require subscriptions or have separate free and paid versions. —P.G.

BOOKS

REFERENCE BOOKS, HANDBOOKS, AND PRACTICAL WORKS ON THE CRAFT OF EDITING

Adin, Richard. *The Business of Editing: Effective and Efficient Ways to Think, Work, and Prosper.* N.p.: Waking Lion, 2014. Practical advice specifically for freelance editors.

Bell, Susan. *The Artful Edit: On the Practice of Editing Yourself.* New York: W. W. Norton, 2007.

Bielstein, Susan M. *Permissions, A Survival Guide: Blunt Talk about Art as Intellectual Property.* Chicago: University of Chicago Press, 2006.

The Chicago Manual of Style. 17th ed. Chicago: University of Chicago Press, 2017. Not just indispensable as a style reference but full of useful information about the publishing process.

Davies, Gill. *Book Commissioning and Acquisition.* 2nd ed. New York: Routledge, 2004.

Dunham, Steve. *The Editor's Companion: An Indispensable Guide to Editing Books, Magazines, Online Publications, and More.* Cincinnati: Writer's Digest Books, 2014.

Eckstut, Arielle, and David Henry Sterry. *The Essential Guide to Getting Your Book Published: How to Write It, Sell It, and Market It . . . Successfully!* New York: Workman, 2010. Much useful information both on finding a traditional publisher and on self-publishing.

Einsohn, Amy. *The Copyeditor's Handbook: A Guide for Book Publishing and Corporate Communications; With Exercises and Answer Keys.* 3rd ed. Berkeley: University of California Press, 2011.

Ennis, Stacy. *The Editor's Eye: A Practical Guide to Transforming Your Book from Good to Great.* San Francisco: Night Owls, 2013.

Germano, William. *Getting It Published: A Guide for Scholars and Anyone Else Serious about Serious Books.* 3rd ed. Chicago: University of Chicago Press, 2016. Smart, knowledgeable, and written with verve.

Gross, Gerald, ed. *Editors on Editing: What Writers Need to Know about What Editors Do.* 3rd ed. New York: Grove, 1993. Though dated in some respects, a highly informative collection of essays by accomplished editors, mostly of trade books.

Guthrie, R. *Publishing: Principles and Practice*. Thousand Oaks, CA: SAGE, 2011.

Lee, Marshall. *Bookmaking: Editing, Design, Production*. 3rd ed. New York: W. W. Norton, 2004. A venerable (if not fully up-to-date) resource, weighted toward design and production but offering a thorough overview of publishing.

Lerner, Betsy. *The Forest for the Trees: An Editor's Advice to Writers*. Rev. ed. New York: Riverhead Books, 2010. Addressed to writers, but includes much astute commentary on the editor's side of the publishing process.

Luey, Beth. *Handbook for Academic Authors*. 5th ed. New York: Cambridge University Press, 2010.

McCormack, Thomas. *The Fiction Editor, the Novel, and the Novelist*. 2nd ed. Philadelphia: Paul Dry Books, 2006. Idiosyncratic, pungently expressed, and shrewdly pragmatic observations by a veteran editor.

Norton, Scott. *Developmental Editing: A Handbook for Freelancers, Authors, and Publishers*. Chicago: University of Chicago Press, 2009. Wry, sensible, and well-organized; excellent advice for any editor involved with manuscripts at a level deeper than copyediting.

Poynter, Dan. *The Self-Publishing Manual: How to Write, Print and Sell Your Own Book*. Santa Barbara, CA: Para, 2007.

Rabiner, Susan, and Alfred Fortunato. *Thinking like Your Editor: How to Write Great Serious Nonfiction—and Get It Published*. New York: W. W. Norton, 2002. One of the most insightful books available on nonfiction writing and editing.

Saller, Carol Fisher. *The Subversive Copy Editor: Advice from Chicago (or, How to Negotiate Good Relationships with Your Writers, Your Colleagues, and Yourself)*. 2nd ed. Chicago: University of Chicago Press, 2016. Not a book of editorial rules but possibly even more useful: guidance from a veteran copyeditor on how to apply the rules and when to bend them.

Sharpe, Leslie T, and Irene Gunther. *Editing Fact and Fiction: A Concise Guide to Book Editing*. Cambridge: Cambridge University Press, 1994.

Skillin, Marjorie E., and Robert M. Gay. *Words into Type*. 3rd ed. Englewood Cliffs, NJ: Prentice Hall, 1974. Overdue for revision but still beloved for its coverage of grammar and punctuation.

Siegfied, Carin. *The Insider's Guide to a Career in Book Publishing*. Charlotte, NC: Chickadee Books, 2014.

Woll, Thomas. *Publishing for Profit: Successful Bottom-Line Management for Book Publishers*. Chicago: Chicago Review Press, 2010.

BIOGRAPHIES, MEMOIRS, AND GENERAL WORKS ON THE PUBLISHING BUSINESS

Athill, Diana. *Stet: A Memoir*. New York: Grove, 2000.

Berg, A. Scott. *Max Perkins: Editor of Genius*. New York: E. P. Dutton, 1978. A first-rate biography of the editor who has (partly thanks to this book) become the icon of literary editing.

Bhaskar, Michael. *The Content Machine: Towards a Theory of Publishing from the Printing Press to the Digital Network.* London: Anthem, 2013.

Cerf, Bennett. *At Random: The Reminiscences of Bennett Cerf.* New York: Random House, 1977. Based on an oral history, the memoir of the founder of Random House.

Clark, Giles N, and Angus Phillips. *Inside Book Publishing.* 5th ed. Abingdon, UK: Routledge, 2014.

Cowley, Malcolm. *The Long Voyage: Selected Letters of Malcolm Cowley, 1915–1987.* Edited by Hans Bak. Cambridge: Harvard University Press, 2014. Cowley, like Max Perkins, was one of the great editors of the twentieth century.

Dardis, Tom. *Firebrand: The Life of Horace Liveright.* New York: Random House, 1995.

Epstein, Jason. *Book Business: Publishing Past, Present, and Future.* New York: W. W. Norton, 2002. An innovative publisher's look at the twentieth-century book business and his own career.

Giroux, Robert. *The Education of an Editor.* New York: R. R. Bowker, 1982.

Gottlieb, Robert. *Avid Reader: A Life.* New York: Farrar Straus & Giroux, 2016. A memoir of a brilliant editorial career at Simon & Schuster, Knopf, and the *New Yorker*.

Greenberg, Susan. *Editors Talk about Editing: Insights for Readers, Writers and Publishers.* New York: Peter Lang, 2015.

Kachka, Boris. *Hothouse: The Art of Survival and the Survival of Art at America's Most Celebrated Publishing House, Farrar, Straus, and Giroux.* New York: Simon & Schuster, 2013.

Korda, Michael. *Another Life: A Memoir of Other People.* New York: Random House, 1999. Possibly the most entertaining memoir of an editor to be found in print.

Kurowski, Travis, Wayne Miller, and Kevin Prufer, eds. *Literary Publishing in the Twenty-First Century.* Minneapolis: Milkweed Editions, 2016. Essays from a variety of editors, publishers, authors, and critics.

MacNiven, Ian S. *"Literchoor Is My Beat": A Life of James Laughlin, Publisher of New Directions.* New York: Farrar, Straus & Giroux, 2014. A biography of one of the best independent literary publishers in America, the founder of New Directions.

Perkins, Maxwell E., and John H. Wheelock. *Editor to Author: The Letters of Maxwell E. Perkins.* New York: Scribner, 1950. Perkins's letters are models not just of editorial insight but of tact in expressing it.

Schiffrin, André. *The Business of Books: How International Conglomerates Took Over Publishing and Changed the Way We Read.* London: Verso, 2000.

Silverman, Al. *The Time of Their Lives: The Golden Age of Great American Book Publishers, Their Editors, and Authors.* New York: Truman Talley Books, 2008.

Tebbel, John. *Between Covers: The Rise and Transformation of Book Publishing in America.* New York: Oxford University Press, 1987. A solid overview from the beginning of American publishing through the 1980s; drawn from Tebbel's four-volume history.

Thompson, John B. *Merchants of Culture: The Publishing Business in the Twenty-First Century*. 2nd ed. New York: Plume, 2012. An inquisitive scholar's study of the current trade book business. An excellent place to begin in seeking to understand the industry.

MAGAZINES AND JOURNALS

Bookforum (www.bookforum.com).

The Bookseller (www.thebookseller.com). Trade magazine of the British publishing industry but with international coverage.

Journal of Electronic Publishing (www.journalofelectronicpublishing.org).

Journal of Scholarly Publishing (www.utpjournals.press/loi/jsp).

Poets & Writers (www.pw.org). Principally for writers but has some coverage of publishing, including a regular feature of interviews with working editors.

Publishers Weekly (www.publishersweekly.com). The trade magazine of American book publishing; its website includes one of the major jobs boards in the industry.

BLOGS AND NEWS SITES

An American Editor (americaneditor.wordpress.com). The blog of Rich Adin, an experienced freelance editor (see his book listed above).

Book Riot (www.bookriot.com).

CMOS Shop Talk (cmosshoptalk.com). A blog from the editors of the *Chicago Manual of Style*.

Doctor Syntax (www.doctorsyntax.net). A blog on books and publishing by the editor of this volume.

Futurebook (www.futurebook.net).

Guardian book page (www.theguardian.com/books).

Jacket Copy (www.latimes.com/books/jacketcopy). The books blog of the *Los Angeles Times*.

Jane Friedman's blog (janefriedman.com/blog/). Commentary on writing and publishing from an astute industry observer.

KOK Edit Blog (editor-mom.blogspot.com/). A blog by the host of the Copyeditors' Knowledge Base (*see under* Miscellaneous Online Resources).

Literary Hub (www.lithub.com).

The Millions (www.themillions.com/).

New York Times books page (www.nytimes.com/section/books). Includes not just the *Times Book Review* but also its other coverage of authors and publishing.

Page-Turner (www.newyorker.com/books/page-turner). The *New Yorker*'s books blog.

Publishers Marketplace (www.publishersmarketplace.com). Publishers Lunch (see below) is the indispensable industry newsletter; its site *Publisher Marketplace* aggregates publishing news from multiple sources, plus other useful tools

....

including job listings; a directory of industry contacts; databases of book deals and reviews; and multiple best-seller lists.

Publishing Trends and its sister blog, *Publishing Trendsetter* (www.publishingtrends .com, www.publishingtrendsetter.com). Like *Publishers Marketplace*, this blog is the online counterpart to a key industry newsletter.

Scholarly Kitchen (scholarlykitchen.sspnet.org/). Blog for the Society for Scholarly Publishing.

The Shatzkin Files (www.idealog.com/). Provocative commentary on publishing from a longtime industry consultant and observer.

EMAIL NEWSLETTERS

Copyediting (www.copyediting.com/publications/newsletter/).

Digital Speed (janefriedman.com/free-newsletter/). Digital media tools and resources.

GalleyCat (www.adweek.com/galleycat/).

Publishers Lunch (lunch.publishersmarketplace.com/). Breaking news and occasional commentary; along with *Publishers Weekly*, the most-read news source in the industry.

Publishing Perspectives (publishingperspectives.com/). International publishing news.

PW Daily (www.publishersweekly.com). Daily news update from *Publishers Weekly*.

Shelf Awareness (www.shelf-awareness.com/booktrade.html). Originally aimed at booksellers, news of books and publishing with a focus on retail.

MISCELLANEOUS ONLINE RESOURCES

AAUP Handbook: Best Practices in Peer Review (www.aaupnet.org/resources/for -members/handbooks-and-toolkits/peer-review-best-practices).

Board of Editors in the Life Sciences website (www.bels.org/).

"Book Publishing Accounting: Some Basic Concepts" by Thomas McCormack (aaupwiki.princeton.edu/index.php/Book_Publishing_Accounting:_Some _Basic_Concepts). A very concise introduction to what publishing people need to know about finances.

The Chicago Manual of Style Online (www.chicagomanualofstyle.org). Online version of the key style reference cited above.

Copyediting-L (www.copyediting-1.info). A listserv "for copyeditors and other defenders of the English language who want to discuss anything related to editing." Its webpage also has a resource list.

Copyeditors' Knowledge Base (www.kokedit.com/ckb.php). Information and links on freelance editing and copyediting.

Copyright and Fair Use site of Stanford University Libraries (fairuse.stanford.edu/). A comprehensive and useful resource for understanding copyright and fair use issues—a good first stop when permissions questions arise.

Literary Market Place / International Literary Market Place (www.literarymarket place.com). American and international directories of publishers, agents, and other industry services.

Publishers Marketplace. *See under* Blogs and News Sites.

EDITING AND PUBLISHING COURSES

As with the resources above, this does not claim to be a complete list, as academic courses and programs are created and changed continually, but I hope it will offer a starting place for readers interested in further education in editing and publishing.—P.G.

SUMMER PUBLISHING COURSES

Columbia Publishing Course at Columbia School of Journalism

CUNY Publishing Institute at City University of New York School of Journalism

NYU Summer Publishing Institute at New York University School of Professional Studies

University of Denver Publishing Institute

Yale Publishing Course

COLLEGE AND UNIVERSITIES WITH PUBLISHING COURSES OR PROGRAMS

Arizona State University: graduate certificates in Nonfiction Writing and Publishing, Scholarly Publishing

Augsburg College: graduate MFA concentration in Publishing

Boston University: graduate programs in Editorial Studies

Drew University: graduate degrees in Book History and Print Culture

Drexel University: graduate and undergraduate programs in Publishing

Emerson College: graduate and undergraduate programs in Writing, Literature and Publishing

Fairfield University: graduate MFA concentration in Editing and Publishing

Florida State University: graduate programs in Publishing and Editing

George Washington University: MPS in Publishing

Hofstra University: undergraduate program in Publishing Studies

Lake Forest College: undergraduate minor in Print and Digital Publishing

New School: graduate program in Creative Publishing and Critical Journalism

New York University: MS in Publishing

Pace University: MS in Publishing

Portland State University: graduate program in Book Publishing

Rosemont College: MA in Publishing

Rowan University: graduate and undergraduate courses in publishing

Sarah Lawrence College: certificate in Book Publishing

Simon Fraser University: graduate and undergraduate programs in Publishing

University of Baltimore, Yale Gordon College of Arts and Sciences: MA in Publication Design

University of Houston-Victoria: MS in Publishing

University of Iowa: undergraduate Literary Publishing Track

University of North Carolina Wilmington: graduate and undergraduate programs in Publishing

University of Toronto: graduate programs in Book History and Print Culture; undergraduate program in Book and Media Studies

OTHER ORGANIZATIONS OFFERING ONLINE OR IN-PERSON EDITORIAL RESOURCES OR TRAINING

American Copy Editors Society

Bay Area Editors' Forum

Council of Science Editors

Copyediting (www.copyediting.com)

Edit*cetera*

Editorial Freelancers Association

Editorial Inspirations

The Graduate School (formerly known as the USDA Graduate School; (www .graduateschool.edu/content/ep-certificates/editorial)

New York University Center for Publishing Studies

Society for Technical Communication

University of California Berkeley Extension

University of California San Diego Extension

University of Chicago Graham School of Continuing Liberal and Professional Studies

University of Washington Professional & Continuing Education

ABOUT THE EDITOR

Peter Ginna has worked as a book editor and publisher in New York since 1982. Most recently he was the founder and publisher and editorial director of Bloomsbury Press, an imprint of Bloomsbury USA. Prior to that he was editorial director for trade books at Oxford University Press and also worked at Crown / Random House, St. Martin's Press, and Persea Books. He developed and taught the course "What Is an Editor" in NYU's publishing program and has written about editorial matters for *Creative Nonfiction* magazine and the Nieman Foundation's website, Storyboard. He blogs on books and publishing at www.DoctorSyntax.net and comments on Twitter: @DoctorSyntax.

INDEX

. . . .

Lightning Source UK Ltd.
Milton Keynes UK
UKOW05f1321221117
313116UK00003BA/10/P